Faith, Hope, and a Lifetime of Beautiful Scars

BEVERLY A. ALTEMUS

Natalee's story: An interrupted life of miracles, Badges of Honor, and
"stump the doctor."

WESTBOW
PRESS®
A DIVISION OF THOMAS NELSON
& ZONDERVAN

WestBow Press books may be ordered through booksellers or by contacting:

WestBow Press
A Division of Thomas Nelson & Zondervan
1663 Liberty Drive
Bloomington, IN 47403
www.westbowpress.com
1 (866) 928-1240

ISBN: 978-1-9736-3397-6 (sc)
ISBN: 978-1-9736-3398-3 (hc)
ISBN: 978-1-9736-3396-9 (e)

Library of Congress Control Number: 2018908240

Print information available on the last page.

WestBow Press rev. date: 08/06/2018

Dedication

To the glory of our unfailing and loving God, for always having a better plan and one more miracle for Natalee.

Your ways, O God, are holy. What god is as great as our God? You are the God who performs miracles; you display your power among the peoples. (Psalm 77:13-14 NIV)

Contents

Part 2. A Mom's Day-by-day Digest of an Interrupted Life with More Beautiful Scars and Badges of Honor

Prologue

If you saw her walking down the street, you would think she was just like any other healthy person. Most people do. Outward appearances can sometimes be very deceiving. Health issues that may be affecting or even slowly destroying someone's life are often times invisible to others.

I started keeping a journal in a narrative format around 1985 for our own family records concerning my daughter's struggles with diabetes and its complications, experiences with her kidney and pancreas transplants, and other health-related trials. As time went on, and her battles with multiple diverse health issues increased, my journal became a diary of the day-to-day frustrations and life-changing challenges that living with chronic illness presents - her *Beautiful Scars*. (Scars remind us that we survived something.)

My daughter's name is Natalee Ann (Altemus) Smouse. People are amazed when they meet her and hear her remarkable story and all she has faced and courageously endured to earn her *Badges of Honor*; of how her challenges have affected family, finances, jobs and daily life. She has been a remarkable inspiration while battling her challenges, never losing faith or hope.

It's hard to put things in the past behind you and to keep them there because that's where they are - forever right behind you. There's always something that can and will inadvertently trigger a memory, good or bad, to resurface. (The bad should make you appreciate the good so much more.) As Natalee and I read back over the notes in my journal it brought back good memories and also some of the challenges and frustrations we'd like to forget, but it also reminded us of how far Natalee has journeyed and how many miracles she has been blessed with many times over in her life.

We pray her story will hearten others to remain positive, to not lose hope and to hold onto unwavering faith in difficult circumstances. Every morning we wake up to is a gift that we should thank God for the moment we awaken, then try to live it to the best of our ability. (Tomorrow is never a given.)

> I can do all things through Christ who strengthens me.
> (Philippians 4:13 NIV)

PART ONE

A Life Interrupted

Chapter 1

Waiting, Bonding and Coping

The definition of *waiting*: Staying in the place where one is without action; in expectation of something; to be in readiness. Nowhere does time go more slowly than while you're waiting, and the business of chronic illness is often times the business of waiting. Over the years, Natalee and I have perfected the art of waiting. Waiting in waiting rooms at hospitals and emergency rooms. Waiting in exam rooms and doctor offices. Waiting for appointments to be scheduled. Waiting for anticipated calls to come. Waiting for test results. Waiting in seemingly endless rush hour traffic. Waiting for Natalee to feel better on a challenging day, and waiting for good news for a change. The idiom "wait and see" has become a mantra. David and I have waited while she has had at least, and if not more than, fifteen surgeries. I think hospitals should have a game room for those who are without action so they can pass the time with some action. (Just in case someone is listening - I vote for Skee Ball.)

We call our time spent together in emergency rooms, waiting and exam rooms our "bonding" time. Waiting, waiting, and more waiting requires patience, endurance...and fun distractions. Little do others around us know we are contemplating rearranging the room we are waiting in to see if anyone notices, or switching places on the exam table after the nurse leaves the room and before the doctor comes into the room. (Not that we ever did those things. *Wink, wink.*) Thank goodness for our Kindle readers to keep us occupied and out of trouble. Checking out postings on Facebook or You Tube on our phones can help pass some time and be entertaining, too. (Although, I think there is an obligatory rule against having fun in a waiting room.)

We have waited in eight hospitals in four cities in Western Pennsylvania - Pittsburgh, Altoona, Windber and Johnstown. For good measure, tally in the many other assorted medical buildings. It adds up to more than I care to count. (On a positive note, I can tell you who has the best cafeteria food or waiting room coffee....and chairs, those ever-present supportive characters.)

Natalee has seen innumerable doctors including several PCPs, various general surgeons, nephrologists and urologists, endocrinologists, gastroenterologists, psychologists, neuro and gynecologic oncologists, medical and radiology oncologists, radiologists, cardiologists, pulmonologists, gynecologists, oncology hematologists, rheumatologists, ophthalmologists, obstetricians, orthopods, internists, anesthesiologists, infectious disease and ENT doctors, and some -ologists I can't remember. If she were able to bill all of them for the time spent waiting to see each one, she'd be worth a fortune! The total of all her medical bills over the years is definitely astronomical. (I guess you could say she's worth a fortune in that regard.)

When Natalee has an appointment with a new doctor, they are usually surprised she is the patient upon first meeting her and even more surprised after they witness her positive attitude and fortitude firsthand. She doesn't look like the person you would picture in your mind after reading over her *War and Peace* length medical history. That history should belong to someone more than twice her age. After reviewing her extensive medical records, many doctors have commented, "You should write a book." Her reply for many years was, "My mother keeps a journal." (Now she says, "My mom did write a book!")

Natalee has had enough CT scans, x-rays and MRIs, she should glow in the dark *and* daylight. She has scars on her head, neck, arms, chest, abdomen and elsewhere from the multiple surgeries and other procedures she has suffered. She has bravely endured being poked, prodded or stuck with needles in and on just about every part of her body. Every body cavity and orifice has been probed or invaded at some point and would make an alien from Planet Rx want to recruit her medical team. (Sorry if that puts a picture in your head of little green men congratulating the docs and techs on a job well done.)

People often ask, "How do you deal with everything?" The answer - prayer and faith. Also, we have learned to take one day at a time. That's all we get anyhow in life with no guarantees. As the saying goes - yesterday is over and done and can't be changed, tomorrow is yet to come and will take care of itself, so we focus on the day at hand. (Control what you can and give the rest to God.)

> "Have faith in God," Jesus answered. "Truly I tell you, if anyone says to this mountain, 'Go, throw yourself into the sea,' and does not doubt in their heart but believes that what they say will happen, it will be done for them. Therefore I tell you, whatever you ask for in prayer, believe that you have received it, and it will be yours. And when you stand praying, if you hold anything against anyone, forgive them, so that your Father in heaven may forgive your sins." (Mark 11:22-25 NIV) Therefore do not worry about tomorrow, for tomorrow will worry about itself. Each day has enough trouble of it's own. (Matthew 6:34 NIV)

We have also learned to find humor even in the worst of circumstances. My friend, Janet, was with Natalee and me one day on a short walk to see the ducks on the Stonycreek River across the street from Natalee's house. Natalee and I were bantering back and forth when Janet remarked, "You two are like a comedy team!" They say laughter's the best medicine and we definitely partake of as many doses as we can. (Maybe more then a little.) Laughter helps ease stress and pain in tough circumstances and fills us with joy.

> ...for the joy of the Lord is your strength. (Nehemiah 8:10 NIV) A merry heart doeth good like a medicine... (Proverbs 17:22 KJV)

Natalee and I have not only laughed together, but we have cried together, made tough decisions together, have driven untold miles to hundreds of appointments together, waited countless hours together, rode dizzying emotional roller coasters of highs and lows together, applauded good news and weathered bad news together, and most importantly - we have simply prayed together. We have also eaten umpteen meals together at Panera Bread on our way home from Pittsburgh. That's one of the things we look forward to most of all. (And I love the French fries in the cafeteria at at Presby.)

> Be joyful in hope, patient in affliction, faithful in prayer.
> (Romans 12:12 NIV)

Natalee has endured all she has with little complaint and great courage. One time when she was going through a particularly rough recovery, she confidently said to me, "God would never give me more then I can handle. (When we trust Him to help us endure) He must think I'm a pretty tough kid."

> Praise be to the Lord, to God our Savior, who daily bears
> our burdens. (Psalm 68:19 NIV)

I read somewhere once that everything in life is a struggle, until it's not. I think of how people struggle everyday to retain what they have while others struggle to obtain what they don't have. We often times take for granted what we have…until it's gone. Without health, nothing else seems worthwhile to pursue, except serving and trusting God. Natalee's health issues make that all too real.

> Let us approach God's throne of grace with confidence,
> so that we may receive mercy and find grace to help us in
> our time of need. (Hebrews 4:16 NIV)

Natalee's strength and resolve during the neverending challenges affecting her never fails to astound me. (I refer to her challenges as the "Cirque du Natalee's Challenges.") The informal definition of *circus* according to *Collins Dictionary* is: A disturbance; setting something in motion. A situation of too much excitement and uncontrolled activity; unintentionally comic.

Prayer, faith, hope, and trust in God are not just words to Natalee, but a way of life. She's not only my tough, wonderful, funny, and beautiful (inside and out) daughter, but my best friend and inspiration. The most important thing we know and rely on above all else is that prayer absolutely works for those who truly believe in God and His Son, Jesus Christ, and who try to live every day according to His Word. We know without a shadow of doubt that miracles happen in spite of stumping a doctor or two. My journal has indeed turned into a book and here is Natalee's incredible story of *Beautiful Scars* and *Badges of Honor* from my perspective....

Chapter 2

The Beginning of "Stump the Doctor"

Natalee's first major health scare occurred in March of 1974, one month before her third birthday. That's when she began testing multiple doctors with what we eventually called "stump the doctor." Over the years, she has unwittingly turned it into an artform, challenging many knowledgeable doctors since then.

I am an RN and was working the 3:00-11:00 p.m. shift at a local hospital when my mother, who was babysitting Natalee, called and said she had noticed a "red rash" on Natalee accompanied by a low-grade temperature. She only observed the presence of the rash under Natalee's arms, on her chest, and in her groin area. I wasn't overly alarmed at the time, since her symptoms were not unusual for a number of common childhood illnesses. I told my mother she should just continue to keep an eye on the symptoms and if they worsened, to call me. ("Wait and see" time.)

Natalee was already in bed and fast asleep when I got home from work. We shared the same bedroom at my parents' house and she slept in a converted crib at the foot of my bed. She slept soundly all through the night. I didn't; waking several times to check on her. Nothing had notably changed since my mother had called me. In the morning, the red areas didn't appear like a typical rash to me. Her temperature was still only slightly elevated. I decided to just continue monitoring the unusual "rash" and her temperature since she had no other apparent symptoms and wasn't complaining about anything. There was nothing more to do than "wait and see" whether anything developed further.

Cause for alarm surfaced later that day when Natalee suddenly spiked a fever over 102 degrees and blistering, angry red areas were starting to appear on the spreading "rash" areas. Now what? (The start of another one of my frequent mantras.) Clearly not so typical, so it was time for an ER visit. No one in the ER who examined her was able to immediately identify the specific cause of her symptoms. Many commented they had previously never seen anything like it. It definitely wasn't one of the common childhood illnesses. The doctors and nurses were stumped. (Which wasn't very reassuring.) I prayed God would reveal to the doctors what was attacking her body and would protect her from serious complications.

> God is our refuge and strength, a very present help in trouble. (Psalm 46:1 KJV)

As a precaution, Natalee was admitted to the pediatric unit in an isolation room. The medical staff proactively started her on injections of a broad-spectrum antibiotic, hopeful it would have some effect until they could make a definitive diagnosis. Our PCP saw her the next morning, and he, too, was totally stumped. No one had the faintest clue what was affecting her or even how serious it could be. I was in panic mode while distressing scenarios ran through my head. (Nurses always think of the worst things that can happen. It's in the job description.) In the meantime, the fiery redness and growing blisters continued spreading all over her body while the fever persisted, and she was becoming more and more listless. It was beyond frightening to watch as the mystery illness spread and continued its attack on her body. I requested time off work to be with her. Fervent prayer was the only reassuring thing I could hold onto at that point.

> Is anyone among you sick? Let them call the elders of the church to pray over them and anoint them with oil in the name of the Lord. And the prayer offered in faith will make the sick person well; the Lord will raise them up. (James 5: 14-15 NIV)

After a couple agonizing days with no noticeable improvement and still not knowing what she was afflicted with, one of the medical residents, who was making rounds for the first time with our PCP, came to see Natalee. After examining her, the resident said when he was in medical school, he had seen a child who presented with the same symptoms and proposed Natalee may have the same malady. Further investigation proved he was correct, and she was diagnosed with staphylococcal scalded skin syndrome (SSSS), a not-so-common syndrome in children that emanates from a bacterial infection. The exposed skin looks like burns or scalded skin, thus the name. The scarlet, paper-like, wrinkled-looking skin develops flaccid blisters. The top layer of skin begins peeling off in sheets when the blisters rupture, which can put the child at risk for serious and life-threatening complications such as sepsis, dehydration, and electrolyte imbalance. Not what we wanted to hear, but it was what we could be facing. To avoid complications settling in, IV fluids were immediately ordered to prevent dehydration and electrolyte imbalance. Natalee was so weak by then she hardly fussed when they inserted the IV needle. (My heart ached for her.)

Where or how she may have contracted the infection was a mystery, but at least the conundrum of what was making her so ill was solved and the treatment was on track. The results of the cultures taken of the ruptured blisters showed the antibiotic that was initially ordered was the antibiotic of choice to treat the infection. So, no time was wasted in that respect. That made it a little less frightening, key word being *little*. I hoped the infection was not something I brought home from the hospital. After coming from work, I was careful and wouldn't let Natalee hug me until I changed out of my uniform and washed my hands. (Being a nurse, I am a germaphobe.) I had to keep reminding myself that kids can pick up germs just about anywhere and I was, in all probability, not responsible for how ill she was. At least I kept telling myself that to try and absolve the guilt I still felt. Even so, she was not completely out of the woods, but her prognosis was looking better and prayers were being answered. (But, we still needed ardent prayer for a full recovery.)

* * *

Excuse the interruption to the story, but I know you're wondering why we were staying at my mom's house. I was divorced from Natalee's father for two-and-a-half years at that time after only three years of being married. My second husband, David, and I had only been dating a few months when Natalee was admitted to the hospital. She had actually met David long before I did. He came to my parents' house one evening with my sister's boyfriend, whom he was friends with. I was at work. My mother was preparing to give Natalee a bath that Natalee didn't want. Before my mother could get her undressed, she escaped and ran downstairs and straight over to David yelling, "Open your legs, open your legs!" She then instructed him to close them tightly around her so she could tell my mother she was trapped and he wouldn't let her go! My parents were surprised she went to him because she was shy around men she didn't know. The only father figure and male in her life at the time was my dad. David came to my parents' house with my sister's boyfriend on several more occasions, but I was at work every time. (I worked all 3:00-11:00 p.m. shift.) My mother said Natalee was inexplicably drawn to him when he came to visit.

Might as well tell the rest of it….

One day my sister asked me to see whether any of the single nurses I worked with would go on a blind date with David. I half-heartedly asked a few girls, but because I didn't know what he looked like or anything about him, everyone I asked declined. (I guess they didn't get the total *blind* date concept!) My sister was disappointed when I told her, so I flippantly said, "If he doesn't mind an older girl, I'll go out with him!" (I'm three-and-a-half years older than he is.) I never gave it another thought until one evening the following week my sister and her boyfriend showed up unannounced at my house with David, and another girl. The next day my sister asked what I thought of him. I commented, "He's not so hot!" But, a girl can change her mind, and yes, he knows what I initially said. We laugh about it now. (At least I do!)

A few nights later, David unexpectantly showed up at my house; alone this time. Unfortunately I had company - a medical resident from the hospital who kept asking me out. I wasn't really interested in going on a date with him, or in dating anyone for that matter. Relenting, I had agreed to have him come to my house one evening, but only as a friend; no date, or at least not in my mind. (I thought maybe I could convince him to stop asking me to go out.) Natalee was upstairs tucked into bed, but it seems she was not yet asleep. She recognized David's voice when I answered the door and invited him inside. He didn't seem deterred that I had a male guest. (They eyed each other warily.) Natalee called for me, and when I went to see what she wanted, she asked if she could say "hi" to

David. Since my other visitor and I were in the living room, David went and sat on the top stair step so Natalee could say hello. (She had quite the imagination and pretended to cut his hair while they talked. He patiently pretended to be her client.)

The waiting game was now on. After a while, and with many glaring glances toward the stairs, my annoyed non-date decided to leave since David apparently wasn't leaving any time soon. (Talk about awkward!) After he left, Natalee went back to bed and David and I talked and found that we had a lot in common, especially music. I decided, if Natalee liked David, he must be okay. He asked me for an official date. I accepted, but with the stipulation he attend church with me on Sunday. He agreed. After I got to know David, the rest is history, especially since I vowed I'd never get married a second time. (Again, a girl can change her mind. Oh, and the resident never asked me for a date again.)

Natalee's biological father and I separated when she was eighteen months old and I divorced him when she was three. He initially moved to Pittsburgh, and to another state several years later. We had bought a house several months before we separated; getting it ready to move into when my world turned upside down. Only Natalee and I moved in, and I suddenly became a single parent with a mortgage. However, we had to stay with my parents on the days I worked. I didn't know how to drive, and even if I did, I no longer had access to a car. My dad was my chauffeur until I learned to drive and bought a used car. (It was also a big help that my parents cared for Natalee, and I didn't have to leave her with a babysitter.)

After David and I married in 1975, he moved into my house with Natalee and me. When she was five he legally adopted her. There was a period of adjustment for Natalee we had to consider before we initiated the process. When the time came for the adoption hearing, Natalee was so excited she could change her last name to David's. She even asked if she could change her middle name to his, but settled for just the last name. She was happy she could now call him her dad - the only dad she has ever known. He has been devoted ever since, going above and beyond for her in every way. When she was younger, many people who didn't know he was not her biological father would comment, "You look just like your dad!" They would both just smile back at them; their shared little secret.

We eventually lost all contact with my ex and he was not part of her life. There was nothing stopping him from contacting her, even after the adoption was complete, but he never did. (Maybe it was for the best at the time.) Serendipity, however, intervened many years later. When Natalee was in college she met a girl at a get-together at a friend's house, and after introducing themselves, Natalee found out her last name at birth was the same as her new acquaintance's. That led to their talking further, and both were stunned to learn they were first cousins. Word of the chance meeting, of course, got back to my ex who eventually contacted Natalee. I never talked about him when Natalee was growing up, but did answer her questions about him when she got older. He was remarried at the time he reconnected with her, and Natalee was surprised to find out she had a half-brother who was twenty-one years her junior.

All that, however, is in the past, and all is forgiven. No sense in keeping old wounds open and digging around in them. They have visited us when they returned to Johnstown to see Natalee, McKenna, and other relatives in the area. We all get along quite well. (People are stunned when they find that out.)

> Do not judge, and you will not be judged. Do not condemn, and you will not be condemned.
> Forgive, and you will be forgiven. (Luke 6:37 NIV) Be kind and compassionate to one another, forgiving each other, just as in Christ God forgave you. (Ephesians 4:32 NIV)

Sorry I digressed, but that part of Natalee's story is part of her history of healing, and badges of honor God has brought her (and me) through. Back to the hospital...

David was genuinely concerned while Natalee was in the hospital and helped care for her like she was truly his own child. The special bond they had developed touched my heart. He and I took turns staying with her day and night. David worked during the day, and came to the hospital after work so I could go home and rest. Not that I would call it much of a rest with my heart and mind still at the hospital, and a maelstrom of a thousand things racing interminably through my head, making it even more difficult to find sleep. (My mind felt like a hamster on an out-of-control wheel. It was a mentally and emotionally exhausting week.) At times like that, I like to picture laying my burdens at the feet of the cross. (The thing to remember after you lay them down is to leave them there.)

> Then Jesus said, "Come to me, all of you who are weary and carry heavy burdens, and I will give you rest." (Matthew 11:28 NLT)

Natalee was very frail and wasn't eating much, which was another concern. Her skin was raw and painful where the blisters ruptured, so even when I held her to try and comfort her, it was not very comforting at all, for either of us. When the nurses came in to give her the antibiotic injections in her thigh, she would pull up her hospital gown to expose her tiny leg for them without fussing or crying. The staff were astounded at what a brave little trooper she was, but Natalee understood the nurses were there to help her, even though they were giving her painful injections. As a nurse, I'd cringe when I'd hear some parents tell their children, "If you don't behave, I'll have the nurse come and give you a shot." That puts a picture in my head of scowling nurses with itchy plunger fingers, wearing holsters wielding giant syringes with ginormous, menacing needles! That's probably how those poor scared kids pictured all nurses; causing them to start screaming as soon as one darkened the doorway to their room! (Nothing like making a child afraid of the person trying to help them.)

Natalee's blistered skin eventually peeled off in sheets… even in her ears, between her fingers and toes, and her palms and soles of her feet. There were no Smartphones or Internet access back then to instantly look up medical information. Through our own supposition we found applying Vaseline to the peeling skin helped it denude more easily, with reduced redness underneath, and she seemed less uncomfortable when touched. In my mind, I still have a picture of a feeble little Natalee sitting in her hospital crib, peeling off some of the loose hanging skin. I feared she would have some scarring, but my fears were abated as the redness eventually went away and her skin healed normally. Many persistent prayers brought her through a scary time without any of the possible serious complications. That was the first stump-the-doctor episode and miracle number one on a long list stumping doctors (and others) and miracles God has blessed her with. (Thank goodness miracles are not one per customer. She would need quite a few more.)

Chapter 3

Never Make a Promise You Can't Keep!

Other than having periodic miserable ear infections, Natalee was a happy and healthy child with an active imagination. Sometimes overactive. Case in point: We had signed her up to join the cherub choir at church when she was four. (She could carry a tune extremely well for her age.) When I went to pick her up after the first practice, I didn't see her anywhere in the church basement among the other kids who were waiting to be picked up. I spotted the choir director coming from the sanctuary upstairs where they practiced. Catching her attention, I asked her if she knew where Natalee was. She looked puzzled and said the only little girl upstairs yet was a girl named Betty. I had a little bit of a panic at that point, but I somehow managed to calmly ask what "Betty" looked like. Yes, the description matched little "Miss Iva Imagination" at her best! Natalee had told the director her name was Betty! The director said she thought her name was Natalee, but that she had been insistent it was Betty. We laugh about it now, but it was not funny at the time. After a little discussion with Natalee, "Betty" was sent on a long vacation, never to return. (And now it's funny.)

The bothersome ear infections resolved once she had her tonsils and adenoids removed when she was eight. The ENT surgeon said her tonsils were enlarged, but he wanted to wait before he would remove them, but I nicely insisted it be done ASAP. Not that I wanted to have her undergo surgery, but I was concerned her hearing could be affected after a few more ear infections, and didn't see the point in having her suffer the discomfort.

So, he nicely agreed. (Truthfully, I suffered along with her when she had them, so I guess you could say I had an ulterior motive.)

Being an inquisitive child, during the initial office visit, Natalee had asked the doctor if she could see her tonsils after the surgery. He humored her with a smile and a promise she could. When it came time for the surgery, she didn't appear nervous about the surgery or the hospital stay. (She had the hospital-stay part down pat.)

The surgery went well, and when it was time for her to be discharged from the hospital, she said she wasn't leaving until she saw her tonsils! (After all, the doctor had promised.) I'm sure when he agreed she could see them he didn't think she would remember and hold him to it. Wrong! She never forgot a promise made to her. The staff were very accommodating, and after some phone calls were made to the lab, the tonsils - now ugly globs in a specimen container - made their debut. Unimpressed, but satisfied she got to see them, we left the hospital. She made no further mention of the tonsils. (Unbeknownst to us, that was the first of multifarious surgeries she would bravely face in her future.)

Chapter 4

A New Challenge…Stumping Mom

Fast forward to when Natalee was fourteen; the beginning of ninth grade. She began complaining of blurry vision and notable increased urinary frequency with urgency. It was easy to attribute the blurry vision to the fact that almost everyone in our family wears glasses. There were no clear symptoms of a urinary infection, but I noticed she was drinking more liquids than usual, so it seemed reasonable to me that maybe she needed to cut back and she wouldn't have to run to the bathroom so often. Then, right before my eyes, she suddenly lost seven pounds in one week. (I was astounded.)

Looking back, the realization of what was really causing those things she was experiencing only came to fruition for me at the end of that timeframe. One day she looked like her normal self; the next day I was stunned by her weight loss. It seemed surreal. How could I explain it away in a presumably healthy child whose eating habits hadn't changed? I couldn't. There is no history of diabetes in either my or her biological father's family, so the possibility of her having diabetes never entered my mind….. until the sudden weight loss occurred. That's when everything finally clicked in my apparently fogged-over brain and I clearly saw the puzzle pieces come together for the big picture to appear. In hindsight, all the symptoms were overtly there - blurry vision, increased thirst, urinary frequency and finally, the significant weight loss. This time the challenge was called "stump my mom." How had I missed it until now? After all, I was a nurse who, ironically, taught patients signs and symptoms of diabetes. I was fighting against waves of being deeply guilt-ridden that I hadn't put two and two together sooner so she wouldn't have had to get to the point of the weight loss and possible serious DKA complications.

There are several risk factors for developing diabetes. One constituent is an autoimmune response, which results when the body's system for fighting infection turns against a healthy part of the body. Earlier that year, Natalee had strep throat on two separate occasions, but close together. In her case, the insulin-producing beta cells in the pancreas, where the body's blood sugar level is regulated, were targeted and irreversibly damaged or destroyed.

In simple terms, when the body can no longer make insulin needed to help cells take in glucose from the bloodstream to burn for energy, the body resorts to burning fat for fuel, thus the weight loss. Without insulin acting as the key, the glucose can't get through the cell walls to be utilized. Thereby it stays in the bloodstream and causes fluid in the cells to be pulled out into the bloodstream and eventually filtered through the kidneys, causing the kidneys to work overtime. The unused glucose is excreted in the urine, and the process cycles back to cause dry mouth and excessive thirst. The high glucose levels cause the lens in the eye to swell, resulting in blurred vision. (It's amazing how one little abnormality occurring in the body, causing things to be out of normal balance, can lead to a chain reaction of much bigger problems.)

The date was November 3, 1985, a Sunday afternoon. One of those exact dates and times that become etched in your mind forever, as does the visual recollection of the event. I was working as a home care nurse at that time when everything suddenly registered in my brain and I finally grasped what was happening to Natalee. I was off that day and took her to my workplace office to test her blood sugar to confirm my suspicion using the glucose monitor we had there. Her blood glucose level was in the high 300s. (Normal fasting level is 70-100, and after a meal is <140.) I was shocked, worried, and relieved at the same time. Shocked that she had Juvenile diabetes. Worried because, as a nurse, I had seen the worst side of diabetes. Relieved that now it was confirmed and she could receive treatment before things became more serious. I called our PCP and relayed the result of the blood glucose reading I obtained. He immediately arranged for Natalee to be hospitalized as a direct admission. We left my office and went home to let David know my suspicion was validated before we took her to the hospital to begin treatment for a life-changing challenge….a new reality. (Praying God will get us through this new challenge.)

> Seek the Lord and his strength; seek his presence continually. (Psalm 105:4 ESV)

According to general statistics, there are around 15,000 children diagnosed every year with Juvenile diabetes (Type I) requiring them to take insulin because the pancreas no longer produces it. Simply put - no available insulin leads to hyperglycemia (high glucose levels in the blood) which, if not remedied, leads to diabetic ketoacidosis (DKA), which causes high levels of blood acids called ketones - a byproduct of the body burning fat for energy when it can no longer utilize glucose. DKA can lead to coma, and even death if not treated. Diabetes is a very complex disease. There are numerous related long-standing complications that can develop over time including neuropathy (nerve damage), cardiovascular and kidney disease, visual impairment, and foot problems to broadly name a few. Sad to say, but too many people don't take having diabetes seriously until an irreversible complication develops. (If I had a dollar for every patient I treated that said, "I wish I would have listened," I'd have a healthier bank account.) When Natalee became one of those statistics, the quality of her life, and even her life itself, like the 14,999 others, now depended on managing the diabetes and its complexities in earnest.

After Natalee was admitted and settled into her room, the doctor didn't waste any time. She was started on insulin and a diabetic diet. I think Natalee was relieved to know what was causing all her symptoms. She accepted her startling diagnosis and came to terms surprisingly well with the changes she would have to make in her diet and learning to give herself insulin. One thing she wasn't very happy about, though, was sticking her fingers several times a day to check her blood glucose levels, but she handled it with very little complaining. (She was always an adaptable kid.)

I think one of the reasons she adjusted so well was that her circle of friends were very supportive. It's hard enough to have a challenging disease and even harder to feel alone with it. One afternoon, one of her friends made sure she got home okay after Natalee had a low blood sugar episode while coming home on the bus after school. Symptoms include shakiness, sweating, confusion, mood swings, headache, and dizziness. If not treated by ingesting sugar or a simple carbohydrate and the level continues to drop, it can lead to seizures or passing out. I was glad Natalee recognized the symptoms early enough and relayed that information to her friend. Natalee carried candy or crackers with her for just such an occurrence and was able to ingest something and reverse the hypoglycemia. (If her level drops too low, she becomes confused as to what she needs to do.) Her friend got off the bus with Natalee, even though it was miles from her own stop, and stayed with her until I got home from work. (Natalee is fortunate to have friends from school and church youth group who have kept in touch with her over the years and have blessed her with their ongoing support.)

From the beginning, we made sure Natalee was learning and taking responsibility for managing her diabetes. David had to also learn to give the insulin and check her glucose level in the event she was unable and I wasn't available. He didn't want to learn at first, so I asked him if he would give her insulin if her life depended on it. He looked at me like I just asked him the dumbest question on earth, and then answered, "In that instance, of course." I told him that her life now depended on it - every day. He learned. All of the patients I gave injections to said I was good at giving them, so I was slightly insulted when Natalee announced she liked it better when David gave her the insulin, but her saying that bolstered his confidence. (I assuaged myself by believing that's why she said it.)

Speaking of responsibility and management, a few weeks after she was released from the hospital, I walked out on the front porch and found Natalee with a few of her friends. They were gathered around her, and I soon found out why. She was checking each of their blood sugar levels with her monitor. The strips she used to apply a drop of blood on and insert into the monitor to get a reading cost around $1.00 each at the time, so I had to close down her little impromptu "clinic" …..and save my wallet from developing cash anemia. (She apparently viewed testing her friends as community service.)

Funny side story: My uncle was in the hospital and his roommate was diabetic. There were no glucose monitors back then. He was given a small paper cup to put a urine sample in for dip-stick testing of his blood sugar level. When the nurse came in to get the sample, he picked up the cup and slugged back the contents saying, "Wait, I think I need to run that through again!" The nurse was horrified. He started laughing and admitted he put apple juice in the cup!

I soon found out it was a whole different ballgame teaching patients about diabetes management and diet as part of my job versus being a mom who had to devise a meal plan and prepare a diabetic diet on a daily basis. In the beginning we weighed and measured all her allowed portions. After a while it became second nature at home, but was always more challenging when we went out to eat.

When eating out, Natalee would give her pre-meal insulin to herself before getting out of the car to go into the restaurant. (No need to have people in the restaurant thinking she was some kind of addict if she injected it at the table, and doing it in the public restroom wasn't very appealing for obvious reasons.) Taking it too soon before she ate, though, could mean a low blood sugar episode if we had a long wait to be seated or her meal was delayed. She took a combination of short- and long-acting insulin. Short-acting insulin can start to lower blood sugar in thirty minutes. One evening, we arrived at a restaurant, and she gave herself insulin before we went inside only to find out there would be an hour wait to even be seated. We had to leave and find another place to eat, which ended up being a fast food place. (Lesson learned: when going to a restaurant, go in and check the wait time before taking insulin.)

Chapter 5

Managing the Disease Versus Being Managed By the Disease

I always reminded Natalee, "You manage the diabetes, don't let it manage you." In all the years she has been diabetic, Natalee has only ever been hospitalized one other time related to her diabetes. She had an episode of hyperglycemia that we couldn't resolve at home when her level climbed into the 600s. She began developing symptoms of DKA, and knowing that worse complications would soon follow if not quickly resolved, we went to the ER for a "bonding" time. She was admitted to ICU. They never did determine what exactly caused the spike; she didn't have an infection of any kind, which can cause an elevation, and was sticking to her diet. (As far as I knew.) I was just relieved she didn't develop more serious complications.

Cheerleading was one of her activities that required making some modifications so she could participate without having hypoglycemia episodes, which can occur with increased activity if not enough food is eaten to keep the glucose level up to normal. As her proud mom, I can brag that she was cheer Captain her senior year and they won the Pennsylvania State championship. (Bragging about your child's achievements is in the Mom's Handbook.) She never felt sorry for herself and never let her diabetes get in the way of what she wanted to do. So far, Natalee was taking charge and managing her diabetes. She identified with it being a part of her, but it was not her identity.

Chapter 6

When in Rome

For her high school graduation gift in 1989, Natalee wanted to go on a two-week tour of Europe with some other girls from school. Even though it was not a trip sponsored by the school, her French teacher agreed to chaperone, coordinated the travel plan, and took her own two children along. I was grateful she volunteered to accompany them because she was also a nurse; one of the reasons we decided to allow Natalee to go on the trip. (The teacher and her family were also trilingual, which was another bonus.)

Readying everything for the two weeks Natalee would be away took a lot of planning. We had to make sure she had enough insulin and monitor supplies to meet her needs, and also verified the locations of hospitals. (But prayed she wouldn't need to visit one.) We slowly adjusted the time of her insulin injections and meals so they would coincide with the time change she would encounter in Rome - six hours ahead of our Eastern Standard time. That way she would already be on her regular schedule when she arrived there, and the time transition would be easier with one less thing for her (and me) to be concerned about. (Prayer was going to get us both through her trip.)

Their itinerary began in Rome at the Vatican on a day that Pope John Paul II held mass. After the mass, her group was one of several factions asked to stay and be blessed by the Pope. Laughing, Natalee commented, "That was pretty good for a protestant girl, but I'll take all the blessings I can get!" (Natalee went to a private Catholic high school and was one of only a few non-Catholic students there.)

I was glad she didn't have any untoward diabetic issues the entire trip and was able to enjoy a wonderful time touring Italy, Switzerland, France and England. (The biggest problem she encountered was ice cubes were not to be found in water or soft drinks.) Looking back, I am glad she got the chance to travel to Europe. As her health issues escalated over the years, going on a trip like that wouldn't be prudent. David and I choose not to travel much either, so we can be available for her. We would be glad to sit through your vacation photos and videos and travel vicariously! We'll supply the popcorn. (And have ice for the soft drinks.)

Chapter 7

A Major, *Major* Change of Plans

In the fall of 1989 it was a leap of faith to allow Natalee to go to college in Erie; three-and-a-half hours from home. She was enrolled as a pre-dental major. In preparation for her college endeavor she had applied for school loans and a received a couple small scholarships. Due to having Juvenile diabetes, she was also eligible to receive some financial assistance through the Office of Vocational Rehabilitation. (Every little bit helped decrease the financial burden.)

While she was growing up, we tried to instill in Natalee that she needed to be *responsible* in all things. She said it was her least favorite word since we reminded her so often; referring to it as the "R" word. (We were evidently nagging positivity... or positively nagging... depending on who you asked.) Natalee had proven to us she was responsible, so we felt confident in letting her go so far away. It was time to let her fly the nest. (An exciting time for her at this stage of her life, but not so much for me.)

Natalee thought she would be taking her car to college with her. When she was a senior I had given her my 1984 Corolla, after I bought a new vehicle. She was to be responsible for the gas and her part of the insurance. The "R' word again. But being a typical teen, there were times she wasn't very responsible. One morning she informed me her car was out of gas and asked if I'd drive her to school. I told her that was what the school bus was for; I wasn't the one out of gas. (I'm calling it tough love.) Instead of taking the school bus, she called a friend for a ride! (New "R" word - resourceful!)

She was very unhappy when she returned from Europe and found we had sold her car; we didn't like the idea of her driving by herself to and from Erie. First, because of her health issues; secondly, she would be traveling alone. There were no cell phones at that time in case of a problem along miles of road with no frequent rest stops or readily available assistance. Also, driving there in winter was challenging in the snow and icy weather for even the most seasoned driver. It took David and me five nerve-wracking hours once in a major snowstorm to pick her up for winter break and five more to drive back home. I had wished winter had taken a break. (Not fun, unless you have sled dogs.)

After she experienced the first few weeks of brutal winter weather in Erie, I was surprised when she called and hesitantly asked me to send her some earmuffs and a scarf. During the winter, I wore earmuffs and a scarf. When we went shopping Natalee would walk several steps behind me and address me as "Mrs. Altemus." My attire embarrassed her - mostly because the fuzzy earmuffs and scarf were not fashion accessories then. She called my look "dorky." I told her looking dorky was better than being cold. Besides, I was married and the mom of a teenaged daughter. Who was I out to impress? (Natalee discovered looking dorky was definitely better than being cold. Chalk one up for mom!)

Before Natalee went away to college, she began having mild symptoms of diabetic gastroparesis (GP for short) and was experiencing occasional bouts of nausea and vomiting. GP is one of those insidious long-standing complications of diabetes and is a form of diabetic neuropathy (nerve damage) causing the stomach to have delayed emptying with resulting fullness, nausea, vomiting, abdominal pain, loss of appetite with possible associated malnutrition, uncontrolled blood sugar levels in diabetics, and abnormal bowel function. Oral anti-emetic medications she tried didn't quell the symptoms, however. Since I was an nurse, our PCP wrote a prescription for Tigan injections I could administer to her when she battled episodes. The injectable Tigan effectively helped relieve the nausea.

While at college, she let the nursing students in her dorm give her the Tigan when she needed it. She was unable to administer it to herself in her hip. The other option was giving it in her thigh, and she was definitely not a fan of that. (Much more painful.) The nursing students gained experience giving an injection, and she gained the benefit of feeling better. Natalee said she taught them a lot about diabetes and GP; things you can't get from a textbook. (I told her she was a living textbook and a lab guinea pig! Little did we know that "textbook" would add multiple chapters, and she would be a guinea pig many more times in the future.)

Because of her ongoing health issues, it was suggested to her by the vocational counselor that she change her major from dentistry due to the amount of schooling she would need to complete and the demands of the job itself. After considering the reality of her medical challenges, and after much discussion, she decided to switch to Early Childhood education and become a teacher - her fallback career choice. We had to trust God had another plan for her.

> The Lord says, "I will guide you along the best pathway for your life. I will advise you and watch over you." (Psalm 32:8 NLT)

Being a teacher seemed to be that plan. Growing up, Natalee was always playing school in her bedroom with her dolls and stuffed animals as her students. One time, "Miss Iva Imagination" came downstairs with her coat on, heading for the back door. I intercepted her and asked where she was going. Her very serious reply was she was taking her class outside for recess. (We always said she pretended for real.) I told her she would have to just "pretend to pretend" to be outside; it was freezing cold and snowing out more than a little! So, she settled for the dining room to be the playground. Looking back, changing her major was a good move in light of what the future held for her. (Besides, she could take her class out on the playground for real and use her imagination to do fun things.)

Was Natalee always the perfect daughter? **No**! She was a good kid who did the usual teenage things like staying out past curfew and dating some guys we weren't overly fond of at the time. Maybe there are some things she did we never knew about (and probably don't want to know), but all in all, she was finding her way to becoming a responsible and caring adult. Over the years, she made mistakes in her life - small and big; some of them painful lessons - but she learned from them. It's a part of life we can all identify with to some degree as we are finding our way. Proverbs 22:6 (NIV) says - "Start children off on the way they should go, and even when they are old they will not turn from it." Natalee may have strayed from the "way" at times, but she always returned. (We are proud of the person she has become in Christ Jesus.)

Chapter 8

Memo: Don't Drink the Water

A month after graduating from college, Natalee and a friend went to Erie to visit friends for a weekend in June. A few weeks later, I noticed the whites of her eyes looked jaundiced. Now what? It was determined she had hepatitis. What I feared. The stump-the-doctor challenge was now finding out exactly what type. After testing negative for types A, B, C, and D, she was finally diagnosed with Hepatitis E, which is rare in the U.S. (Of course, if anyone could contract that type it would be Natalee.) It's acquired through ingesting contaminated food or water. Natalee obviously didn't get the memo a contaminated water alert was in effect while when she was there. She spent a few days in the hospital and the rest of the summer at home recovering.

Natalee had been hired full-time that summer as a "popsicle packer" at the local dairy processing plant, but after being diagnosed with hepatitis, she had to give up her job. A few months later, fully recovered, she applied and was hired full-time at a preschool. The start of her teaching career. (Little did we know how short-lived a career it would be.)

Chapter 9

And Two Shall Become One

Jumping ahead to January 21, 1995 - Natalee got married. She and Jimmy knew each other most of their lives. He only lived a couple blocks away. They began dating in 1990 and became engaged in 1991. Before they got engaged, she made Jimmy ask David for her hand in marriage. (Of course, simply for his own amusement, David gave him a hard time.)

By this time, her GP had contributed to her being a "brittle" diabetic, making it hard to control the high and low swings. David and I had a serious conversation with Jimmy about Natalee's health issues when they got engaged and discussed how it could affect her, and their, future. Dating someone with chronic health concerns is a far cry different than living with someone with multiple ongoing health issues. (So he eventually found out.)

Natalee was working at a Montessori school, teaching three and four year olds - who could impressively read and do math. (I could probably count to ten and say my ABCs at that age....no longer impressive.) She loved teaching, loved the children in her class, and wanted to have a child of her own one day. She had been advised by her doctor, however, that getting pregnant could pose a significant risk for her. At church one Sunday morning that October, Natalee surprised us and revealed she was expecting. Her due date was Memorial Day! We were overjoyed, but at the same time concerned for her due to her increasing health issues. (Sad to say, the warnings were predictive, and all too soon we would begin her ongoing association with doctors and hospitals in Pittsburgh.)

Chapter 10

Surprises All Around!

On the morning of April 2, 1996, Natalee had an appointment to see her OB-GYN. She was seven months pregnant and hadn't been feeling well for the past week. It was always difficult to tell if her symptoms were from her GP acting up, the pregnancy, a combination, or if it was something else entirely. It was determined to be the something else - her blood pressure reading was too high, and she had some fluid retention. Jimmy had accompanied her because they had plans for her birthday after the appointment, but there would be no celebration as planned. The doctor sent her from her appointment straight to the hospital to be admitted.

It wasn't until the next morning that she was diagnosed with toxemia, also known as preeclampsia. Without question something consequential. If not treated, preeclampsia can lead to serious complications and even be fatal for the mom and baby. The only "cure" for preeclampsia is delivering the baby. Being diabetic compounded things for Natalee, the antithesis of the news we wanted to hear. (Time for prayers.)

Natalee remained in the hospital several days with no changes. Knowing her OB-GYN doctor always made early rounds, I went to visit Natalee before I went to work on the morning of the fifth, hoping to be able to talk with him. I was concerned she wasn't feeling any better and felt transferring her to Magee Hospital in Pittsburgh, where they could better manage a high risk pregnancy, was in order. After voicing my concerns, I was relieved when the doctor said he had already considered it and would make arrangements. She met the criteria warranting transferring her there due to the preeclampsia, the fact she wasn't due for two more months, and she was a Juvenile diabetic. So, I called off work, went home, rounded up the troops, and got ready for what was an uncomfortable two-hour ride with her via ambulance to Pittsburgh. (Usually, no "civilians" were allowed to ride along, but since I am a nurse, they let me ride with her. David, Jimmy, and Jimmy's mother followed motorcade-style in the comfort of our car.)

On arrival to Magee, Natalee was admitted to the ICU labor and delivery unit. The nurses there were assigned one-on-one, and her nurse was always in the room, which was very reassuring. Jimmy was permitted in the room, and they allowed me to also stay after I played the "I'm an RN" card. (Hey, whatever works!) Initially, they were just closely monitoring her blood pressure, blood sugar levels, and any other problems. The plan was to induce her in the morning - barring any urgent complications.

David, Jimmy and Jimmy's mom went back home for the night since Natalee wasn't in labor, and in good hands with her blood pressure and blood sugars currently under control. I was elected to stay with her, and they planned to return in the morning. They felt, since I was a nurse, I would understand more of what was going on. Lucky me. I had to sleep in a semi-sitting position in a ubiquitous uncomfortable visitor chair. The staff at least offered me a pillow and blanket. I was only able to sleep a few hours cobbled together in restless bouts. (The nurse card doesn't always work in my favor.)

Natalee had a fetal heart monitor encircling her very roly-poly abdomen, and we were able to hear the baby's heartbeat when things were quiet. The nurse in me, who never worked in OB, grew concerned at one point when I became cognizant of pauses in the rhythmic heartbeat. I was reassured by the nurses that pauses happened when the baby hiccuped! It was a long night, but the staff were very friendly and duly competent; making us both a little less anxious by checking on Natalee frequently. At one point, a very affable anesthesiologist came to insert an epidural line for pain management, so Natalee would be more comfortable when labor started. After she completed the procedure, she decided to sit and chat with me. (I guess she didn't realize I wasn't working the night shift, too.) Even though I was really tired, I did enjoy talking with her. It made the night go by faster. (The rush of adrenaline from the next day's events would keep me wide awake!)

The next morning was "D" day - "D" for Delivery. Natalee was induced with an IV-administered medication called Pitocin, which is a synthetic form of the hormone produced naturally in the body to trigger spontaneous labor. It was the day before Easter - cold and lightly snowing outside in the morning with intermittent sunshine later on. Natalee was not concerned with the weather, though, as active labor began. Due to the excess fluid from being preeclamptic, she was ordered a Swan-Ganz catheter to monitor for heart failure. (The catheter is inserted though the right jugular vein to the right side of the heart and progresses with the natural flow of blood into the pulmonary artery leading to the lungs.) To complete the conglomeration of medical paraphernalia, she also had two peripheral IV lines, one in each arm. I'm sure she felt like a human pin cushion. (Or a marionette!) Each line was connected to an amalgam of monitoring and delivery devices mounted on multiple IV poles standing like sentrys beside the hospital bed, each steadily humming away with lights winking, and Natalee safely positioned in the midst of them. As a nurse, I was used to seeing people with tubes everywhere and hearing machines making a cacophony of sounds, but when Jimmy arrived, he was taken aback for a minute when he entered the room and saw Natalee in the center of the morass of tubes and equipment, along with a bevy of doctors and nurses. The look on his now pale face conveyed pure shock, and in spite of the fact his body language imparted run away to anywhere but here, he hesitantly entered and found a place at the bedside to be the caring husband and expectant father.

This was one time humor didn't take Natalee's mind off things. She didn't like my idea of naming a boy Peter Robert, and a girl, Esther Bonnie. (It was Easter weekend after all.) Looking over at me, her face conveyed what she thought of that idea - *Really?* Then she concisely stated, "Not. Funny. Mom!" A moment of laughter in tense times can keep you from going crazy, but I surmised forthwith that being attached to multiple tubes, machines beeping all around you, and the pain of being in active labor pushed her past the limit where laughter was possible. I quickly made a note to self....do not deliver any further humorous thoughts out loud. (Pun intended.)

We were told the baby was presenting face first, making labor and delivery more difficult; adding another dilemma to the situation. The longer Natalee was in labor, the greater the risk and distress on the baby and her. After seven long hours of labor, her blood pressure and blood sugar levels were rising. On top of that, she was just plain exhausted. The doctor decided she was not going to be able to deliver normally without further undue stress and increased risk for both of them, so an emergency C-section was decidedly the only option to ameliorate the deteriorating situation. A very anxious Jimmy was allowed to go to the OR with her. I saw a hint of trepidation on his face, but he bravely followed as Natalee was whisked away. (Being a nurse did not get me access this time, however.)

David, myself and Jimmy's mom gathered in the waiting area and expectantly waited for news (pun intended), knowing Natalee and the baby were in good hands with the doctors and our prayers.

Take-out menus were available at the information desk, and since we hadn't eaten lunch, we ordered a pizza for delivery (no pun intended) so we didn't have to leave the waiting room. The only labor involved was dialing the phone! (Sorry, pun intended.) After what seemed like an interminably long time, Jimmy came down the hall looking relieved and declared, "It's a girl!" He assured us Natalee and the baby were both stable. They hadn't known beforehand if the baby was a boy or girl as none of the prior ultrasounds were able to confirm it either way. She had an ultrasound on arrival at Magee, and the tech told her it looked like a girl, but just in case the tech was wrong, Natalee didn't tell any of us. We only got a brief glimpse of the new arrival as they wheeled her incubator to the NICU. She was perfect and beautiful! They named her McKenna Berlyn Smouse. Instead of our "Memorable Memorial Day Baby," she was our "Memorable Early Easter Surprise." (My dad had difficulty remembering McKenna's middle name, so my mother tried giving him a hint - "a city in Europe." Certain he had it correct, he confidently replied, "Paris!")

Unbeknownst to us, things had gone further downhill with Natalee's vital signs during the C-section; enough that Jimmy was asked to sign papers stating who to save, mom or baby, if it got to that point. I can't imagine being there, witnessing what was happening and having to make that immediate heart-wrenching decision while in a heightened emotional state. (Now I'm glad I wasn't permitted in the OR.) We could have lost one or both of them, but God had other plans.

Even though McKenna made her debut two months prematurely, she weighed seven pounds! High birth weight babies are common in mothers with diabetes. If the diabetes is not well controlled, the fetus is exposed to high glucose levels. The baby responds by secreting higher amounts of insulin, which causes an increase in tissue and fat deposits, making the baby's weight higher than normal. (I couldn't imagine how much she would have weighed if she were a full term baby.)

The next morning, Easter Sunday, when David and I returned to the hospital to see Natalee in ICU, the same nurse was there from the day before and granted us special permission and ID bands to go into the NICU to see McKenna. We were elated since only fathers were allowed and given ID bands. (I was later told permission was only granted for us to see McKenna because - you guessed it - I'm a nurse.)

After a week, Natalee and McKenna were discharged and rode home together via ambulance. Natalee returned to her house, but McKenna was transferred to our local NICU because she was two months early and she needed bili light phototherapy to treat the jaundice she developed, which usually disappears in days to a few weeks. We were all feeling sad not being able to bring McKenna home to her almost finished nursery, but at least she was in the local NICU and we could visit her there.

After making numerous trips to Pittsburgh, working full-time, and visiting the local NICU in the evenings once Natalee and McKenna returned to Johnstown, David and I were only in our house long enough to eat and sleep. On top of that, we now had to rush to ready the nursery for McKenna since her early arrival caught us off guard. We were in a serious time crunch in our limited spare time. David was doing the construction work, and I was doing the decorating as a gift. After three weeks of this schedule, our spoiled, four-pound, black poodle, Balki, was not acting like his usual adorable self; requiring a trip to the vet to make sure he wasn't sick. We were surprised when the vet said he was just neurotic due to us not being home very much. Poor little guy was as glad as we were when our schedules returned to normal. He got back to being adorable once he no longer felt abandoned. (Where's a doggie psychiatrist when you need one?)

McKenna's early arrival foiled one surprise and led to another one.

Invitations had already been sent out at the end of March for a surprise baby shower on April 21, however, we had to tell Natalee about the shower so she could prepare to attend. She was still struggling with some lingering fluid retention and decreased energy. Jimmy brought her to the shower after everyone was there already so she wouldn't have to be there any longer than necessary and get overly tired. She was upset that she couldn't fit into her regular clothes and had to wear maternity clothes and an old pair of unlaced sneakers. Her feet were still too swollen to fit in her shoes. McKenna was still in the NICU, and many of the people who came to the shower weren't aware Natalee had delivered McKenna already. The shower was still a surprise of sorts - on some of the guests! (We proudly displayed pictures of McKenna on the cake table so everyone could see our precious little miracle.)

McKenna continued doing well and was discharged home after two weeks in the local NICU. By that time Natalee was feeling stronger and able to care for her without too much help. David and I also crossed the finish line in record time, and the nursery was ready and waiting for her. More miracles and answered prayers! (Time for a long nap!)

Chapter 11

An Eye for an Eye

Diabetic retinopathy causes leakage of the small blood vessels in the retina, located in the back of the eye, and can lead to distorted vision and blindness in advanced stages. Natalee was diagnosed with it in 1997 when she saw her ophthalmologist after "floaters" appeared in her vision. He told us that she needed to have laser surgery to hopefully remedy the problem, but that she had a 50/50 chance of losing her vision. Not the best odds, but not the worst either. Natalee, per her usual, took it all in stride and was holding on to faith that everything would be okay. (As an added measure, I had people from nine different churches praying for her.)

> Now faith is the substance of things hoped for, the evidence of things not seen. (Hebrews 11:1 KJV)

Her ophthalmologist referred her to another ophthalmologist from Pittsburgh for the surgery. He came to see patients on scheduled days at an office in Johnstown, which was equipped to perform the laser surgery. I was very glad we were spared traveling to Pittsburgh for an office visit and surgery. Natalee was instructed to be there at 8:00 a.m. the day of the surgery. On arrival, she was handed the usual registration and pre-surgery forms to fill out. When those were completed, a tech took her to a room that had a special camera that took pictures of the inside and back of the eye. I was allowed in the room with her, and it was very interesting to see the pictures displayed on a big screen. When that was completed, we were sent back to the waiting room that was gradually filling up with more patients. More time went by, and I was wondering when she, or anyone else for that matter, would be called to see the doctor. (At least the waiting room chairs were a little more comfortable than the usual ones.)

It would have been nice to be forewarned that we would be there half the day. Since no one told us we would be there that long, we had taken McKenna with us. I was glad we took her infant safety seat in with us so we didn't have to hold her the whole time. It was a good thing she was a pleasant baby, not only for our sake, but for others in the waiting room, too. (Babies are like fish in an aquarium, people like to watch them. Mostly the pleasant ones.)

The doctor and his nurse had driven in from Pittsburgh, arriving at 11:00 a.m., and immediately readied for surgery. I was thankful Natalee was the first one to be called. I was permitted to be in the room while they did the procedure. First, the doctor put drops in her left eye to dilate her pupil. That was the easy part. Next part, not so much. In my mind I can still see her standing against the wall…yes, standing with the back of her head against the wall while he numbed her eye. I don't know how she tolerated having a big needle (at least it looked *really* big to me) stuck into her eye socket to inject the medication, or why she didn't pass out. I still cringe when I think about it! (Gives me shivers up my spine, too!) I could see how uncomfortable she was. I was uncomfortable just watching!

Next, she was seated in front of the laser machine in an upright position with her elbows resting on a table with attached hand grips she could hold to help steady herself. Instructions were given for her to sit perfectly still during the procedure. No problem. (I would have been frozen in place with fear!) She placed her chin and forehead on a support like you do for a regular eye exam, and the nurse who assisted the doctor helped steady her head from behind. I couldn't see what device was used to hold her eye open and was just as glad I wasn't able to see it. (I don't like anything to do with eyes. When I get something in my eye, well, let's just say the world is ending!)

Funny side story: When I was working on a med-surg unit in the hospital, we had an elderly confused patient who had an artificial eye. One evening, as we were readying him for the night, we noticed his artificial eye was missing. The frantic search around his bed and in the garbage can began, ending with no luck. Returning to finishing his evening care, as we started to turn him in the bed to freshen the sheets, to our relief (and amusement) there was his artificial eye….stuck between his shoulder blades staring back at us! Now the problem was which of us was going to put it back in its proper place. (I can tell you it wasn't me!)

Back to Natalee's eye surgery…

At one point during the surgery the doctor noticed Natalee was beginning to feel some discomfort by the way she was squeezing the life out of the hand grips. I also noticed and was feeling her pain. He asked if she wanted another injection. Her response was an emphatic, "NO, thank you!" I really don't know how she tolerated the pain, but she did. For her, having another tortuous injection was worse than the laser procedure, and she just wanted to get the surgery over with as quickly as possible. She persevered through the rest of the surgery somehow, knowing she would have to go through it again on her right eye in six weeks. (She earned a Badge of Honor for bravery for enduring the pain all the way to the end of the procedure.)

The second laser surgery evoked less anxiety for her, mainly because she knew what to expect, even though she wasn't looking forward to it….. especially the big needle in the eye part. (We were also prepared for the long wait this time.)

Her local ophthalmologist saw her every six months afterward for several years and was amazed there was no visible scar tissue from the surgery. The only ongoing residuals Natalee has after both surgeries are poor low-light and night vision. (We attributed the positive outcome to all those prayers. More miracles!)

Five years after the surgeries, it was discovered she had a small clot on her left retina, called a retinol vascular occlusion. The clot causes a small blind spot in the center of her visual field if she is only looking with her left eye; right eye closed. It has not gotten any worse over the years. There is no treatment that can reverse the blockage other than treating the underlying risk factors and to detect and treat any complications which, in her case, would be related to her diabetes and high blood pressure. (The best treatment of all is, of course, prayer!)

Chapter 12

The Invisible Monster

In the midst of being a new mom, and dealing with her daily diabetes and increasing GP struggles, she had started and was the director of a daycare/preschool at our church Monday through Friday. Natalee also signed on to coach cheerleading at one of the local high schools. She didn't let GP and diabetes incapacitate her ambition and goals in life.

By late 1999 into early 2000, however, her GP had exacerbated exponentially and began interfering with everyday life. (A daily juggling act....and most times a struggling act.) Around that time, the church decided they no longer wanted a preschool in their building, so it was closed. Disappointed, but not to be deterred, she took a position teaching at another preschool. As her GP continued to progress, there were many mornings severe symptoms caused her to be late for work. Sometimes she still managed to go to work, but her symptoms escalated as the day went on and were acute enough she was unable to finish her work day. At those times, she was too ill to even drive herself home, so two of us would have to leave work to bring Natalee and her car home. She continued trying to work in spite of not feeling well in some capacity most days, always pushing her limit. By June of 2000, when she couldn't keep a dependable schedule and was missing too much work, she accepted she had to resign from her job. Things worked out, however, in her favor for the time being. Since enrollment was currently down, the director laid Natalee off, so she was able to collect unemployment rather than quit her job. That in itself took away some of the stress she was feeling. Now she just had to be patient and "wait and see" what was going to happen next.

> Wait for the Lord; be strong, and let your heart take courage; wait for the Lord! (Psalm 27:14 ESV)

Patience is the ability to accept trouble or suffering without getting upset. It's difficult to be content in undesirable and uncertain circumstances. Fear is one of the devil's tools he uses against us, but God works things out for our good when we trust Him. It's hard to let God be in control when in our own flesh we think we have a better plan. We want answers right now for that plan to come to fruition and to make everything okay in short order, but we had to be patient and wait to see what His plan was for her as she went forward. (Now was the time for a leap of faith and trust.)

> When anxiety was great within me, your consolation brought me joy. (Psalm 94:19 NIV)
> The heart of a man plans his way, but the Lord establishes his steps. (Proverbs 16:9 ESV)
> Submit yourselves therefore to God. Resist the devil and he will flee from you. (James 4:7 KJV)

Natalee's medication cupboard was replete with just about every available prescription medication on the market to aid stomach motility, but none of them were effective in controlling her GP episodes. There was increasing disappointment with every new drug she tried, and the options were running out. We researched motility drugs online; enticed by one that looked very promising - unfortunately it was only available for use in Canada and Europe and not yet approved in the U.S. We mentioned it during a visit to her gastroenterologist, and he agreed it was worth pursuing. With the doctor's help we were able to get it from Canada via mail order. After everything we learned about it, we were very hopeful it was *the* magic pill. This medication was her last available hope. We were elated the day it arrived. Albeit, it, too, was ineffective. (Talk about feeling like a deflated balloon; but we were grateful she at least had the chance to try it.)

Natalee was also prescribed various oral anti-emetic meds, but only a few were remotely successful in lessening the frequency of the nausea and vomiting while the ongoing delayed stomach emptying wreaked havoc with her blood glucose control. She had constant fatigue from lack of proper rest when the GP symptoms kept her up at night and persisted throughout the day, only allowing cat naps. The struggle with episodes of extreme blood sugar fluctuations also took a toll on her. Her food tolerance was limited, thereby putting her nutritional status in jeopardy. She began losing weight she couldn't afford to lose. (I think about how hard it must be to wake up everyday and not feel well. Depressing in every sense of the word, making it easy to fall into despair.) We were all hanging on to faith and trusting in His plan, but being patient was proving to be more and more difficult.

Even with good management, for some people, diabetes and the myriad of possible complications related to it can be a life-altering, life-threatening, life-cheating monster that never lets you forget it can have control over you instead of you having control over it. Monster GP was virtually running her life at this point with adversarial uncontrolled diabetes contending to be a close second. Her day was at their mercy. It was difficult to watch Natalee go from someone active and vibrantly full of life, to never feeling well; spending many days lying on the couch being miserable while caring for McKenna and her home the best she could. We tried not to think about the growing elephant in the room - the worst that could happen if her GP progressed. Complications are esophageal hemorrhage, poor nutritional status eventually requiring tube feedings, increased food intolerances, and intestinal obstruction. For Natalee, the associated difficulty controlling her blood sugars was the most frustrating aftermath. The hardest part was realizing and accepting she may not ever live a "normal" life and have a decreased quality of life with a shorter life expectancy. We didn't really talk about the elephant taking up residence in the corner of the room, but recognized it as a reality. Dwelling on it wouldn't change anything. (One of the people I loved most in this world was miserable and only prayer could make any difference.)

One day, Natalee and I had planned to go shopping, *if* she felt well enough. I arrived at her house to pick her up and let myself in when she didn't answer my knock on the door. I called out to let her know I was there. She answered back that she was upstairs, but didn't sound quite like herself. Concerned, I went upstairs to see if she was okay. Through the open bathroom door I saw she was down on her hands and knees throwing up into a small garbage can that was in front of her. She held up her index finger and calmly said, "I'll be with you in a minute!" When she was finished, she brushed her teeth, changed the garbage can bag, and we went shopping! That was her reality, but she never complained. (Her resilience and strength to not let GP win the battle was inspiring.)

> God is our refuge and strength, an ever-present help in trouble. (Psalm 46:1 NIV)

I must admit I am the antithesis of Natalee. When I am sick for five minutes, I am ready to die. (Okay, maybe longer than five minutes. Six, maybe.) In that situation, I have to remind myself Natalee doesn't feel well a majority of the time, and what I may have to endure lasts a modicum of time in comparison. Then I feel guilty for being such a baby. Inspiration develops when I think of her, and I steel myself to hang in there because she does it every day.

Natalee repudiated the idea of an insulin pump to help with diabetes management for many years, but relented when GP made control more difficult. She finally accepted it was something that could help regulate her levels better than insulin injections. Her PCP initiated the paperwork necessary to make sure she was a candidate for a pump, but it had be approved by her insurance. (Next we did what we do best - we waited.)

When the long-awaited pump arrived, Natalee went to a class to learn how to program it. There was a learning curve for calculating carbohydrates she ingested so she could cover them with the appropriate amount of insulin, but she is a quick study and was soon an expert at it. She still had occasional high and low swings due to her GP, but was better able to manage them with the pump, which gave her a continuous basal rate of insulin - much better than taking intermittent injections during the day. She only had to bolus insulin when she was able to eat or needed to correct a high reading. After having the pump for a while, she wished she had gotten a pump sooner! (Hindsight is 20/20.)

During those same years, she had three benign outpatient breast lumpectomies. Just a blip in the overall big picture. There was another elephant lurking, however, that needed to be faced. This one was too impending not to acknowledge.

Chapter 13

Disqualifying Deprivation

While laid off from work, Natalee had to face the undeniable elephant in the now crowded room - that she may possibly never be able to go back to work again if her GP remained uncontrolled and continued to worsen. On her own, she applied for temporary disability, but was denied. (No surprise there.) She didn't meet the criteria for eligibility without presenting her case. The next step was to hire an attorney. The process was long and required her to see numerous doctors who evaluate people with disability claims and determine, after only one short office visit, if they are eligible. The doctors indubitably know nothing about the people applying except what they may have read in a report sent to them ahead of an appointment. (At least that's how it appeared to us as she went through the process.)

One of the doctors Natalee was sent to see asked her why she was there to see him on the day of the appointment. (Hmmm) It gave Natalee the impression he never read any of her medical records or reports sent to him beforehand to even know why she was there. She explained how her health issues and GP symptoms were affecting her life and why she was applying for temporary disability. After the physical exam, he assured her he would "give her a good report."

The psychologist she was sent to see had a sparsely furnished, but otherwise cluttered office, and no office staff. Natalee felt a little uncomfortable being there alone with him. She said he asked her some very bizarre questions, and as part of the exam, he asked her to mail two letters in the postal boxes outside of his office building - an in-town and out-of-town letter - to see if she knew which mailbox to put them in! He watched her mail them from his second floor window. Natalee said the whole appointment was a ten on the creepy meter and very weird. She thought maybe *he* needed to see a psychologist or psychiatrist! Maybe he just needed letters mailed and didn't want to leave his office. (We'll never know.)

At last, she was scheduled for the disability hearing in March of 2001. I was requested to write down my observations of Natalee's disabling issues to be presented by the attorney at the hearing. It was an emotional exercise. I was caught off guard when instead, I was requested to read it outloud to the judge. Another emotional exercise. (It was a draining and heartrending day.)

At first, I got the impression the judge didn't really believe how ill Natalee was, and I was worried. The judge was seeing her for the first time, and was the arbiter of this life-changing decision outside of our control. He was very matter-of-fact as he literally barked a succession of questions at her. Never smiling once, he was intimidating to say the least, adding to the stress of the day. (He was definitely no Judge Judy. At least she's entertaining.) It was obvious, though, that he had read her medical records and considered the recommendations from the "disability docs" she was sent to see. All but the one we found to be reprehensible from "Dr. Good Report." Natalee's attorney asked to have his "good report" disregarded because he wrote "in his opinion" Natalee didn't have GP! (Even though Natalee had testing to prove she did.) His "opinion" was thankfully discounted.

A vocational counselor was present during the proceedings, and after all the testimony was given and the reports were reviewed, she was asked to render her thoughts. She told the judge, in light of the findings, she felt Natalee was unable to hold *any* job and recommended the disability be granted. The judge stated, even though she only applied for temporary disability, he felt she was too ill to go back to work and adjudged permanent disability. (That was a big surprise, and relief.) Some people would have been overjoyed at having permanent disability granted, but Natalee instantly burst into tears. The realization she was probably never going to be able to work again at a job she loved became a truth she had to face. A heavy veil of loss was present in the room. Sitting in that stark courtroom, my heart ached for her and the seeming finality of the changes in her life plan, but there was no point in obsessing about an unsure future she couldn't control, it was in God's hands. (One less elephant in the room, at least for the moment.)

It was shocking when word got back to us that a few people had made the comment Natalee was "just a freeloader on society" when they found out she was on disability. They, of course, never saw her when she was having severe GP episodes, or struggling to get her blood sugars back to normal levels and coping with the after effects. They didn't witness the sleepless nights. They didn't know there were days she couldn't keep any food down. They didn't have to live on a shoestring income, struggling to pay bills. That was her reality, but she didn't complain or let others know the extent of her struggles. She suffered in silence. Only leaving home when she felt "well" (a relative term we use), so others only saw her on her "good" days. (Another relative term we use along with "normal.") She would have gladly traded them places and gone back to work in a heartbeat.

It was a seriously discouraging time for her. I could see her teetering on the slippery slope of the precipice of depression and prayed she wouldn't slide off into the darkness of despair. All I could do was helplessly watch as she grappled with the changes in her life, and pray. All of this was taking a toll. Divorce became inevitable after seven years of marriage. (Jimmy and Natalee did remain friends, however.) She and McKenna continued living in their house and he went back to living with his parents. Natalee focused on being a mom and trying to live a normal-for-her life on the days she wasn't feeling too ill to do much of anything. Little did we know that additional serious medical issues would complicate and jeopardize her health and future even more with a literal circus full of unanticipated elephants waiting in the wings of the Cirque du Natalee's Challenges. (I'm glad we're not prescient because dealing with the present is tough enough at times without stressing about unforeseeable and unwelcome future events.)

> When times are good, be happy; but when times are bad, consider this: God has made the one as well as the other. Therefore, no one can discover anything about their future. (Ecclesiates 7:14 NIV)

Chapter 14

More Monsters and Elephants, Oh, My!

The possibility of Natalee having kidney failure as a complication of diabetes was one of those elephants in the room you know could be a future problem but choose to ignore it for the moment; hoping it doesn't create a problem one day. When that elephant decided to suddenly come to the forefront of Natalee's life, we found ourselves on a whole new journey. Not only would Natalee be dealing with the challenge of impending kidney failure, but facing future dialysis or the possibility of a transplant.

We never expected kidney failure would complicate Natalee's life in her early thirties, and progress so rapidly. In my mind, even the possibility was years away. Little did we know at the time, two of the medications she had been prescribed - one for the joint pain due to tenosynovitis, and a newer motility drug she tried - caused her kidney function to deteriorate. (Both medications are now off the market, but sadly for Natalee, not soon enough.)

Natalee developed puzzling intermittent generalized swelling in early summer of 2004. One day, an increase in the swelling was making her especially uncomfortable. She assumed the high heat and humidity that day was a contributing factor, but when it hadn't subsided by the next morning she knew it was time to go to the ER. (It seems things of an emergency nature with Natalee always seem to happen on a weekend.) The results of the blood work the doctor ordered showed Natalee's kidney function was abnormal. An unexpected shock, and not a good sign. He was very concerned and suggested she make an appointment with a nephrologist ASAP. (It was time to confront the elephant that we didn't want to acknowledge so soon.)

We soon learned the nephrologist we chose was the right doctor she needed at the time. (God definitely led us to him.) Showing great empathy toward Natalee, he took a special interest in her case. In September, he suggested we look into a living kidney donor program since her GFR had alarmingly declined from 48% to 32%. (GFR measures the Glomerular Filtration Rate or how much blood passes through the tiny filters in the kidney each minute to filter waste.) We had naively thought we had sufficient time to explore living donation, but we were clearly wrong. (Without a doubt, time was not on her side now.....but God was.)

...This I know: God is on my side! (Psalm 56:9 NLT)

In November, we were dealt a bombshell when blood test results showed her kidney function had acutely decreased to below 9%. The failure was irrevocable. End-stage renal disease (ESRD) had taken a fervent firm hold. Natalee was told she needed to find a living donor in the next few months. The only other option was dialysis, but the nephrologist said it would be better if she found a donor before dialysis was necessary. Life expectancy for diabetics on dialysis is half that of non-diabetics on dialysis. Statistically less than 25% of diabetics on dialysis live more than ten years, and death is mostly attributed to an acute cardiac event. On hearing the surreal news, overwhelming silence filled the room and time seemed to stand still. (Natalee cried for two days afterward. I knew, without question, what I needed and wanted to do.)

We were told there are reportedly, on average, over 100,000 people on just the kidney transplant waiting list with more than 15,000 kidney transplants performed each year. If you do the math, that leaves a boat load of people drifting in an endless sea of dialysis, hoping for a transplant lifeline. Wait time for a cadaveric organ is three to five years and up to ten years for some who are a hard match for various reasons. Success rate is higher if the kidney comes from a living donor. (More sobering information for us to digest.)

The harsh actuality of what she was facing was very real to me as a home care nurse who took care of people in that exact position. Too many times I had witnessed firsthand some of them succumb to the disease. Having memories of how they struggled is difficult to deal with when you have a child that could be facing the same outcome. The statistical elephant was now a reality and firmly rooted. Natalee was not oblivious to it, but she preferred not to feed it with worry. None of us did. Instead, after a few days of self-pitying depression, and after contemplating her situation, she rallied and elected to live life one day at a time, trusting God, and not stressing about what may happen tomorrow. (We had a mission to complete with God's help.)

> May the God of hope fill you with all joy and peace as you trust in him, so that you may overflow with hope by the power of the Holy Spirit. (Romans 15:13 NIV) The Lord delights in those who fear Him, who put their hope in his unfailing love. (Psalm 147:11 NIV)

At the time, we only knew a little about kidney transplant. As we navigated our way through the process, we learned there are more transplant stories than most realize. Most interestingly, we discovered many people have no idea where transplants are performed, the process involved, or what organs and tissues are even able to be transplanted. Statistically, kidneys are the most transplanted organ. Other much needed organs for transplant are liver, lung, pancreas, intestines, lung, and heart. On average there are around 120,000 on the waiting list for an organ and sadly more than twenty of those waiting die each day. One donor can save eight lives and also improve the lives of up to fifty others through tissue and eye donation. The number of those needing a transplant grows daily and the name of a hopeful person is said to be added to the list about every ten minutes. (Staggering numbers.)

People were very surprised to learn what we experienced prior to and after the transplant surgery. (Many people thought we just went to the local hospital, had routine surgery to remove my kidney and transplant it into Natalee, and ….voila, end of story! (Boy, if only!) They were flabbergasted upon learning the degree of endless testing a donor must complete prior to surgery. A few people absurdly commented they thought it was terrible those needing a transplant sit around hoping for someone to die so an organ will available for them. The reply to that untrue characterization is a big "ABSOLUTELY NOT!" Not one person we met who was waiting for an organ was morbid enough to wish for, want or will someone to die so they could have a transplant. They were, however, hopeful and extremely grateful that others were willing and generous enough to donate so they could have a chance for a better life when the call finally came that an organ was available for them. May God bless all those who are registered donors with many thanks to unselfish living donors. Also, thanks to the families who make the decision to donate the organs and tissues of loved ones who have unexpectedly departed. (Altruism at the highest level.)

We are fortunate to live seventy miles from a top-rated transplant center at UPMC Montefiore/ Presbyterian Hospital in Pittsburgh, Pennsylvania. Natalee's nephrologist contacted the center to give them information about Natalee to start the ball rolling. It wasn't long until Natalee was contacted by the Starzl Transplant Center there to begin the process for living donation and transplant. (We were on the clock now; preparing for the race ahead.)

> Do you not know that in a race all the runners run; but only one gets the prize? Run in such a way as to get the prize. (1 Corinthians 9:24 NIV)

Thus began our journey....a race with time to the finish line. (Along with prayer, maintaining a sense of humor was paramount to keeping our sanity.)

Chapter 15

Ready, Set, Go!

The first step in the living donor process was the qualifying round to identify two possible donors to be tested. Donors cannot have heart disease, high blood pressure, diabetes, cancer or other illness that can preclude them from donating. I was eligible to be tested; first qualifying hurdle cleared. My friend, Barb, who lives in San Diego, also immediately volunteered to donate and qualified. (It's an intriguing story how Barb and I met. I will elaborate that whole amazing story later on.)

Donors have to match the blood type of the recipient. Natalee, Barb and I are all A+, so match one confirmed. Second qualifying hurdle easily cleared. The next needed match involved tissue typing and antigen matching. Results took three V-E-R-Y L-O-N-G weeks, eating up valuable time. The long awaited results confirmed we were both matches. Third and last qualifying hurdle cleared.

Next was to let the transplant center know which one of us was going to be the donor. (Of course, that donor was unquestionably me.) Even being a nurse didn't prepare me for all that was entailed when I entered the race. When my assigned transplant coordinator called and gave me a laundry list of required testing, I said something to the effect, "You've got to be kidding me!" She seriously assured me she wasn't. (You could paint me flabbergasted.) Many hurdles to clear to get to the finish line; now seemingly farther away than anticipated. The lengthy list left me a little thunderstruck. I prayed I would clear all the hurdles in record time and sprint to the finish without being disqualified. I was officially waiting on the starting line to begin the race. (I soon found out doing a year's worth of actual laundry, by hand, in one week, per se, would have been less grueling.)

Chapter 16

Testing, Testing......and More Testing

Did I mention testing?

Natalee had her own laundry list of testing, too. We never imagined how long all the testing was going to take once I was deemed the dedicated donor. It is said slow and steady wins the race, but we were in a race with time that wasn't on Natalee's side, so we each tried to schedule and complete the required testing as quickly as possible. Any required tests that Natalee may have had done and were recent enough to be accepted, were faxed to the transplant center. That shaved off some precious time. Some of the testing for Natalee included: a colonoscopy, kidney ultrasound, Pap smear and gyne exam, cardiac exercise test stress test, a 24-hour urine, and TB test. There was ongoing blood work which included testing for viruses. Sometimes up to twenty-two vials of blood were taken at a time! (It makes me dizzy to think about it!)

In addition to all the testing, Natalee was scheduled for an all-day consultation at the transplant center. We met with the transplant team's Medical Social Worker (MSW) to discuss any family concerns, any psychological issues, and what support systems we had in place. It was no surprise when she told us we both needed to make living wills. (Reality check: we had made living wills years ago.) Our meeting also included a discussion regarding the insurance coverage for the testing and surgeries. Most of the testing I had was ordered directly by the transplant center and paid for by Natalee's insurance, as was my hospitalization and surgery. Natalee had Medicare disability insurance, and the ESRD part of her insurance was the payer. (I was so focused on all things leading to the transplant, I must confess I never thought about who was going to actually pay for everything, but was enormously relieved when the MSW gave us the news.)

Natalee's surgeon met with us to discuss the actual transplant procedure and focused on answering any concerns or questions we had. Following that, we viewed an interesting and enlightening film about kidney transplant. (Even if popcorn would have been offered it was not on David's favorite movie list.) I also got to meet my coordinator in person, who had only been a familiar voice on the phone. (Funny how people never seem to look like what you picture in your mind after only hearing their voice on the phone.) It was a long and tiring day, but a few steps closer to the goal nonetheless.

Trying to get the laundry list of testing I had to complete while working full-time literally took the starch out of me. My exacting list included: a gyne exam and Pap smear, a mammogram, 24-hour urine for Creatinine clearance, and a 3-hour glucose tolerance test. Then came the ever-dreaded colonoscopy followed by an EGD, a renal CT angiogram, carotid Doppler, ECHO cardiogram, TB test, chest x-ray and EKG, a cardiac exercise stress test and, of course, more blood work. (There were a few more that seem to have escaped me.) Oh, and lucky me...*not*....there is one test I wish I could have escaped! I had to have an "extra" test called a voiding cystourethrogram due to having Fibromyalgia with irritable bladder. They needed to check for reflux (backup) of urine into the ureters and kidneys, which can cause damage. The test is an x-ray of the bladder, urethra and ureters done while the bladder is emptying, and it was the most humiliating test I ever had to endure. (Yes, I said while the bladder is emptying.) Let's just say, after a catheter was inserted to fill my bladder with sterile water, then removed, I developed a sudden case of bladder shyness when it came time to "perform." It's hard to empty your bladder on demand with a tech and radiologist in the room. (I felt like I was in a bad parody of *The Princess and the "Pee"*; laying on a pile of blankets on an x-ray table. My head kept telling my bladder - *This is just wrong*.) A girl I went to high school with was the x-ray tech assigned to me and was patiently waiting for "showtime." All of a sudden she disappeared from the room.

Reappearing with a pan of warm water, she grabbed my hand and stuck it in the water, and well, you know the result! (YUK!)

There were a few more tests I'm sure I forgot to list, but you get the gist....there were loads, and I definitely felt like I went through the wringer trying to get them completed ASAP. The race was becoming a grueling marathon, one hurdle at a time. (When all was said and done, for me, the surgery was easier than all the testing, testing, testing that made me extremely tired, tired, tired.)

I also had to spend a day at transplant clinic to see a film and meet the transplant team who would be involved in my upcoming surgery. David accompanied me. We met with a psych nurse who was to evaluate how I felt about being a donor and living with one kidney. (I figured God gave me a pair, so why not share!) The surgeon who would be performing my surgery, called a nephrectomy, spent an hour going over the surgery in graphic detail. (David was a little disconcerted and green around the gills between that and the movie. Medical stuff is not his thing.)

When almost all of our tests were completed in late January, our case was presented at a meeting of the entire transplant team. They evaluated all the test results and made sure everything was in order to proceed. Everything had been approved thus far, and a surgery date was set. The finish line was in sight. We were nearing the goal - so we thought. Big disappointment slammed us causing a delay in the race. I had a false-positive reading on my exercise stress test, so I had to have a repeat test. (I get tired just thinking about it.) Key word to that test was *stress* because the second test was also questionable. Now I was headed for a cardiac cath to confirm my heart was okay to withstand the lengthy surgery. The surgery date was postponed a week due to a problem in scheduling my cardiac cath locally any sooner. A delay of another week followed when Natalee also had to schedule a repeat stress test resulting in her having to have a cardiac cath, too. (Like mother, like daughter....like it or not.)

To add to the delay, and much to Natalee's dismay, she had to have a few dialysis treatments. The dye used for the cath had to be flushed from her system via three successive days of five-hour-long dialysis treatments because her failing kidneys could no longer rid her body of the dye. In order to receive the dialysis, she had to have a temporary Tesio catheter inserted - a tunneled vascular catheter radiologically guided into the large jugular vein in the neck and advanced to the right atrium of the heart for taking and returning blood during dialysis. She was very uncomfortable after the procedure; experiencing pain and nausea lasting for several days. The catheter, which was not very flexible, protruded several inches from the exit site in her neck and upward toward her jaw making it unbearable for her to move her head or to relax in any position the first few days. When the Tesio wasn't removed after the three days of dialysis, Natalee was not a happy camper. Even though she had adjusted to its presence, her displeasure was because she was not allowed to shower with it in place. The good news was that the race was thankfully still on, even though Natalee and I both broke stride for a moment. (At this point, the finish line to the "big day" couldn't come soon enough.)

The holdups were emotionally and mentally exhausting. One day, we were up; the next day was a downer knowing an abnormal cardiac cath result could have eliminated me as a donor and end the race we were urgently running with the goal so close to being achieved. Waiting for the cath results was extremely stressful. As challenging as it was, we tried to keep a positive attitude, and stay healthy. (Faith and prayers were our best friends while we waited.)

> Be strong and courageous. Do not be afraid or terrified because of them, for the Lord your God goes with you; he will never leave you nor forsake you. (Deuteronomy 31:6 NIV)

Chapter 17

The Good, the Bad, and the Ugly

In preparation for the "big day" and extended stay in Pittsburgh, arrangements were made for McKenna to stay with Jimmy and his mom until David returned home once Natalee and I were able to manage post-op on our own at Family House. It was hard to imagine all the things that were going through McKenna's head at the time. She knew her mother was very ill and needed a kidney, but we never talked about the life-threatening aspect with her. (Like Dr. Phil says - never discuss adult things with children.) One time David started telling McKenna about something going on with Natalee when she turned to him and with a serious face said, "My little head is already too full. I can't take in anymore or my head will explode!" From then on it was best to just answer her questions and not volunteer more information than she could handle.

She was in third grade at a Christian School, and her very caring teacher met with her each day before class to get an update on Natalee and offer support to McKenna. (A true blessing.) At prayer time each day, she had the class pray for Natalee. I remember the day McKenna came home visibly upset and said a girl in her class nastily commented to her, "I hope your mother dies!" We were all shocked at how mean, ugly and hurtful those words were coming from anyone, let alone an eight-year-old at a Christian School. McKenna usually took everything in stride for someone her age, but that was unnecessarily cruel. She understood that some people are just not nice people, and it's best to ignore them. (And pray for them.)

But I tell you, love your enemies and pray for those who
persecute you.... (Matthew 5:44 NIV)

My co-workers and some of our close friends blessed us with gifts of
money to help pay for our expenses in Pittsburgh. We were very grateful
for their support and generosity, but more so for their pledge of prayers.
Not everyone was supportive though......

David lost his job over Natalee's transplant. His boss was going to
lay someone off, so David volunteered to be laid off, even though he had
worked there faithfully for seven years and had the most seniority. He
needed the time off, and we looked at it as saving another employee with
a young family from being laid off. In late April, David called to find out
when he might be called back to work, but his calls were not answered or
returned. He later found out his boss hired someone else in spite of the
fact David was a very loyal and dedicated employee. The saddest part was
not the loss of his job, but that no one from his workplace even called to
see how the surgery went or how Natalee was doing. Looking back, losing
his job at the time was a blessing. (God always has a plan, even if we can't
see it right away.) David was able to be there for us throughout the kidney
transplant and the many trips to clinic. (One of the hardest things to do
is to praise God when things aren't going well in our lives.)

> ...giving thanks always and for everything to God the
> Father in the name of our Lord Jesus Christ... (Ephesians
> 5:20 ESV) I will bless the Lord at all times - His praise
> shall continually be in my mouth. (Psalm 34:1 KJV) But
> I will keep on hoping for your help; I will praise you more
> and more. (Psalm 71:14 NLT)

We knew firsthand that God would supply our needs until David
found another job. At one time David worked in the coal mines. In the
late 1990s his mine permanently shut down. Eventually his unemployment
ran out, and I was only working in the hospital part-time, which created
a financial burden for us. On the way home from church one Sunday
we were talking about all the things we could no longer afford to buy
at the grocery store. Things we wished we could purchase, but were not

necessities at the moment. After we were home for a while, there was a knock at the door. A neighbor stood there with two big paper bags full of groceries in his arms. They were a blessing from his church on the next block. When we unpacked the bags we were very surprised. *Everything* we had talked about on the way home from church was in those bags, and so much more! (Lots of praises and thanks to God that day!)

Also during that time, I remember standing in the kitchen holding a bill for $20.00 in my hand. I was telling God I didn't know how we were going to pay it on time and praying about it. The next day when I got the mail there was a plain white envelope addressed to us. No return address. When I opened it there was folded newspaper inside. I couldn't fathom who was sending us newspaper, and why. I took it out and inside the newspaper was a $20.00 bill! (I was glad I didn't just throw away the newspaper without looking inside.)

> And my God shall supply all your need according to his riches in glory by Christ Jesus. (Philippians 4:19 NKJV) ...your Father knows what you need before you ask him. (Matthew 6:8 NIV)

It was heartbreaking and frightening to watch as Natalee looked and felt more ill as valuable time was quickly slipping away, especially with the surgery now being put on hold twice. We felt like we were stalled - running in place - but we never lost sight of the finish line. We were trusting God, to again supply our needs and get us to the goal soon. (As far as I was concerned, the goal would not be complete until I actually left the OR minus a kidney and it was functioning in Natalee.)

Chapter 18

A Funny Thing Happened on the Way to a Transplant

When Natalee still lived at home, she was always bringing one critter or another into our household. She had a conglomeration of pets at any given time: a black rabbit named Bugs E. Bunny, hermit crabs, mice and gerbils, a white rat named Jasmine and a bearded lizard, to name a few. (The mice were stinky, the gerbils were returned to the pet store after the little cannibals ate their babies, and the lizard was just plain mean. Jasmine, "Jazzy" for short, was a real sweetheart and loved dog cookies.) I used to cringe when Natalee came home bearing a new cage with a new addition to her ragtag zoo. And yes, snakes were on her list of acceptable pets. She owned several over the years. (I am envissssioning you shhhhhuddering about now.)

Natalee had a 3-foot-long ball python named Imhotep at the time of the transplant. My mother was helping me clean Natalee's house days prior to departing for Pittsburgh. My mom was deathly afraid of snakes... and most critters. I was elected to dust near Imhotep's aquarium and must have bumped the latch on the lid. You guessed it, Imhotep eventually discovered the lid was loose. She decided to take advantage by escaping and going on an excursion of her surroundings outside of her glass house. That evening Natalee noticed Imhotep was missing from her enclosure. Finding her became paramount before we had to leave for our extended stay in Pittsburgh. My mother was planning on coming the following day to help finish cleaning. I called her and made up some excuse why she didn't need to come in the morning, not wanting to think about what would have happened if my mom would have been the one to find Imhotep! (*Hello, 911...*)

The evening before we were to leave for the "big day", David and I were at Natalee's, sitting in the living room talking. At this point, we had exhausted our search in every nook and cranny we thought Imhotep could have slithered into. (David was not fond of snakes, but helped search.) It was a concern having to leave if we couldn't find her since she wouldn't have water, heat or food. We were discussing where she could possibly be when Natalee's dog (a Keeshond) all of a sudden started whining and excitedly running back and forth between what Natalee called the "front room" and the living room. Curious as to what had Keesha Bear so wound up, we went to check it out. Keesha led us to a box of books Natalee had previously packed; ready to donate. Much to our surprise, and relief, there was Imhotep peeking out of the lid as if to see what all the commotion was about. We never thought to look in the box because we didn't think she could fit through the narrow gap between the folded lid flaps. Poor thing was cold; missing her heat lamp. Natalee put her back in her nice warm environment and made sure the latch was tightly secured. One less thing for us to worry about for the moment. (I think I saw Imhotep smile and heave a sigh of relief as she settled into the warmth of her abode.)

Chapter 19

The "Big Day"

At last the race was on again and the surgery was scheduled for February 28, 2005; another memorable date. (We named it the "Transplantiversary" date.) The surgery was also the day before David's and my thirtieth wedding anniversary. (Nothing like celebrating with a romantic dinner of hospital food, and me in my eye-catching, open-backed hospital gown.)

The day before the surgery Natalee was admitted to the ICU. In the evening, she was given a drug called Campath, which knocks out the body's immune system and stays in your system for up to fifty-six days to decrease the risk of rejection of the transplanted organ.

The morning of the surgery I was admitted through the ambulatory surgery department and was as ready as I could be before heading for the last hurdle and the ultimate finish line. I had great confidence in the doctors and OR staff and wasn't the least bit nervous or scared. (Prayer and faith were on my side.)

After being given pre-op meds, the last thing I hazily remembered was being wheeled into the brightly lit operating room and sliding onto the operating table with help from several masked OR staff. Thank goodness I floated off to twilight-land oblivion soon after and didn't remember anything else. (I love anesthesia!)

David also had a big stake in the race, betting on a big win-win for Natalee and me. The "big day" was a very long day for David, mentally and emotionally. It still evokes feelings of sadness in me when I think about him waiting patiently, all alone. Physical exhaustion saturated him while he waited in an unforgiving less-than-comfortable chair for slowly-passing hours on end while the surgery took longer than expected. The stress of knowing *both* "his girls" were in surgery compounded it. I'm sure all those harrowing hours with nothing to do, trying not to entertain anguishing thoughts, was difficult. (Nothing is as frightening as what one's mind can conjure.)

> And the peace of God, which passeth all understanding,
> shall keep your hearts and minds through Christ Jesus.
> (Phillipians 4:7 NIV)

Chapter 20

Prize Awarded: A Journey of the Heart: from Mom, with Love

My laparoscopic surgery only required three small keyhole incisions for the insertion of the various instruments the surgeon would be using to free the kidney and for the very important telescopic instrument he used to see what he was doing. Another incision of four to five inches was made through which my left kidney, its blood vessels and the attached ureter were removed. (Hard to believe such a big operation could be done through such small incisions with great precision.)

Natalee had been prepped in the same manner I was readied, but was not brought into the adjoining OR until they were ready to remove my kidney. Her single incision was eight to ten inches wide, angled on her lower left abdomen above her left groin area. My kidney was placed into the area, the ureter was connected to her bladder and the blood vessels joined to hers. The surgery, we were told, could last as short as four hours or as long as twelve if complications arose or the unforeseen happened. Of course, the unforeseen happened due to a problem with connecting the blood vessels - one vessel was too short. A matching blood vessel graft from a cadaveric organ donor had to be used to reattach the kidney, causing a delay. When the surgery was completed and Natalee crossed the finish line, she went to the recovery unit for a short while, then back to ICU.

Natalee and I were very grateful for David's devotion to us as he endured the agonizing hours of waiting for news in chairs not designed for comfort. Around 7:00 p.m. he was finally informed the surgery was over and all went well; the crushing weight of the last twelve hours lifted, replaced by welcome relief. He was directed to the room I would be assigned on the transplant floor when I was released from recovery. David was there waiting for me (in a more comfortable chair) when I arrived; looking exhausted, but reassured when they brought me into the room and he saw me smiling at him. He left me long enough to check on Natalee once we were informed she was back in ICU. When he returned to my room, we called McKenna to give her the good news.

The surgery part was a breeze since I was blissfully asleep and unaware. (I *really* love anesthesia!) It wasn't time for celebration just yet, though. The next phase was contending with the immediate post-op recovery. I had a very distended abdomen from the insufflation of CO_2 gas to blow up my belly during surgery so the surgeon had adequate room to visualize the removal of my kidney. (I felt like an overinflated beach ball ready to explode.) The importance of getting out of bed and moving about was key post-op, but my body wasn't so sure. In fact, it was positive it wasn't and let me know it. Standing up straight was out of my comfort zone and current ability. I held a pillow tightly against my abdomen for support while trying to attain and maintain being upright. (That pillow was my newest supportive friend.)

After three days, Natalee was moved to a room across the hall from my room. She was happy she was sans Tesio and using her insulin pump again. (The Tesio had been left in place as a safeguard in case she would need dialysis should the transplant not begin to function right away.) The endocrinology team readjusted her insulin pump settings since anti-rejection medication can increase insulin requirements. Daily blood work was drawn to gauge Natalee's kidney function and the level of the anti-rejection drugs so the dose could be adjusted when needed. If the level was too low, rejection could occur. Too high could be toxic.

So much to be thankful to God for - we sprinted to the goal line and won the race. Natalee received her prize - a functioning kidney. We were both doing well. Many prayers answered! (Big sigh of relief here.)

Chapter 21

A New Lease on Life

The newly transplanted kidney can begin to work as soon as it is connected in almost all cases involving a living donor. If it doesn't, the recipient may need to have dialysis for a short period of time until it does. We were told in some cases it can take up to three weeks, especially in those receiving a cadaveric kidney. Natalee's new-to-her kidney started to work without delay, and it was truly an astounding dichotomy of extremes to see how she went from having a sickly gray pallor to looking pink and healthy immediately after surgery. (An awesome miracle.)

In case you're wondering if her native kidneys were removed during the transplant surgery. They weren't. The non-functional native kidneys eventually atrophy or waste away. It would take a much more extensive surgery to remove them, and put the person at greater risk for complications. (You can get some really funny looks when you tell people you have three kidneys, then say that only one works.)

Natalee was bombarded daily with intensive teaching regarding the sixteen new medications she was now prescribed. The unbelievable total cost of all these combined was from $5000-$10,000 a month and covered by her insurance, which was a real blessing. (Keeping a transplant healthy is expensive.) We bought a large see through cosmetic bag that fit all of her medication bottles - a small pharmacy - she carried with her in a backpack. A book of instructions was given to her outlining critically important new information to learn and remember to keep the new-to-her kidney healthy.

In the backpack, she also carried her post-op log book. For six weeks, she was to measure and record her fluid intake and urine output. Taking a "toilet hat" everywhere was rather repulsive, but necessary. (For obvious reasons, it was excluded from joining the other necessities in the backpack and stayed in its own opaque plastic bag.) Natalee managed to drink the required three liters (3.17 quarts) of fluid a day and was to continue ingesting that much for several months to keep the kidney hydrated. (I felt bloated just watching her drink all that liquid. It was a wonder she didn't slosh when she moved and her back teeth weren't floating.)

I was discharged on the fourth day post-op and went to stay at Family House with David. Meeting and talking with others there who were in the same boat, so to speak, provided some solace in the midst of lives being upended. We shared stories, and Natalee's wasn't the most challenging one we encountered. I even learned how to heat tortillas on the gas stovetop burners from a Mexican guy who was there with his brother who had been waiting a year for a heart, and now also needed a liver. (Unfortunately, we never learned the outcome for him.)

A week after the surgery, Natalee joined David and me at Family House, where Natalee and I claimed the queen-sized bed in the room. Air mattresses and extra linens were provided for additional family and visitors staying overnight, but David wasn't fond of sleeping on the air mattress. McKenna loved that part. (It was a grand adventure for her - like camping indoors.) David made sure Natalee and I got settled and were able to manage on our own before going home to a real bed a few days later.

Natalee had daily clinic visits at the transplant center at 6:30 a.m. (Which meant an afternoon nap for sure!) Once checked in, she waited to be taken to a triage room where the nurse drew blood, checked her vitals and reviewed her medications. Shortly after, she was taken to one of the exam rooms. Each had four semi-reclining, comfortable patient chairs with personal TVs. For visitors, there were the usual omnipresent uncomfortable chairs. We waited two to three hours for the lab results to come back and for the doctor to discuss them with us. In the meantime, we had the option to stay in the exam room or leave the clinic and go to breakfast in the café or cafeteria. Napping sounded better and what we chose to do. (Sleeping while sitting up in uncomfortable chairs is a skill I perfected over time.)

Talking and sharing information with others we met at clinic who had transplanted organs made the time go faster. A few we met had second and even third transplants, nevertheless, none of them ever complained about their lot in life. They chose to meet their challenges head-on because the only options were a life on dialysis (for those needing a kidney), long hospital stays with complications, or even death. They remained hopeful, not wanting to fall into the dark abyss of despair and depression. I heard an analogy comparing it to being on a train heading through a dark tunnel. We don't jump off and throw away our ticket and possibly suffer a worse fate. We need to trust the engineer and have faith we will come out of the darkness. Those we met who came through that darkness had more living to do in spite of their struggles. (God is the ultimate engineer to get us through dark times.)

> ....God is light; in Him there is no darkness at all. (1 John 1:5 NIV)

On the first few clinic visits, Natalee's blood work indicated she needed IV fluids. (It was hard to imagine she needed additional fluids after guzzling three liters a day.) The infusion added two hours to our clinic visit. (More time for me to bond with the tortuous chairs while cutting into afternoon nap time on a nice soft bed!) As she improved, her clinic visits were gradually decreased to three times a week, then to twice a week.

In April, when clinic visits decreased to weekly, David brought us home. Clinic visits were scheduled every Tuesday and occasionally on Friday if they felt she needed a follow-up. Over time, clinic appointments had longer spans between visits, but she continued to have blood work drawn locally every Monday and results were faxed to clinic. If adjustments were needed in her medications or her treatment plan, her post-op coordinator phoned her with instructions. Things were definitely looking up for a change. Even her GP symptoms had mysteriously lessened somewhat after the transplant. (Natalee wasn't complaining.)

There are times when something triggers my memory and I am transported back in time. I envision a complete mental slide show of the "big day" and all that led up to it just like it was yesterday. I thank God that we were blessed with that opportunity. It wasn't easy by any means, but faith, prayer and a great medical team brought us through it all to the miraculous outcome. (Another elephant defeated.)

> Oh give thanks to the Lord, for he is good, for his steadfast love endures forever! (Psalm 107:1 ESV)

65

Chapter 22

Be a Hero, No Cape Needed

Would I recommend being an organ donor? In a hummingbird's heartbeat. I can now say I gave life to Natalee....twice! (We joke that I gave her my "coffee kidney" because after the surgery I lost my taste for coffee, and Natalee gained one!) Seeing her feel better and look healthier post-op was worth it all. We were blessed through this whole extraordinary process in so many ways. One of our hopes is that Natalee's story will encourage others to be heroes - organ donors - giving others the gift of life. (No cape or super powers needed!) Organ donation not only changes the lives of organ recipients, but of those who love them and share in their lives, too.

Through Natalee's transplants I learned that there are several agencies involved in organ transplant. It's not as simple as "first name on the list, first served" as many people think. The Network for Organ Sharing (UNOS) coordinates transplants in the U.S. The National Organ Transplant Act of 1984 (NOTA) helps maintain fair distribution of organs. When an organ is available, the donor's information is entered into a computer system to locate a recipient who would be a good match with consideration to waiting time, urgency of need and geographic location. There are eleven regions across the country under the Organ Procurement and Transplantation Network (OPTN) that is managed through UNOS. When there is a death in a hospital, the Center for Organ Recovery and Education (CORE) assists in obtaining authorization from the family of the deceased for donation and organ recovery. CORE then sends information about the donor who meets the guidelines to UNOS so a match can be made and arranges for the harvesting of the donor organs. A tissue sample is typed and matched to find a prospective recipient. When a match is found, CORE notifies the recipient's transplant surgeon who then decides to accept the organ or not, taking many factors into consideration. If accepted, the recipient is notified. (A mind-blowing process from start to finish and carried out with great precision, time being a critical factor.)

Although Natalee now had a functioning kidney, she still had to face the challenges related to her diabetes, GP, and keeping the kidney healthy. Life for her was much better right now, but even so, Natalee's health was capricious and her story doesn't end here. Far from it. (There always seemed to be one more elephant wanting to join the Cirque du Natalee's Challenges.)

Chapter 23

Divine Providence - A Friend in Need is a Friend Indeed

Here is the part of the story I promised to tell you about the extraordinary way Barb and I met:

It was a dark and stormy night….. (Not really, but it sounded very dramatic to start with.)

It was really just an ordinary warm, sunny day. I was searching online for information regarding diabetic gastroparesis (GP) since it was affecting Natalee more and more. As her mom and a nurse, I wanted to upskill myself with any new information on the subject, if there was even any out there. (Sad to say, but there is no real cure.)

During my optimistic search, I came across a web page designed by a young girl who had idiopathic (unknown cause) GP. On her page, was a lot of information about her personal struggles living with debilitating GP and several links to information about the disease. She had also set up an E-group. You could correspond with those who posted contact information to either share knowledge, offer or gain support, and empathize with others in general.

I chose two people whose information inexplicably drew me to them from the many choices on the list. Truth be told, I was a little leery about contacting a complete stranger and giving them information about myself and Natalee, but I decided to be brave and send an email hoping I would get a reply. (And I prayed it wouldn't be from some crazy person!)

In those initial emails, I introduced myself and briefly recounted Natalee's trials with Juvenile diabetes and her eventual life-changing GP challenges. Only Barb responded. Her husband was a diabetic with GP and other health issues. At first, we shared what it was like to feel powerless while watching a family member contend with GP, diabetes and other serious health concerns; discussing what current treatments they were prescribed - what worked and what didn't. As we started feeling more comfortable with each other we began sharing more personal details about ourselves and our families. In other words, she was not a crazy person and obviously didn't think I was one either. (Or maybe we're both crazy!) Soon a long-distance friendship blossomed. That was over seventeen years ago, and now she has unquestionably become my adopted sister. Together we have enjoyed sharing many good times in our lives, supported each other through trying times, and have been each others sounding board over the years. (Barb refers to it as our "sharing a cup of tea" long distance.)

When Barb learned Natalee needed a kidney, much to our later amazement, we found out she had immediately contacted the transplant center at Montefiore to be tested. She hadn't mentioned that little fact to me, though, and I was totally dumbstruck when my coordinator relayed to me in a phone call that Barb was a match. Say what? That was definitely a color-me-surprised moment. (What color you ask? Tickled pink, of course!) I knew for certain Barb was one truly remarkable friend indeed. (I thank God every day for sending her into our lives and for her selfless generosity.)

Chapter 24

A Memorable Meeting

A year after Natalee's transplant, she and I had the opportunity to meet Barb in person. Barb was one of the chaperones for her youngest son's class trip to several notable places in the Northeast. One of their planned destinations was Gettysburg, Pennsylvania. Gettysburg is only a two-and-a-half-hour drive from Johnstown, so after discussing their itinerary with Barb, Natalee and I made reservations to stay at our favorite historic B&B - The Brickhouse Inn - in Gettysburg. We would meet the evening their group was to arrive for a night's stay at a hotel a few miles from the B&B.

Natalee and I arrived in Gettysburg in the early afternoon, did some sightseeing, shopped for souvenirs, and had a great dinner at a place David and I have returned to when we visit Gettysburg. (O'Rourke's has *the* best coleslaw.) We then relaxed at the B&B until it was time to meet Barb. (A non-medical bonding day with Natalee for a change.) Arriving at the hotel, we were excited for the bus to pull into the parking lot soon. The bus, however, pulled in later than expected; around 10:00 p.m. Natalee and I intently watched while a multitude of tired-looking adults and kids trickled into the hotel lobby dragging their suitcases and duffle bags as we waited with growing anticipation for Barb to appear. When we eventually spotted each other, a rush of excitement ensued. Meeting face to face was beyond words. We had hugs all around, met her son, took multiple pictures to remember the occasion, and talked nonstop until after midnight. Before Natalee and I left the hotel, plans were made for Barb to text us in the morning so we could meet up with the tour bus when they arrived on the battle grounds to begin their exploration.

In the morning, Natalee and I had a wonderful gourmet breakfast at the B&B. After we checked out, we drove to the place Barb texted they would begin the battlefield tour. Barb joined us in our car so we'd have more time together, which was too short to begin with; their group would only be there until the whirlwind visit was completed, then they were heading straight to D.C. Our brief day together made me feel even more bonded to Barb. It felt like we had known each other forever. (A very memorable and fun day I'll always cherish.)

A few years later, I was overjoyed when Barb was able to visit us for a week in June. It was a fun week and over way too soon, but another wonderful memory to file away.

Barb is kindhearted, upbeat and a wonderful friend. How do you thank someone who so unselfishly offered a kidney to your only child in her time of need? I feel God led me to pick her name from all the people on that list to contact, then led her to respond. Her unconditional friendship has been a true gift and wonderful blessing.

Several years after we first met, her husband unexpectantly passed away from complications related to his health issues. He was only in his fifties….way too young. Barb officially retired in 2016, but now she has a new job - helping care for her growing number of beautiful grandchildren. (I am praying she can visit me again one day.)

Chapter 25

Full Circle

The evening before the "big day" a church group had graciously come to cook a spaghetti dinner for those staying at Family House. Not having to make dinner for ourselves was one less thing to have to think about with our minds preoccupied with the surgery. David and I gratefully got our food and sat down at an empty table. I noticed a woman who was by herself and asked if she would like to join us.

We introduced ourselves and she said she was from near Hershey, Pennsylvania. Her twenty-something daughter was waiting for a rare five-organ transplant. (Includes stomach, small and large intestine, liver, and either a pancreas or spleen.) They had been in Pittsburgh waiting for the past fifteen months. Her daughter was to the point she was unable to eat solid food; sustained by tube feedings. (If you could call being a mere sixty-six pounds being sustained.) Being on and off the transplant list due to frequent hospitalizatons related to various complications compounded her chances for transplant. To say she was in dire need of a transplant was an understatement. Her life was truly hanging in the balance.

Waiting for five organs is a monumental test of patience, perseverance and faith. It is difficult to find five viable, good quality organs from the same donor that would be a match. Size constraints limit the chances even more. There are very few programs world-wide that offer five-organ transplants. People don't realize the sacrifices that go along with waiting for a transplant, let alone one of that magnitude. It affects the whole family dynamic. They mentioned that their Christian faith sustained them through the long wait, disappointments, and life-threatening times. (I don't know how anyone would get through all that without the Lord.)

> The steadfast love of the Lord never ceases; his mercies never come to an end; they are new every morning; great is your faithfullness. (Lamentations 3:22-23 ESV)

I asked what her daughter's name was, and when she told me, I was absolutely floored. It was the same uncommon name as the girl who had the GP web page where I found Barb's contact information. Very interesting, but how could it possibly be the same girl? The possibility would have been astounding. I asked her if her daughter had a web page about GP with an E-group. Imagine my momentary wide-eyed, open-mouthed surprise when she answered "yes" with a quizzical how-did-you-know look on her face.

I explained to her how I met Barb through the E-group. I told her Barb offered my daughter a kidney and was a match, but I was going to be the donor in the morning. It was an unforgettable emotional moment. Knowing how I met Barb and now meeting her and her daughter here, what seemed like chance or coincidence to some people, we believed was destined to be and all these circumstances came full circle by divine intervention.

After we finished eating, she invited me up to their room so I could meet her courageous daughter. We stayed in touch after Natalee's transplant and received the good news that the gift of a life-saving five-organ transplant became available in 2006 and was successful. Incredible! More wonderful life-saving miracles. (God's timing is perfect.)

Chapter 26

Transplant...Take 2

FYI: The pancreas is located behind the stomach. It has two functions:1) The exocrine pancreas - 95% of the pancreas - aids in digestion. 2) The endocrine pancreas releases the hormone insulin. That little non-functioning 5% is Natalee's nemesis.

Natalee was interested in receiving a pancreas transplant and saying good-bye to diabetes, finger sticks, glucose monitors, food limits, pumps and uncontrolled blood sugar levels and the after-effects. It was a viable option open to Natalee, but she would have to wait several months after her kidney transplant before she could be on the active list for a pancreas transplant.

In the meantime, looking ahead, she decided to take an online college course and get a pharmacy tech degree. I guess taking a small pharmacy of meds sparked her interest. She completed the short course, and now all she needed was to be well enough to someday hold at least a part-time job. (Life may have had her down at times, but she never let it count her out entirely.)

The pancreas transplant was unlike the living-donor kidney transplant process. There were still certain tests required and to keep up to date for this transplant: a yearly cardiac stress test, EKG and chest x-ray, mammogram and various blood work studies to name a few. Natalee thankfully didn't have to rush to get them completed this time since most of those were currently up to date. So, in May of 2006, another adventure began, but with no tiring marathon race involved. We soon found out we were in for an adrenaline-inducing roller coaster ride filled with emotional highs and lows of anticipation and disappointment. (I, for one, do not like roller coaster rides, and this one proved to be a wild one.)

Chapter 27

Talk About an Adrenaline Rush!

The first time Natalee got a call from her transplant coordinator to tell her a donated pancreas was available was a high-octane, take-your-breath-away moment and just plain scary at the same time due to not knowing what exactly to expect. Sort of like the feeling you'd get jumping into a murky ice cold lake off a speeding boat crashing through the waves, not knowing how deep the water was....once you took that dive it was time to sink or swim. (Taking that leap and swimming with the flow seemed to be the option for the chosen adventure she was now facing.)

Natalee received the call later one evening and promptly called me on her house phone while she had the transplant coordinator on her cell phone. She was only given minimal information about the donor and the cause of death. In just a few brain-scattering minutes, she had to make a decision that could change her life. (No pressure!) Because we had some reservations and questions about something we were told about the donor, the coordinator said she would contact the doctor and have him call right back to discuss our concerns. In just a few minutes, he called back. After we spoke with him, we decided to pass and let someone else have the chance for the organ. Maybe we were being overly cautious, even though there was nothing that would prevent the organ from being used, but that was the split-second decision we made. We couldn't focus on if it was the wrong decision; the moment had passed and we had to move on. On a good note, now we were more prepared for the next call and what to expect. (However, every time the phone rang, it gave Natalee and us an adrenaline rush of anticipation as our hearts went racing into overdrive wondering if that could be "the call"....or not.)

Once the phone rings and the voice on the other end says an organ is available and the person accepts, there is no time to waste; only a small window of time exists that the organ can be preserved and viable. Thus, a go bag and non-perishable food items took up residence in David's vehicle in case one of the life-changing calls was accepted by Natalee and a drop-everything-and-rush-to-Pittsburgh trip resulted in a transplant and extended stay in Pittsburgh. (Exciting and nerve-wracking at the same time.)

The second call came one quiet evening, turning it into frenzied chaos within minutes. Having no real concerns or questions, in no time flat, David was racing Natalee off to Pittsburgh for a possible transplant. (Key word always being *possible*.) High anticipation, to say the least. But this time was not to be, and it was determined the donor pancreas was not what they considered 100% when examined. So, they returned home feeling tried and let down, but it wouldn't be the first time. Just one of many crestfallen twists and turns on the roller coaster ride that wouldn't be letting up so we could breathe every time the phone rang until Natalee received a transplant.

Over that summer, Natalee had a few calls that came close together; others were weeks apart. We were thankful most calls came in the evening when we were home from work. The ones that came when David or Natalee were out somewhere made things more stressful and hectic. Rushing to return home, then getting ready before making the mad dash to the hospital took up precious time. There was a literal smorgasbord of calls regarding available organs. One donor organ was from as far away as Arkansas, one from Ohio, one from New Jersey, and another from here in Pennsylvania. Most of the donors were young, in their twenties or thirties. Heartbreakingly, one was a twelve-year-old boy from Connecticut. An air of excitement when the calls came energized us, knowing there was a possibility of the transplant actually happening. There was also heartfelt deep sympathy for the donor and their family, mixed with gratitude beyond measure for their life-saving gift. (It's paradoxical that the death of one gives life to another.)

David still did not have a job at the time and was the one who dropped everything to take Natalee to Pittsburgh when she received calls. (A real blessing of sorts for us in that respect, but definitely not financially.) In early August, the homecare agency and affiliated hospital I worked at for over twenty years was acquired by another hospital. I was hired by their homecare at my current salary, but I was otherwise a new employee with no paid time off, so I was only able to go along if it was my day off, and there was someone to take care of McKenna on very short notice. (Needless to say I didn't go along very often.)

There were only two calls Natalee turned down. The other five organs didn't qualify as 100% or weren't totally compatible for her for various reasons. Natalee and David made all five trips to Pittsburgh at the drop of a hat, only to return home disappointed again. The anticlimactic aspect never got any easier and the roller coaster ride of high expectation resulted in a momentary dispirited low each time she was sent home to wait some more.

> Why are you cast down, O my soul, and why are you in turmoil within me? Hope in God; for I shall again praise Him, my salvation and my God. (Psalm 43:5 ESV) I am counting on the LORD; yes, I am counting on Him. I have put my hope in his word. (Psalm 130:5 NLT)

When a call came and the organ was turned down by Natalee, it was offered to the standby person. Natalee was the standby person twice. She received a call to alert her that a pancreas was available, but was told that there was another person ahead of her whose need for the organ was either more pressing or they may have needed both the kidney and pancreas from the same donor. Both times she received a call back saying they were sorry she wouldn't be getting the organ; the first person it was offered to had accepted. Even so, Natalee was glad that someone else was able to have a much needed transplant. She continued trusting God that her time would come. (Good thing we were masters of waiting.)

When Natalee arrived at the hospital each time she received a call, no time was wasted. Many times Natalee already had an IV started and other prep initiated when it was decided she was not going to receive the transplant. On a few occasions, she even got as far as being ready to be taken into the OR for surgery only to have it canceled. That's the part she disliked the most about the whole process - being physically, mentally and emotionally ready to have the surgery, only to be sent home. It's like going to your birthday party, anticipating, but never receiving the most wonderful gift you were hoping for and having the whole scenario repeated time after time. (I could see why she was losing enthusiasm as each successive call came.)

One of the calls came in the early evening when McKenna was on a weekend trip to an amusement park with her Girl Scout troop. We were scheduled to pick her up in a couple hours when they were due to return. Natalee accepted the offer. I was off work and able to go along, but in order to do so, arrangements for picking McKenna up had to be hastily made. I called my friend, Janet, at the last minute and prayed she and her husband were available to help us out. It was a blessing to have such good friends, always willing to drop what they were doing when we needed them. We left our key to Natalee's house so they could stop by for McKenna to pack things she'd need to stay with them. However, we had no way to let McKenna know of the juggling act going on and that she'd be staying at Janet's house. I can't imagine what went through McKenna's mind when she saw Natalee and I weren't there to pick her up, but Janet and Rick were there instead. I'm sure it gave her a jolt of panic; wondering why we weren't there, where we could be or what could be wrong. I look back and think how disruptive and stressful it was for her. Our hopeful jaunt to Pittsburgh turned out to be a no-go again and we didn't get back home until late, so we picked McKenna up in the morning. (Janet had a pet rabbit, and I'm sure it helped McKenna take her mind off of everything that was transpiring.)

The *possibly* Lucky #7 call came when Natalee was visiting friends out of town. Since they were closer to Pittsburgh, they hurriedly drove her to the hospital and David met them there as soon as he could. It was another disappointing no-go, so they returned home deflated and frustrated once again. (We were all hoping to get off this wild roller coaster ride, but #7 wasn't her lucky number.)

Chapter 28

A Gift from a Hero

Natalee said she thought she would pass on the next call. She was getting discouraged making trips to Pittsburgh in a rush of expectation. We persuaded her to accept the next offer just in case it was *the* one.

Natalee accepted the eighth call in the early evening of September 27, 2005; another hopeful trip to Pittsburgh. When they arrived at the hospital the doctors and staff were waiting and ready for her. She was immediately prepped for surgery and by 8:30 p.m. she was in the OR receiving a new-to-her pancreas. After seven no-goes, this was the much awaited moment we had been praying for the past six months. The donor was a thirty-six-year-old male from Altoona, Pennsylvania. That's all we were told about him. We are forever grateful to him (and his family) for the gift of life he donated. (Another memorable date and time of life-changing events in Cirque du Natalee's Challenges.)

> Rejoice always, pray without ceasing, give thanks in all circumstances; for this is the will of God in Christ Jesus for you. (1 Thessalonians 5:16-18 ESV)

David called me as soon as he got the official word the surgery was indeed going to take place. It was hard having to remain home and go to work in the morning and not be there with Natalee, but I knew she was in good hands at the hospital - especially in God's. It was the first time in our lives that I wasn't by her side for our "bonding" routine. I was, however, glad David was available to be with her for the transplant, her post-op stay in Pittsburgh and for the follow-up trips to clinic after her release from the hospital. (David - our dependable Rock.) Another long, lonely and stressful wait for David of watching the minutes and hours on the clock slowly tick away as he occupied the time in prayer - a calming balm to soothe the soul. He was fortunate to have reserved a room at Family House on such short notice; thankful he didn't have to drive back home that night and would have a comfortable place to unwind from the day's event. (God was watching over both of them.)

After David called and we said prayers, I tucked McKenna in for the night and assured her that her mom would have a new pancreas shortly. It was hard for me to find sleep, though, until I heard from David that all went well. The much awaited call came just after midnight. Natalee was in recovery and doing well. A huge relief for all of us. I waited until morning to tell McKenna. She was excited we could visit Natalee on the weekend and stay at Family House. (Staying at Family House was like a stress-free mini vacation for her.)

It was important to make sure McKenna was cared for without upsetting her life any more than it already was at times. I'm sure she felt like she was dancing "the Crazy McKenna Shuffle" that went like this - In the mornings, I would take her down the street to get on the school bus in front of her house. Then I'd go back home and get ready for work. Her other grandmother got her off the bus after school in front of Natalee's house, then took McKenna home with her. I picked her up on my way home from work and took her to my house for the night. In the morning we started the dance all over again. (Of course, you have to have refreshments at a dance, and root beer floats were our choice.)

Other than taking an additional immunosuppressant drug, Natalee's general post-op course was basically the same as for the kidney, minus drinking all that liquid and toting "the hat" around. She came home from Pittsburgh after three weeks - going to outpatient clinic as before and continuing weekly blood work. It was freedom for her to be able to eat what she wanted, when she wanted, and have normal blood sugar levels. She didn't miss taking insulin, pricking her fingers several times a day or having to deal with the effects of high and low blood sugars; although GP was still an unrelenting problem flaring up at times. Even so, she had an excellent recovery from the surgery with no major problems....with either transplant....until March of 2006 when faith and trust would be tested again.

> So, if you are suffering in a manner that please God, keep on doing what is right, and trust your lives to the God who created you, for he will never fail you. (1 Peter 4:19 NLT)

Chapter 29

A New Dreaded "R" Word

Acute organ rejection is not uncommon and always a possibility, but treatable. It is the consequence of a recipient's immune system attacking the graft as a foreign body, meaning to destroy it. Risk is highest in the first three months, but can occur months to years after transplant. Knowing what symptoms to report to the doctor, keeping up to date with the required blood work, and taking the medications as prescribed were all vitally important.

Elevated pancreatic enzymes can indicate rejection, and when her blood results noted indications of rejection in March of 2006, Transplant called her to come to Montefiore and be admitted right away. Now what? She wasn't having any of the notable signs of rejection we were instructed to watch for and report. We were blindsided, when seemingly out of nowhere, the results of a pancreas biopsy confirmed she was in acute class II rejection. The kidney was thankfully not affected. (Now we had a new dreaded "R" word - rejection. There was nothing positive about it; it was just positively frightening.)

We were told there are three types of allograft rejection: 1) Hyper acute - occurs in minutes after a transplant due to unmatched antibodies. Although it is very rare due to the extensive screening before transplantation even occurs. 2) Acute - occurs within one week to 12 months and is reversible. 3) Chronic - occurs over years; an immune response against the organ, slowly damaging it. It is irreversible, eventually resulting in graft failure.

Standard treatment for acute rejection is administration of an IV corticosteroid. Natalee was given daily doses of Solumedrol IV for three days. (Her new best friend.) Increasing the anti-rejection medications to further block her immune system was also part of the treatment plan. It was very scary knowing rejection could have led to the loss of the graft had she not been so closely followed by the transplant team. Losing the pancreas would also have meant going back to a diabetic management regime of insulin, finger poking and a strict diet, and she was thoroughly enjoying her freedom from that daily challenge. We were greatly relieved when she responded to the treatment and the rejection was reversed; grateful for the expertise of the transplant team and doctors at UMPC, and most of all for the answers to the prayers of all our friends and relatives that got her through this alarming setback. She remained in the hospital for three weeks with another birthday celebrated in the hospital. We brought Natalee some fancy birthday cupcakes, but unfortunately her GP prevented her from enjoying any. (Insert very sad face here.)

In the ensuing months, after a third rejection scare was reversed, we thought she was out of the woods since she had no futher transplant related complications....until April of 2007 when things took an unbelievable turn. Life is truly fragile and change for the worse can come all too quickly. (She would need more miracles, we just didn't know how big of a miracle it would be.)

Chapter 30

An Unexpected Tragedy

Along with the roller coaster ride of dealing with rejection, another unexpected issue totally sent us reeling. Without any significant warning signs, McKenna's father committed suicide on June 12, 2006. I was with Natalee when we gave McKenna the news of his death. She had just come home from a fun vacation at the beach with Jimmy's sister and her family. Telling her that her dad was gone was one of the hardest days of my life, and I know it was for Natalee, too. Natalee and I were at a loss for words as to how to even begin to explain his death to McKenna, so I looked up information on the internet on how to broach the subject. There were several articles on how to tell a child of a parents' death/suicide. It was definitely much easier to read about how to tell McKenna than it was to actually deliver the shocking news face to face. She quietly listened and then very matter-of-factly said, "I'm going out to play now." She quietly walked out of the room without looking at us, and went outside. That threw us a curve. We hadn't thought to search for any articles on how to handle McKenna's reaction, so we let her go outside to play with her friends for the time being. My heart was unbelievably hurting for her. I wanted to gather her in my arms and tell her everything would be okay. Kids have their own way of coping and processing information, though, so we had to let her work through hers until she was ready to ask more questions and express her feelings. I really think it was such shock she didn't know how to react; denial seemed to be her first response to the pain and sense of loss that was invading her sense of being. (It's somethng you never truly get over.)

> May your unfailing love be my comfort, according to your
> promise to your servant. (Pslam 119:76 NIV)

Her dad's plain square bronze cremation urn is on the tall chest of drawers in her bedroom. One day the four-year-old neighbor boy spotted it and curiously asked her what was in the intriguing sealed box. McKenna replied without explanation, "My dad." He thoughtfully paused, then seriously asked, "Where's his eyes?" Wow! His response both amused and baffled me, making me wonder what goes on inside kids' heads that he would ask that instead of asking how he fit in the box or why he was in there. I frequently wonder what thoughts McKenna keeps inside her head, sealed up tight like the cremation urn, after losing her dad and watching her mom struggle with ongoing unrelenting illnesses. McKenna saw a therapist on and off for many years to help her cope with Jimmy's death and Natalee's chronic illnesses; to hopefully discuss and work through and declutter those things she keeps bottled up inside her head. (Sometimes I think my mind needs decluttering.)

Chapter 31

The Start of the Endless Summer

Natalee developed a small ulcer in her mouth in early April 2007. Even with topical treatment, it spread until her whole mouth was filled with extremely uncomfortable ulcers. For most people, ulcers should clear up in a week or two on their own and are rarely a sign of anything serious, but for Natalee, it was a genuine concern due to her being immunosuppressed to prevent rejection. (The ironic rock and hard place.) She was eventually seen at Transplant clinic due to weight loss from not being able to eat due to the increase in the degree of ulceration and mouth pain. On top of that, much to our surprise, her lab results showed a depleted white blood cell (WBC) count of only 0.7 and normal is greater than 4500. Now what? Being overly immunosuppressed and not having enough WBCs to fight infection contributed to the level the ulceration had progressed. No way now could her body fight any infection off on its own. Consequently there were several things to be addressed and concerned about. (One being the elephant - Mr. Rejection - trying to come out of the shadows.)

Due to her low WBC count increasing her risk for further infection, Natalee was admitted to UPMC Montefiore in reverse isolation. She had to be briefly taken off her anti-rejection medications so the ulcers could be resolved. Doing so allowed her to heal, and she was eventually released with a normal white cell count. The ulcers were no longer a threat and she resumed her immunosuppressant meds. (So far, so good....so we thought.)

Chapter 32

Through the Revolving Door

Natalee was back in Pittsburgh again a few weeks later for a biopsy of the grafted pancreas after developing *possible* symptoms of rejection once again. The biopsy confirmed the beginning stages. She was admitted and treated with her dependable friend, Solumedrol IV, to halt the rejection and was allowed to return to home when the treatment proved to be successful. Another bullet dodged. At least for the moment....

She was only home a few days when her blood work showed an elevated Creatinine (CR) level, indicating a decline in kidney function. Now what? (Not good news is what.) After a kidney biopsy confirmed acute rejection in that allograft, too, she was readmitted to the hospital. (Definitely not good news.) When she arrived on the unit where she was always admitted - her third stay in a short span of time - she was greeted by the staff all lined up to welcome her back, applauding her! (I wondered if she was going to be presented with an award for the most admissions so close together.) This time, she was started on treatments of Thymoglobin, an IV immunosuppressant, to try and reverse the rejection in both grafts. (Prayer, however, was going to be foremost in the line of defense against this frightening new challenge.)

It was confirmed the rejection of her kidney was antibody-mediated type rejection - her body was forming antibodies against the donor kidney, attacking it and causing damage. Plasmaphoresis, an exchange of blood plasma to rid the body of the antibodies, was ordered. A machine, similar to dialysis, separates and removes the plasma portion of the blood where the antibodies are located and replaces it with good plasma or a plasma substitute. Natalee had a double-lumen central venous catheter (a PICC line) inserted to receive the treatment. (It can be left in place for an extended period, which she liked better than a Tesio.)

After another lengthy hospital stay Natalee was to be discharged home on June 20. She was to have a much disliked Tesio catheter inserted at a local hospital to replace the PICC line. The plasmaphoresis treatments would continue locally as an outpatient to try and save the kidney. It was confirmed by then that the pancreas graft had fully rejected and Natalee was back to square one - taking insulin and following a diabetic diet. Certainly devastating news, but not something we were unaware could happen. Transplants are not always a sure thing; no guarantees. Disappointed, but per her usual, she accepted being back to finger pricks, diets and insulin; thankful she was free of the diabetes for almost two years. (Time to forge ahead and focus on saving the kidney.)

Much to Natalee's frustration, the local hospital could not schedule inserting the Tesio for another week, so her discharge was canceled and the catheter was inserted the next day at Montefiore with treatment to start the following day. (She just wanted to come home.)

During the administration of the anesthesia to have the Tesio inserted, Natalee said she had a sharp abdominal pain and a feeling like "water being squirted" into her abdomen. The anesthesia she was given took effect right away and she wasn't able to report what she felt to anyone at that time. Afterward she mentioned it to the doctors, but no one could figure out what caused the sensation or fleeting pain. (A stump-the-doctor mystery for the time being.)

Chapter 33

The Very Most Horrible Scariest Nightmarish Day of Our Lives

Thank goodness things worked out like they did, causing her to stay in Pittsburgh. (God intervening.)

Natalee began having intermittent minor rectal bleeding along with continuing nausea and cramping in her abdomen. The bleeding was thought to possibly be hemorrhoidal at the time, but they were still checking and trying to figure out what was causing her problems. All avenues of finding the cause came up with negative results. A few days later, she was to possibly (there's that word again!) be released if she felt well enough and her diabetes was in control with taking insulin again.

A little while after she returned from a plasmaphoresis treatment the day she was to be discharged, she began having intense intermittent acute abdominal pain, accompanied with cramping. Natalee was in the bathroom when she began feeling like she was going to pass out. She rang the emergency bell for help. The nurse barely got her back to bed before Natalee did pass out. Her blood pressure had dropped to an almost imperceptible 70/40. Her color was turning cyanotic - a blue/gray skin color from lack of oxygen related to decreased cardiac output. Emergency measures were immediately instituted and one of the doctors present on the unit rushed in to examine her. Accompanied by other staff, he pushed the bed with her in it straight to the ICU. Her life was hanging in the balance at this point. (Little did anyone know it was a precursor of things to come.)

Once Natalee arrived in ICU, the GI docs came to see her, thinking she might have had GI bleeding from all the steroids administered to her in the past few weeks. They did an emergency EGD, but nothing abnormal was noted in her upper GI tract, so they decided to prep her for a lower GI endoscopy to see if they could determine where the bleeding originated from. Before they were able to take her for the lower GI, one of her post-transplant doctors came to see her, even though she was off that day. She had stopped in on the 12S unit and asked where Natalee was when she didn't see her name on the board. When she learned what happened, concerned about what they told her, she immediately went to the ICU. After reviewing all the facts, the puzzle pieces came into focus for her and triggered her memory. She remembered a post pancreatic transplant patient elsewhere who presented with the same symptoms Natalee was having. She called the surgeon who had performed Natalee's pancreas transplant in September 2005 and discussed with him what she thought was happening. He came at once to the hospital (also on his day off), and it was decided to go ahead with emergency surgery to find and repair the source of the bleeding. Thankfully, she wasn't stumped and played her hunch, which turned out to be correct. (God intervening again.)

While all this was going on, David and I were on our way to Pittsburgh, hoping she would definitely be released. En route, we got a call telling us they were moving Natalee to ICU due to abnormal bleeding. Say what? It normally took us two hours get to the hospital, but we ended up having to take a detour due to road construction, so it took way longer. As time dragged on my anxiety level was out the roof not knowing exactly what was going on with Natalee. I was vibrating in my seat. (Good thing David was driving.) My mind was racing, emanating in my heart hammering in my chest, culminating with my pulse furiously tap dancing a percussive rhythm in my ears. Being a nurse, I, of course, thought of every possible awful cause. It was a helpless feeling, but not hopeless. At least I had to keep reminding myself of that. I had to depend on faith, prayer and the expertise of the doctors. It seemed like we would never get to the hospital, time seemed to be moving slower than the crawling claustrophobic crush of bumper-to-bumper madness. I needed to be with Natalee NOW. McKenna, fortunately, was with her other grandmother and spared witnessing my evident overwhelming anxiety. We weren't going to call them until we got to the hospital and talked with the doctors and knew more about what was happening. (I couldn't put McKenna through that emotional turmoil.)

Arriving at the hospital, I felt like I had a cold stone of foreboding sitting in my stomach and a one-ton anchor sinking into the depths of my soul as they ushered us into the room to see Natalee. She was alert enough to know we were there. Overall, the tenor in the room was dire. IV fluids were being delivered at a wide open rate to keep her blood pressure up, and she had been given 4 liters, yes, *liters*, of blood to replace what was turning out to be a major exsanguination. In the back of my mind I knew that one liter is equal to 1.06 quarts, and the body holds about 6 quarts of blood. Loss of more than 40% can lead to the need for immediate resuscitation or death can occur within five minutes. (I really didn't want to think about it. *And still don't.*) She was going into hypovolemic shock, which can lead to decreased cardiac output and blood clots, loss of blood pressure and organ failure. I do not like horror movies and now I was living one - horrified down to my bones. I saw what I will never be able to unsee - Natalee possibly hemorrhaging to death before my eyes, and there was nothing I could do to stop it. I can't begin to explain all the thoughts and feelings that were running through me. My inner feelings were numb, and I didn't quite believe my outer reality was really happening. My lungs felt too inelastic to even breathe. It was a terrifying nightmare, but I was awake. David was off to the other side of her and thankfully couldn't see all the blood, but he was equally dazed with overwhelming fear and helplessness.

Fear can cripple and action needed to be taken, and the doctors methodically did just that. Things were happening quickly all around her, but it seemed like slow motion. I lost count of all the doctors and nurses buzzing around her doing all they could to remedy the situation and keep her alive. The whole scene was surreal, a visual that will forever live etched vivid in my mind in an unwelcome movie in high definition.

After what seemed to me like an organized mad scramble to prepare for the surgery, she was quickly on her way to the OR. We kissed her and told her we loved her and silently availed God's mercy as they wheeled her out of the room to the OR, praying we would see her again. (McKenna couldn't lose another parent.) We still did not, however, let McKenna know what was happening. I felt a stab of guilt penetrate my heart for not calling to let her know the situation; even so, I couldn't put that emotional burden on her until we knew the outcome of the surgery. We needed a miracle…. a really, *really* big one. (*Only* God could pull her through these desparate insurmountable odds.)

My thoughts were too disseminated to focus on any one thing. A kaleidoscope of pictures of Natalee's situation ran through my head. David and I spent the time waiting by calling family and friends to ask them to fervently pray for Natalee's critical situation. The distraction appeased our worried imaginations for the time being. I even called my ex. His number was in Natalee's phone that I now had for safe keeping. At the time, we hadn't spoken since the night he called David to ask him to adopt Natalee. I'm sure he was shocked I was calling, but probably knew I would only be calling with bad news since he and Natalee kept in touch and he knew she was in the hospital. He said he and his wife would be praying and asked to be kept up to date with her condition. Time seemed to stand still while David and I finished waiting in silence, too numb to talk, quietly praying for another much needed life-saving miracle. (I was trusting God for one more.)

The surgery lasted a couple hours and both doctors came to talk to us afterward. We were buoyed by the news that she made it through surgery. I felt like I could breathe again. They said if they had not taken her to surgery when they did, she would have hemorrhaged to death in just a short while. The source of the hemorrhage was a ruptured iliac artery. An iliac artery aneurysm occurrence is less than 1% of all aneurysms and are difficult to detect on physical exam. I wonder if what she called the "water squirting in her abdomen" feeling was the beginning of a leak leading to the rupture? Something no one would have guessed. It was explained to us the failed pancreas caused a type of pseudo aneurysm, forming a growing hematoma that ruptured where the iliac artery was connected to supply blood to the grafted pancreas. The doctor told us they repaired the iliac artery and removed the grafted pancreas. Natalee had a total of ten *liters* of blood to save her life, which is almost twice what her body normally had circulating. (God bless blood donors.) We later learned there were only about forty reported cases worldwide of iliac artery rupture after pancreas transplant at the time of this happening to her. Aneurysm rupture has a very high mortality rate, but Natalee miraculously beat the odds. (What can I say, Natalee loves being a statistic; just glad she wasn't on the high mortality list for this one.)

> But He said, "The things that are impossible with people are possible with God." (Luke 18:27 AMP) Behold, I am the Lord, the God of all flesh; is there anything too difficult for Me? (Jeremiah 32:27 AMP)

It came up a few days later in conversation that Natalee's heart had stopped during surgery and how close she came to dying. I must have looked shocked - like a ton of bricks just fell on me. David said he remembered the doctor telling us that they "lost her" during the surgery, but with the trauma and drama of all that transpired I may have not absorbed or processed that information when the doctor told us. I was living in a very limited reality at the time and apparently only heard that she survived the surgery. (The thought of how close Natalee was on the brink of death rattles me to the core to this day.)

If Natalee had been sent home June 20, the local hospital would have been stumped and not known what was happening to her in time. She surely would have died before we could have gotten her out the door and on the way to Pittsburgh. If her doctor hadn't shown up on her day off and inquired about Natalee, took the initiative to go to see her in ICU, then played her hunch as to what was causing the bleeding, the outcome may have been quite different. The other surgeon being available to answer the call and agree to give up his day off to assist in performing a difficult surgery was not just by chance. Their dedication is beyond noteworthy. There is no way to adequately thank her doctors and other staff for all they did so that we still have our daughter. And thanks most of all for God's intervention; He was surely watching over Natalee for so many disparate events to come together; answering a plethora of prayers, and blessing Natalee with a *gigantic* miracle. Even the doctors recognized all this as a miracle. (Most of us don't value life as much as we should....until it's threatened.)

I read a statement I saw online that the biblical author, John Piper, wrote regarding Romans 8:28 (NIV) - "And we know that in all things God works for the good of those who love Him, who have been called according to His purpose." He wrote, "We will have everything we need in this life, including painful things necessary to bring us to glory." I must remember *need* doesn't equal *want* and we *need* to be believers in Him first, and obedient to His word foremost. He will bring us through painful times when we truly seek Him. Despite her daily sufferings, Natalee doesn't look at all her painful times as a punishment, but those times bring her closer to God and wanting to be used to bring Glory to Him for the victories and miracles He has provided her.

> Blessed is the one who perseveres under trial because, having stood the test, that person will receive the crown of life that the Lord has promised to those who love Him. (James 1:12 NIV)

Natalee spent another week in the hospital, continuing treatment to reverse the kidney rejection she was still facing. In addition, the endocrinologists continued seeing her regarding regulating her insulin and diet while she was being reacquainted with having diabetes. She was released seven days after surgery and began outpatient plasmaphoresis three times a week locally. David and I shuffled work schedules to get her there and back home until she was able to drive herself. (Hopefully life would soon return to "normal"….whatever that is!)

Chapter 34

More Battle Scars

On the evening of July fourth, Natalee began having persistent pain in her lower rib cage area and abdomen. (Sigh. Now what?) She called Pittsburgh, and one of her doctors was the doctor on call and instructed her to be seen in the ER at UMPC Presby the following day unless the pain got worse, then she was to go there right away. The pain didn't intensify during the night, so David took her to Pittsburgh in the morning, and she was admitted. I had to work that day while vivid flashbacks of her previous nightmare were still fresh in the back of my now-what racing mind. Not a good day for any of us. (McKenna included, since she would be shuffled around again.)

It was determined Natalee had a post-op abdominal infection and/or fluid in the abdomen. IV antibiotics were ordered along with continuing the plasmaphoresis. She was discharged in a few days on the IV antibiotics and was ordered home care nurses from the agency where I worked to assist with them and report her progress to Pittsburgh. (I was not her nurse in that instance, just her mom.)

Natalee went back to outpatient transplant clinic for another kidney biopsy on July 13, and received a call after the results came back that the biopsy confirmed ongoing rejection. So, back to Pittsburgh for readmission to receive an amalgamation of IV meds - Thymoglobin, Solumedrol, and IVIG (intravenous immunoglobulin G which is given to people with immune deficiency) - to hopefully reverse what was now T-cell rejection of the kidney. (T-cells are a type of lymphocyte and are part of the immune system.)

After a week, there was no progress in reversing the rejection, so it was decided to stop all treatment because it was only making her more immunosuppressed and susceptible to infection. (The rock and the hard place decision.) It was a paralyzing realization when she was told her kidney might continue to function for two months or even up to two years. She was looking at dialysis whenever it did stop functioning, but could be eligible to be on the transplant list for another kidney. She was discharged from the hospital; back to square one. (The post-op infection had resolved, so that was good news at least.)

When Barb learned Natalee's transplant was in rejection, I told her we would never ask or expect her to donate her kidney for Natalee to have another transplant. Barb was working full-time and raising four children alone while endeavoring to make ends meet. I know, if her circumstances were different, she would volunteer again in a heartbeat. (I'll always be beyond grateful for her willingness to give Natalee a kidney without hesitation the first time around.)

Chapter 35

Becoming a Frequent Flyer

Natalee was only home a short time when the abdominal pain returned and she began spiking a fever. (Now what?) A CT scan revealed what was either a hematoma or an abscess, and on July 31, she was readmitted to the hospital. (All these admissions felt like being stuck in a revolving door, without the fun.) Natalee had an ultrasound for visualization of the area so a drain could be placed into the affected area to remove the fluid in the pocket that had formed causing a localized infection with pain and pressure in the area. (Natalee said she should have had a zipper placed in her abdomen for easier access.)

A few days later the drain was removed after confirmation there was no more fluid in the pocketed area, but she decided to play a few rounds of "stump the doctors." Even though she was on IV antibiotics, she continued spiking a fever on and off. Although the blood cultures were negative, a big concern was that she might still become septic due to her depressed immune system. Because she was so immunosuppressed, it was decided to lower her Prograf dose and take her off the Cellcept (both immunosuppressants) in hopes her body could help fight the infection. Since the fevers persisted, an oral antibiotic was added to the IV antibiotics to hopefully prevent a generalized sepsis. Instead, in true Natalee fashion, she developed an elevated blood pressure that persisted requiring a change in those medications, which eventually brought it down to normal levels. If it's not one thing, it's another. Everything is a juggling and balancing act. (Definitely her circus and her monkeys.)

She had been hoping to be home in a few days, but again complications kept her hospitalized longer. We all had to have faith God had a plan and focus on going forward with hope for a better day. Sometimes I am baffled at how she stayed so positive being in the hospital almost the whole summer - tired of never going outside, eating repetitive hospital food three meals a day, being bored, not seeing McKenna or family very often, enduring poking and prodding, confined to one room and not having a "life." She was just plain tired at this point - tired of being a "frequent flyer" of hospital admissions.

It wasn't easy for us, or McKenna either, trying to live our "normal" lives and wonder what was going on with Natalee at the hospital; only able to visit on our days off. Frequent phone calls had to suffice. From past experience we knew things could change in a heartbeat, so that concern was always in the back of all our minds. (Another always present elephant in the crowded room of "What now?") While all this was going on with Natalee, we were able to hire Natalee's neighbor to care for McKenna during the day when we were at work. (At least that was something consistent in her inconsistent life.)

Looking for any hidden pockets of infection before allowing her to come home, Natalee had a CT scan from her head to her toes. She was to be released if her temperature remained normal and she had no other problems. (Key word in that sentence: *if*.) "If" won out, however, and other disappointing and scary news was going to keep her in the hospital longer.

The CT showed a scary development - a small pocket of fluid near the iliac artery, so she had another procedure to insert a drain into the area. (She needed that zipper in her abdomen for sure.) It was decided to discontinue the Prograf so she could fight the infection on her own, but that put the kidney that was still functioning at greater risk for complete rejection. (Alas, a rock and even harder place to be.)

McKenna was hoping Natalee would be discharged before school started so she could spend some time with her. By this time her whole summer was spent with Natalee's neighbor during the day, and then with us in the evenings and nights. She missed her house and her own bed, but most of all, she missed her mom.

Finally! On August 15, Natalee was released after not having a fever for 24 hours. The IVs had been discontinued and the Tesio catheter had also been pulled because it wasn't being used any longer. Just a needless source for infection at that point. She was so excited she could actually take a shower again. (The things we take for granted.)

It would take a while to adjust her insulin now that she was out of the hospital and eating regular meals and was a little more active. She hoped that when she started feeling better she could get an insulin pump again. Things were starting to get back to "normal." (Hopefully.)

Chapter 36

Maybe We Should Just Move to Pittsburgh

August 24 was clinic day. Her CR (Creatinine) level was up to 3.4 (normal is 0.6 to 1.2), and her GFR was down to 16%. (Increased CR levels in the blood indicate poor kidney function.) Now the doctors would be watching her lab numbers very closely to see when dialysis would be warranted and let her know.

We knew firsthand things can change drastically in a short amount of time and by August 29 her GFR dropped to 12%. Dialysis was a nearer reality. Not the news we wanted to hear so soon. On the good news side, her blood sugars were more regulated without her having hypoglycemic episodes. (Any progress, even if it's just a little, is cause to be thankful.)

Natalee would need to have surgery to have an AV fistula created for future dialysis. An appointment with the vascular surgeon was scheduled for the middle of September for mapping the fistula. Mapping involves using a Doppler - a machine that uses sound waves to show underlying images to locate veins and arteries, which are then marked for the actual surgery once they are visualized. A fistula is not viable for three to four weeks after the surgery, and I didn't feel, with the way her GFR was rapidly dropping, that she could afford to wait that long for dialysis to start. We contacted the doctors in Pittsburgh about possibly having a Tesio inserted ASAP to begin hemodialysis before she got symptomatic. It was a viable option, but not one Natalee was looking forward to having to endure. (And not being able to shower again.)

On September 6, when Pittsburgh got Natalee's weekly lab results, she got a call to come to UPMC Montefiore to be admitted. Now what? Her white blood cell count was low (1.0), CR and BUN (Blood Urea Nitrogen) levels were elevated, and her GFR was only 6% - all critical levels warranting dialysis to start ASAP, before she got into serious jeopardy. (Sigh.)

David and I both left work early to take her to Pittsburgh after we made arrangements for our friends to pick up McKenna for us. It was a recurring scenario - McKenna was on another field trip with her Girl Scout troop. We told Janet and Rick where to pick up McKenna. I'm sure when McKenna saw them she knew right away something was wrong with Natalee involving another hospital stay. Too much drama for one little girl to have to contend with. (And no family available to comfort her as only family can do.)

Natalee was admitted into reverse isolation due to her low WBCs increasing her risk of infection with no way to fight it. She was started on Neupogen injections subcutaneously to stimulate an increase in her white count. Her red cell count and hemoglobin were also seriously low, precipitating the tiredness and shortness of breath she'd been having. The concern of a very low red cell count is it can trigger a heart attack. (Something else on the growing prayer list of things to be apprehensive about.)

A Tesio catheter was inserted the next morning, and later that evening they took her over to Presby for a three-hour dialysis treatment. She was to possibly be discharged that day, but due to the continued nausea, vomiting, and pain that bloomed like fireworks on the fourth of July from the anesthesia and Tesio placement, as usual "possibly" was the defining word and she remained in the hospital. Vein mapping for fistula placement was done the next day. She said, "My arms look like I ran through a room of crazed preschoolers with markers!" We had not been informed as yet if they planned to do the actual fistula surgery there or if we were to keep the appointment for the next week with the vascular surgeon at Bon Secours hospital in Altoona. ("Wait and see" time.)

The next morning, she had another dialysis treatment via the Tesio. Later in the day she was given two units of blood to boost her H&H. She was feeling and looking better already. (Prayers at work.)

Natalee's voice was sounding stronger. A good sign. Her Creatinine level dropped from 6.4 to 4.3 after two dialysis treatments. She was still having some degree of nausea, but had an improving appetite. The doctor was in to see her in the morning, and since arrangements hadn't been made for dialysis at a center in Johnstown yet, she had to stay to have a treatment in the morning and then possibly get to come home. ("Possibility" was a state we seemed to live in and entertain all too frequently with "Waitnsee" our hometown.)

Things seem to get done more slowly over the weekends in hospitals, even large ones. However, Natalee's social worker was excellent at making all the arrangements we needed and definitely went the extra mile. She had everything taken care of to make a smooth transition to home, and the next morning, Natalee was discharged with arrangements made to begin dialysis three days a week at a local dialysis center we chose. A four-hour treatment was scheduled before we left Pittsburgh and hopefully she would no longer be the "frequent flyer" of hospital admissions. (We all needed a break.)

Natalee definitely wanted to get back on the transplant list for another kidney ASAP, but not a pancreas. Now we are on a new journey, learning to adjust to a new "normal" and hoping for a smooth ride ….(for a while at least.)

A Mom's Day-by-day Digest of an Interrupted Life with More Beautiful Scars and Badges of Honor

Chapter 1

Preparing for Dialysis

Sept. 13, 2007 Natalee continues having unrelieved nausea since her hospital discharge; doubting that it's still a persisting side effect of the anesthesia. (I'm wondering if it could it possibly just be her GP or even a case of gastritis?) Her PCP ordered a CT scan of her abdomen, and changed her anti-ulcer medication to see if that will give her any relief.

To add to her misery, she's back to square one - adjusting insulin injection doses multiple times a day to try to regulate her glucose levels. It will be a day of rejoicing when she is able to get an insulin pump again so she can gain better control. She's also looking forward to being rid of the bothersome Tesio as soon as she has a viable fistula for dialysis, hopefully in the near future. One bright spot is that she is feeling stronger and less tired after adjusting to being on dialysis. (She's even able to drive herself there and home.)

Sept. 14, 2007 McKenna had the day off school today and had to spend four hours at the dialysis center and then an hour at a PCP appointment with Natalee. Right now waiting at dialysis is somewhat of a novelty for her, but I'm sure that will wane with time. At least they have TV for her to watch and a big comfy couch for her to hang out on. (Sadly, it has become part of life on days she has no school and David and I are working.)

After work today, David and I picked up Natalee and McKenna and went to Altoona to see the vascular surgeon who will be creating the AVF, a virtual lifeline, in Natalee's arm. They usually create it in the less dominant arm, but Natalee's veins are poor and her pulse is weak in her left arm, making it necessary that it be created in her dominant right arm so her circulation won't be further impaired in the left. Like me, she is ambidextrous, which will come in quite handy for her while her arm is healing! (Pun intended!) Each of us do some things left-handed, some right-handed, and some with the hand that's handiest. (Sorry!) Natalee told me about the time she was holding a sleeping McKenna with her left arm, and filling out some papers using her right hand while waiting for an appointment. When her left arm got tired, she switched McKenna to her right arm and continued writing with her left hand. A woman in the waiting room looked puzzled and finally asked Natalee, "Weren't you just writing with your right hand?" Natalee laughed and explained she could write with either hand. (I think the woman was relieved she wasn't hallucinating.)

Instead of one surgery to create the fistula, the surgeon said it will take two because he will have to use a deeper vein to first create the fistula, and then, when it is "grown", he will have to move it closer to the surface for accessibility. To create a fistula, a slit is made in both an artery and a nearby vein which are then connected at the slit so some blood from the artery leaks into the vein, making it grow larger. This way blood can be circulated from the person, through the dialysis machine, and returned through the same site via one needle that is placed into the arterial side of the fistula and one in the venous side. The blood is circulated through a special filter (an artificial kidney), and fluid dialyzer (dialysate) detoxifies it before it is returned to the body. The machine monitors the flow of blood while it is outside the body.

AVFs can be created in the upper or lower arm or the upper leg, and are considered the best option for dialysis. They are less expensive to maintain, have lower complication rates, and have a longer life-span - some lasting up to 35 years. Natalee is scheduled for surgery September 19. Another day off work for me. Natalee tells people, "Instead of going to the beach for a vacation, my mom goes to hospitals and doctor offices!" (No wonder I never have a tan!)

Before we left the vascular surgeon's office, he introduced Natalee to an elderly gentleman in the waiting room who had a AV fistula created recently. He was very willing to let Natalee palpate the area and see the tiny incisions in his arm. I know it made her feel more at ease about having the surgery after being able to see the result and feel the fistula. (Fistulas have a whooshing, "buzzing" sound called a "bruit", and a very prominent pulse called a "thrill" that feels like it's vibrating to the touch.)

Sept. 19, 2007 Up early for the AV surgery today. My taste for coffee returned, and I was glad the waiting room had really great coffee to keep me awake. (Same old pervasive chairs, though.) Natalee will be able to return to using her arm tomorrow, within reason. She is to return for a checkup in two weeks, but for now, we were instructed to keep an eye on her circulation in the arm and report any changes. (One step closer to saying good-bye to the Tesio, and hello to a shower!)

Sept. 27, 2007 The phone rang late in the evening; a sound we don't like to hear after 9 P.M. It's generally not good news. A very excited Natalee was calling to say she felt the "thrill" in her fistula for the first time and felt a small bump in the area - the developing fistula. (It was not good news.... it was *great* news!)

Sept. 29, 2007 Yesterday, was Natalee's follow-up appointment with the vascular surgeon. The sutures were removed, and the site is healing nicely. The doctor was pleased with the growth of the fistula, and Natalee is scheduled to return in two weeks to have the growth rechecked. The second surgery to move the fistula closer to the surface will be scheduled soon. (I've lost count the times Natalee has been under general anesthesia or twilight sleep.)

Natalee has been doing well with dialysis all except for an occasional drop in blood pressure at the end of her treatment. Intradialytic hypotension occurs when there is too much fluid pulled during dialysis and the blood becomes too "dry." When her pressure drops, she has to stay longer at dialysis and be given a small amounts of saline solution to raise her pressure again so it is safe for her to drive home. The saline is counterproductive, putting fluid back into her that she can't get rid of until her next treatment, but it is necessary.

Her uncontrolled blood sugars are the biggest problem now, especially when her GP interferes with her food intake and absorption. When her GP doesn't cooperate she can only manage to eat one meal a day without feeling sick, and sometimes she can't eat anything at all. It's hard to keep control while taking scheduled insulin injections when you can't count on eating regularly. With a pump, she would only need to give herself insulin to cover the carbs she eats, when she is able to eat, and to correct high readings. Natalee is hoping things are in order soon to get another insulin pump. (The high and low swings in her levels are taking a lot of out of her.)

Chapter 2

Transfusions and Wigs

Oct. 5, 2007 Natalee received a call from one of her doctors and was told she was to go to the hospital ASAP to be admitted due to a low H&H and WBC count. David picked McKenna up and took her to our house while Natalee and I headed to a local hospital for a "bonding" time. No one at the hospital admission office knew anything about orders for a direct admission, and told us we had to go to the ER. More blood work was done, and we had to wait to find out the results, and if she was to going be admitted...or what. (So, frustrating.) I was on call for work and had to leave at 9:00 p.m., but no decisions had been made yet. Later on, Natalee called me and said they were going to give her two units of blood and send her home - reasoning that her count "wasn't that bad." The problem now was that the blood would run until 3:00 a.m. The usual juggling act ensued: David got the call she was being discharged at 4:30 a.m., but when he got to the hospital he had to wait for her to finally be released at 5:30 a.m. By then it was time for him to get ready to go to work on only a few hours sleep. I got McKenna off to school, and then readied myself for work. (No happy jugglers in this circus.)

Oct. 10, 2007 This evening we went shopping to get Natalee a wig. Her hair is thinning at a fast rate, presumably from the side effects of the Thymoglobin she received. She bought two wigs that are styled similar to how she normally wears her shoulder-length, almost black hair. She was apprehensive about getting the wigs and felt people would know she was wearing one. As we were paying for them, the sales person revealed to us that *she* was wearing a wig! (That we both were surprised is an understatement.)

Oct. 12, 2007 I think Natalee's hair loss has been more traumatic for both of us than any of her surgeries. I guess it's because it is something more visible than a surgical scar on her body she can hide; her hair is part of her identity. (I reminded Natalee that all the glamorous movie stars wear wigs and hair pieces and she's definitely a "star" in my book, literally!)

A mysterious spike in her temperature has been occurring in the evenings. Blood cultures were drawn today at dialysis to make sure an infection is not brewing since her WBCs are so low, increasing the risk of infection. ("Wait and see" time.)

Natalee was informed that Pittsburgh called the dialysis center and they are setting up some of the tests she will need to be on the active transplant list for a kidney. Again, there are a myriad of tests she has to have done regularly that will be ongoing up and until she would get a kidney. One step at a time, one day at a time…can't look beyond that right now. We will hope and pray she has acceptable test results with no major setbacks. (Knowing how well she looked and felt after the first kidney transplant keeps us hopeful she'll be able to get another kidney.)

Oct. 16, 2007 Tonight Natalee had what's left of her rapidly thinning hair cut short. It's sad to see her losing it. The hairdresser, who is new to us, wasn't sure at first if Natalee had a wig on when we arrived. Fooling her made Natalee more confident in wearing it. (A small victory in the midst of a big trauma.)

Oct. 17, 2007 Today Natalee had a follow-up appointment with the vascular surgeon to check the progress of the developing fistula. He felt the area several times then commented the pulse was weak and added that he never encountered this before. Natalee and I told him about "stump the doctor" - that if something rare could occur it would happen to her. He scheduled her for the second surgery to move the fistula closer to the surface and felt that would correct the problem. (Praying it does.)

Chapter 3

Now What?

Oct. 26, 2007 All I can say is, "Now what?" Another new doctor to stump is what. Natalee was sent to see a local neutropenic oncologist regarding the ongoing low WBCs. He is ordering a bone marrow biopsy to determine the source of the problem. Natalee is definitely not looking forward to another painful poking procedure.

Nov. 1, 2007 Today was the dreaded bone marrow biopsy. It was very painful, more so because the doctor had difficulty getting a sample from her posterior hip bone. The doctor said he " never had such a problem." Natalee told him about "stump the doctor." (She should just carry a sign saying "I stump doctors. Welcome to the club." Then hand him a membership card.)

She had to lay on her side during the procedure with one arm up by her head. When the biopsy was completed, she was asked to turn over. Her wig somehow popped off and landed on the floor! She said no one missed a beat or blinked. The nurse picked the wig up, handed it to a mortified Natalee, casually pushed over the bedside table and flipped open the mirror so Natalee could see to put her wig on straight. Natalee said, "I guess you see *that* a lot!" The nurse matter-of-factly replied, "Yes, we do!" Natalee was just glad the biopsy was over. (I could say she flipped her lid over it.....but I won't.)

Nov. 8, 2007 Natalee received a call from the neutropenic oncologist to say he wants to see her tomorrow and possibly repeat the bone marrow biopsy. (That is one poking procedure she is definitely not wanting to repeat after the last experience.) The result of last weeks biopsy was shocking, showing virtually *no-zero-nada* white cells and very few red cells being produced. It's very disappointing her levels have not improved with the injections she has been receiving to boost cell production. I marvel at how she faces all this and stays so positive and upbeat. I can't even explain how much I hurt for her having to go through all this pain and emotional turmoil. (She should be enjoying life - teaching, and being a mother who can enjoy doing things with her daughter.)

It takes a lot of strength to get up day in and day out and face a normal everyday life. It takes even more strength to face another day with chronic illness in the picture, not knowing what unwanted challenges will present themselves today or the next day, or what life-changing news, good or bad, a simple phone call will bring. I often hear people say that life isn't fair. Maybe it isn't fair, but it is what you make of it. (Choices.)

I especially worry about McKenna, who is now eleven... and a half. At her age, the half is very important. *(At my age - not so much.)* She continues to deal with more than most adults face in a lifetime. (She should just be able to be a kid with no worries.)

Yesterday, I met with one of my friends for lunch and said out loud what I think about all the time - I may outlive my daughter. (The behemoth elephant in the room.) I remember what the mother of the daughter who had the five-organ transplant told me as she cared for her daughter who was at risk of and even close to dying several times. She shared with me she had come to terms that her daughter might die. Only those of us with very ill children could even understand how a mother could accept that, or even say that out loud. Truth be told, it's ratcheted into the back of my mind, even if I don't say it out loud. I live with that elephant every day and try to keep it contained in the far reaches of my thoughts. Often times I have to remind myself not to dwell on foreboding and negative thoughts, but on the positive fact that Natalee is still here with us, fighting on. We must all seize the day given to us with alacrity and make the most of it while we can and above all - look to and trust God. How people survive without God in their lives is a mystery to me. (I would crumple like cellophane in a fire without God to lean on.)

Nov. 9, 2007 Stump-the-doctor time again. (Here's your membership card!) The neutropenic oncologist looked at Natalee with disbelief and said, "There's *nothing* in your bone marrow, it's empty. I've never seen anything like this before." Natalee startled the doctor when she started laughing, but sometimes the laughable and the dreadful closely reside in the same strange space. Natalee quickly explained to the doctor why she was laughing when he looked quite taken aback. What else can you do after facing so many doctors that have said "I've never seen this before." It becomes so absurd it's laughable. Natalee tells people her purpose in life is to be a guinea pig to help doctors figure out what to do for puzzling medical problems. (She may be onto something.)

New plan: a blood transfusion is ordered for tomorrow and arrangements are being made for her to see a hematology oncologist in Pittsburgh at the Hillman Cancer Center for further investigation as to what is going on. The big worry right now is Natalee contracting an infection she can't fight off without white blood cells to lead the charge. Hand washing, Clorox wipes and hand sanitizer - our good old reliable friends - and avoiding others with anything contagious is the protocol for now. (And much prayer.)

Right now I'd like to pull the covers over my head and hope to wake up to find all of Natalee's never- ending trials were only a bad dream. I go to bed thinking about her. I wake up the same. One day is no different than any other; it's mentally and emotionally exhausting. In my heart, I truly believe in "Let go, let God", but sometimes it's just really, *really* hard ....my mind doesn't seem to have an off switch. I try to appear positive on the outside to others, but inside myself I fight daily to be rid of the negative thoughts that are waiting in every corner of my mind, ready to engulf me if I let them.

> It is true that I am an ordinary weak human being, but
> I don't use human plans and methods to win my battles.
> I use God's mighty weapons, not those made by men,
> to knock down the devil's strongholds. (2 Corinthians
> 10:3-4 TLB)

I feel sad more than anything. Sad watching Natalee go though all she does knowing there is nothing I can physically do to make her well. Sad that McKenna has to see her mother struggle every day with one ailment or another and has had to grow up faster in so many ways. I know it is a constant worry for McKenna, wondering what will happen to Natalee next, and if or when she'll be in the hospital again. Frankly, knowing Natalee could die from all her health problems is far too big a burden she is faced with every day. (Especially since she's already lost her dad.)

It's sometimes hard to talk with people who haven't had to go though another person's inveterate struggles. After a while, people slowly start pulling away because they no longer know what to say, or they just don't want to hear about your "situation" anymore. People don't truly understand the full scope of it all - the toll it can take financially, mentally and emotionally. I read divorce rates are reportedly high - a staggering 75% - in couples with chronically ill children due to challenges beyond those of an average parent. We are so blessed that David has always been rock solid and right there for us, and God is on our side because we are on His. Looking back, I now see that David would always be there for us since he came into our relationship when Natalee was ill with SSS. He could have walked away then since we were only dating at the time. (We are blessed that he didn't.)

There are so many normal, everyday things and other personal issues we have to cope with along with all Natalee's problems. One of the hardest is not having any other family support. Thank goodness we have great friends who let us know they care. The Greek philosopher, Euripides, said this: "Friends show their love in times of trouble, not happiness." (So true.)

Nov. 10, 2007 Natalee went to a local hospital today for two blood transfusions starting at noon, and we finally left for home after 9:00 p.m. So much for our Saturday, but at least she feels better after being transfused. I asked myself why visitor chairs so detestable? I decided it's so visitors are not encouraged to overstay their welcome. (Then again, who would want to anyhow?)

Nov. 12, 2007 Feeling good after the transfusion didn't last long. Last night, Natalee had trouble sleeping due to chest heaviness related to the excess fluid circulating in her post transfusion. Good nurse that I am, I didn't realize until today that Saturday is not a good day for a transfusion. I was too focused on other concerning things going on with her. Sunday, Tuesday or Thursday would be better days for transfusions so she would have dialysis the following day to rid her of the excess fluid. Live and learn.

(Unfortunately Natalee had to live with being very uncomfortable while we learned.)

Nov. 14, 2007 The surgery to move the AVF closer to the surface went well yesterday. Dialysis can begin using the fistula in a month, barring any complications. Natalee is counting down one long month until she can get rid of the Tesio and take a shower! (Prepare for a major celebration to follow.)

Chapter 4

An Unexpected New Challenge

Nov. 27, 2007 God answered our prayers for good weather today for our trip to Hillman Cancer Center in Pittsburgh; always a bonus. The hematology oncologist she saw is very nice and impressed us with his knowledge. After reviewing her records, he told us she has Acquired Aplastic Anemia, probably immune-mediated, airing what I had already suspected. Another bone marrow biopsy is scheduled for next Tuesday at Hillman to confirm the diagnosis. (Natalee's facial expression showed a lack of unbridled exuberance, confirming she was not thrilled.)

Hearing the diagnosis out loud made it an actuality we didn't really want to have to acknowledge or hear verified. Severe Aplastic Anemia (SAA) is rare and can be fatal if not treated. Very scary. (I have cared for patients who died from it. One more elephant in the room to face.) It's also known as bone marrow failure. Stem cells, from which all three types of blood cells (red, white and platelets) develop in the bone marrow, are being destroyed; no manufactured cells are being released into her bloodstream. With treatment, there is a 75-85% five-year survival rate; a higher survival rate is associated with those who are younger in age. (Hey, Mr. Statistic… Natalee is younger and Queen of beating the odds with God on her side.)

The first treatment considered was immunosuppression, but Natalee is obviously already immunosuppressed. The next option would be a bone marrow transplant. A donor would have to be an *exact* match, unlike a donor for other transplants. In the meantime, the injections of medications specific to stimulating the WBCs will continue along with transfusion support. The transfusions are needed to keep her counts up and prevent further serious problems. On the other hand, transfusions cause the body to produce antibodies that are counterproductive with transplants. (Sigh.)

She is scheduled December sixth, for a kidney transplant evaluation. I wonder if she still needs to do that right now because she can't get another kidney until her Aplastic Anemia is addressed. (There are no current prospects on the horizon clamoring to be a living donor either.)

Right now we all just feel tired and numb. For now, focusing on finding out all we can about this new development and prepare to hit it head-on is the foremost issue to tackle. Natalee looks more ill every day, and truthfully, thoughts that she could succumb to the statistics before any treatment could be effective are trying to cloud my mind. I try not to think about it and to be thankful for answered prayers that have gotten her this far. (In the meantime, all we can do is continue to have faith and pray.)

> This is my command - be strong and courageous! Do not be afraid or discouraged. For the Lord your God is with you wherever you go. (Joshua 1:9 NLT) Don't be afraid, for I am with you. Don't be discouraged, for I am your God. I will strengthen you and help you. I will hold you up with my victorious right hand. (Isaiah 41:10 NLT)

Nov. 29, 2007 Researching SAA is frightening. Associated problems can develop, including irregular heart rhythms, an enlarged heart with heart failure, infections, and bleeding related to decreased platelet counts. In hindsight, Natalee had been exhibiting many of the symptoms over the past few months. It's always a matter of connecting the dots correctly to get the full picture, and time is always of the essence. Her counts are still too low, so she had two blood transfusions today.

I received an email from my amazing friend, Barb, in San Diego. I'm not surprised that she is already checking into how she can be tested to be a bone marrow donor for Natalee. I am so blessed to have such a wonderful and giving "adopted" sister. (Everyone needs a friend like Barb!)

Natalee doesn't have the energy or feel well enough to do much of anything. McKenna is such a great little helper with laundry, basic cooking and cleaning up. She is so grown up in many ways for age eleven (and a half), but she has had to be. I seriously need to try to find a cleaning person for Natalee. That's too much to expect McKenna to manage. She needs to be an eleven-and-a-half-year-old girl and do things kids her age do. To add to my own already full plate, my elderly mother, who lives alone in a two story house, needs more help now. (More to balance on already overloaded spinning plates.)

Dec. 4, 2007 Due to a snowstorm, we had to cancel the bone marrow biopsy in Pittsburgh today. (This is one time Natalee was overjoyed to see a snowstorm.)

Natalee is happy regarding the prospect of *possibly* having a bone marrow transplant soon. (*Possibly* and *if* are two words we hear all too often....meaning it could or could not happen, so don't count on it.) On the other hand, Natalee is unhappy about the fact she has the fistula now for dialysis and they haven't used it yet. In a moment of frustration, she commented, "I hope I didn't get this fistula for nothing!" (The Tesio remains in place, which means she still can't fully shower.)

When I am hurting or having a bad day I think about how Natalee endures all this with grace, courage, and humor, and I am humbled. I have nothing to complain about in comparison. She has been an inspiration to everyone who gets to know her. During the many hours of our "bonding" time spent waiting in doctor offices, clinic appointments and the ER, we usually joke and carry on. People who don't know us probably think we are either nuts, annoying, or just plain weird. Those who get to know Natalee eventually see what I see....someone who can have joy and be positive in spite of her circumstances. Yes, there are times when she is down, but she gets over it quickly. On and off, she has taken anti-depressant medication, but that was mostly when GP started taking over her life and she could no longer work. Incredibly, she no longer takes anti-depressants, but relies on peace from the Lord.

> The Lord gives His people strength. The Lord blesses them with peace. (Psalm 29:11 NLT) Now may the Lord of peace himself give you his peace at all times and in every situation. The Lord be with you all. (2 Thessalonians 3:16 NLT) I am leaving you with a gift - peace of mind and heart.

And the peace I give is a gift the world cannot give. So
don't be troubled or afraid. (John 14:27 NLT)

Today I asked Natalee what she wanted for Christmas from me and
her dad. She seriously replied, "Nothing." I asked her why, and she replied,
"You and Dad have done more than enough for me already." I know she
appreciates everything anyone does for her. Someone in my family made
an insensitive comment directly to Natalee - that it was terrible we did so
much for her, as if she asks, expects or demands it. Natalee never asks for
anything from us. (We do things for her simply because we love her, and
we can.)

Chapter 5

Why is it Always Something?

Dec. 6, 2007 Transplant called and mentioned again that the more blood transfusions Natalee has before being transplanted, the higher the risk for rejection due to antibodies. That's a gigantic rock and extremely hard place when her counts are so critically low. I can't even write what I am feeling in regard to all this. All we can do is continue to hope, pray, trust, and take a day at a time. (I am convinced God has a better plan.)

Natalee called at 9:00 p.m. She has a temp of 102+, but no other symptoms. Now what? I told her to call Hillman in the morning to see if they will do the bone marrow biopsy scheduled for tomorrow while she's running a fever. (I sincerely doubt they will, so right now I am mentally preparing for a change of plans.)

Dec. 11, 2007 After multiple calls back and forth to Pittsburgh, the biopsy is postponed. However, the doctor wanted her to come there for blood work. After explaining traveling there just for labs is too far and too taxing for her, arrangements were made for the blood work and a chest x-ray to be done locally. Her WBCs are still critically low, but they want to try and keep her out of the hospital, if possible. We should be used to delays and changes in plans, but it doesn't make it any easier. Natalee says I sigh a lot. I wonder why? Sighing is defined as a sound of comfort for the moment. (Big sighing pause here right now.....inhale deeply then exhale slowly.)

Dec. 13, 2007 It seems like every day lately there is something untoward happening. Today Natalee got a call that her scheduled colposcopy procedure was canceled due to freezing rain and hazardous road conditions. It will have to be rescheduled…. *again*. More delays. She wasn't feeling all that well anyway, so I guess it's for the best. I keep reminding myself to let God be in control….I sure don't feel like Natalee or I have any control right now. (If I could only shut my overloaded mind off. I'm still looking fruitlessly for the off switch.)

Dec. 15, 2007 McKenna and I went Christmas shopping today. Natalee is unable to participate due to feeling beyond tired, short of breath, weak and dizzy - all related to her low blood counts. Plus, she can't be out in a crowd for fear of catching something her body can't fight off. Most of her day is spent resting on the chaise feeling useless.

When McKenna and I arrived home, Natalee was asleep on the chaise. She doesn't bother to wear a wig around the house, and it's still shocking for me to see her without it. She told me she feels like a terrible mother because she can't do all the things she once did with McKenna. (I told her she is a great mom where it counts…..loving and supporting McKenna.)

I still need to find someone reliable to help Natalee with housework. No luck so far. With my work schedule and everything else on my overly full plate, I just don't have the time or energy. David and I are still in the process of remodeling the house my Aunt Gert left us so we can sell our current house and move where we will have more room. Our decision was based on two facts - 1) the house is close to my mother, and 2) the real life factual elephant in the room is all too frequently reminding us Natalee and McKenna may have to permanently live with us someday if Natalee becomes too ill to function in her own home. I know that sounds negative, but it's the reality of the situation. I can't even explain the gambit of emotions I feel in this situation. Sometimes I scare myself that I can talk about her illness so matter-of-factly. People probably think it's cold, but it's something I can't pretend is not there and one that our little family must face. On the other hand, I just want to fall apart; I feel so tired and overwhelmed at times. As her mom, I just want to make it all better right now. (Isn't that a mom's job?)

Chapter 6

Sanity

Dec. 16, 2007 Natalee has been too weak, too dizzy, and short of breath with any activity to be driving. David will take the time out of work to take her to dialysis M-W-F, and I will pick her up between visits to my assigned patients. (Back to the juggling act.)

Dec. 18, 2007 During the day, I have work and other things to take my mind off everything for a while, although it really never leaves my mind. Nighttime remains the enemy. (Has anyone seen my sanity?)

If truth be told, as much as I don't want to even have the thought, I am afraid Natalee won't make it to Christmas. She looks and is quite ill. Looking in Natalee's eyes today, knowing tomorrow could be the day you dread is beyond comprehension, especially since we faced almost losing her a few months ago. I can't come to terms with that thought, and have to keep that negative feeling at bay and try hard to be positive, trusting God for another miracle. I think of how the Apostle Peter was able to get out of the boat and walk on water to Jesus, *as long as he kept his eyes on Him.* When he took his eyes off of the Lord for a second and saw the circumstances surrounding him, he began to sink. Jesus then said to Peter,"O you of little faith, why did you doubt?" Then Peter cried out for the Lord to save him in his distress, and He did. (I need to keep my eyes solely on Jesus and not the surrounding stormy circumstances so my negative thoughts don't cause me to sink into a depthless void of doubt and despair.)

Tonight was McKenna's Christmas program at school. I know McKenna understands why Natalee can't be there, but it's still disappointing for them both. She should have been able to be there to enjoy seeing and hearing it for herself. (I wanted to cry, but had to be strong for McKenna.)

Chapter 7

More of the Same

Dec. 19, 2007 Today I was to take Natalee to dialysis at 10:00 a.m,. but was called to go ASAP to see a patient with a problem. I had to call David to leave work right away and take her. (Being late for dialysis throws everyone else's schedule off.) Thank goodness he was able to leave work as soon as I called. I decided to request Friday off work so I could take Natalee to and from dialysis without having to let that interfere with my job, or David's. (My boss is extremely understanding for now, but I don't want to take advantage of her goodwill.)

Dec. 22, 2007 My goal today was to clean house for Natalee. (I never did find a reliable cleaning person. The old adage "If you want something done, do it yourself" is applicable in this instance.) Natalee spent the entire day on the chaise. She looked miserable, but she never once outright complained. (I think she is too weak and tired to even complain.)

Later this evening, I spoke with Natalee, and she sounded a little better which allows me to mentally clear out unwelcome negative thoughts running through my head and replace them with positive ones. (I am hanging on to hope and faith.)

> Trust in the Lord with all your heart and lean not on your own understanding. (Proverbs 3:5 NIV) May the God of hope fill you with all joy and peace as you trust in him, so that you may overflow with hope by the power of the Holy Spirit. (Romans 15:13 NIV)

Dec. 28, 2007 At dialysis today, her nephrologist said he conferred with the neutropenic oncologist here and also with the hematology oncologist in Pittsburgh. It was decided that Natalee would have to be transfused. Her levels were too critical to ignore, making a transfusion requisite.

Dec. 29, 2007 Transfusion today. Natalee received a call at 8:30 a.m.to let us know they were ready for her whenever she could get to the hospital. We got there at 10:00 a.m. (Sneaking in a little sleeping-in time!) She was ordered three units, so we never got out of there until 9:00 p.m. The blood was infused slowly to prevent acute fluid overload or other reactions. She did well, but said she felt "full" and will have to sleep sitting up on her chaise in the living room tonight. (I pray the transfusions give her a much needed energy boost.)

Jan. 3, 2008 Natalee said she had a good day today and was actually able to make a full meal and clean up the kitchen afterward. She hadn't slept more then six hours the past few nights due to her restless leg syndrome, and the additional excess fluid added in didn't help. Last night she finally slept well all night after having *twelve pounds* of fluid removed at dialysis yesterday. (Congestive heart failure can occur from fluid overload and I worry how that much excess circulating fluid could affect her heart.)

Natalee applied for transport to and from dialysis, but again, lots of paperwork and a slow process. I hope we hear soon if she is eligible. (It's a concern how much longer our workplaces will be supportive of us leaving work to take and pick her up.)

Jan. 7, 2008 Today they used her fistula at dialysis for the first time. She was looking forward to finally being able to have it accessed, but said it was painful and made her nauseous when the nurse inserted the needles. (They have a much larger bore than the kind you get an injection with.) She was given a script for xylocaine gel to apply to the fistula beforehand to numb the area. Most dialysis recipients apply it then cover the area with saran wrap to give it time to work before they come in for treatment. Natalee commented that she is now an official member of the "Saran Wrap Gang." The Tesio will remain in place for a few more weeks before it will be removed….a precaution to make sure the fistula is working successfully. That will mean another trip to Pittsburgh. We were told no one here will remove it because it was inserted in Pittsburgh. (We know prayer can change things!)

> ...The prayer of a righteous person is powerful and effective. (James 5:16 NIV) In the morning, Lord, you hear my voice; in the morning I lay my requests before you and wait expectantly. (Psalm 5:3 NIV)

Chapter 8

Praying for a Better Plan

Jan. 10, 2008 Hematology oncologist appointment at Hillman today. A bone marrow biopsy is scheduled for the 22nd. (She would have rather just gotten it over with today!) It was disappointing that we have to wait some more to find out if anything changed after receiving the injections to boost cell production. She was told the National Donor Registry is searching for a bone marrow match for her. Right now they do not want to have anyone get tested as a donor. He said she may *possibly* not need a transplant if her cell levels show improvement with the second biopsy. That would be a fantastic miracle, for sure. (Trusting God for *His* better plan,)

We were told the doctor's plan is for Natalee to have a stem cell or T cell transplant by phoresis (intravenously) at Hillman if the cell numbers aren't improved. After researching, I found when stem cells are collected from the donor's bone marrow and transplanted, it is called a bone marrow transplant. If the stem cells come from the bloodstream, it is called a stem cell transplant. Stem cell transplants are more common. (Hoping and praying for God's better plan instead.)

Natalee's WBC count is up, >2 now, so that was encouraging news. (At least for someone who had <.01 not long ago.) Seriously low red blood cells are also causing her to feel more tired again, which is a major concern. (The doctors were astonished she can function at all and questioned how she even walked into the building today on her own!)

Jan. 15, 2008 Today was the l-o-n-g awaited day.....the Tesio catheter was removed. Arrangements were made for Natalee to have it removed here instead of having to return to Pittsburgh - by the power of prayers being answered! Natalee was ecstatically happy she can fully shower again, and that's putting it mildly! (Insert humongous celebration here followed by a long hot shower!)

After the Tesio was removed, she was scheduled to have a CT scan of her head due to the dizziness she was having so frequently and ongoing complaints about her ears hurting. After the CT scan, the tech looked concerned and asked, "Do you have implants in your eyes or something?" As it turned out, Natalee was permitted to leave her wig on. Apparently there are tiny wires on the inside of the wig. You guessed it....that's what showed up! I guess you could say when they were "wigged out" when they saw the scan result. (Sorry, had to go there! I rolled my eyes, too.)

Today was a sad memory day. My dear friend, Barb, held the funeral for her husband today. I wish I could have been there for her in person. She understands why I couldn't, and knows my heart, my thoughts and prayers are with her. (I did talk with her on the phone, which I hope was of some comfort to her.)

Jan. 22, 2008 Bone marrow biopsy day at Hillman. Natalee was feeling anxious about it since the first one she experienced was so painful. Her anxiety was building, and she was feeling more and more nauseated from it as we were en route. We were partway to Pittsburgh already, but I asked if she wanted to cancel and go back home. She stoically replied, "No, I just want to get it over with."

The tech who did the biopsy today was very proficient with no complaint of discomfort from Natalee. We will find out the biopsy results at her next appointment. We are praying for a miracle that she will not need a stem cell transplant. God has gotten her this far, with quite a few miracles so why not hope and pray for one more? (I'm working on totally letting go and letting God.)

Jan. 28, 2008 Saturday McKenna went to a school dance for 6-8th grade students. It was a semi-formal dinner dance, and McKenna invited her long time friend, Ben, she's known since early grade school. David and I were McKenna's chauffeurs, and Natalee felt well enough come along. It was a big day of many firsts for McKenna, and we were so happy Natalee felt "well" enough to take part, especially since it was an important event for McKenna and Natalee to share as mother and daughter - McKenna's first "date," dance, and corsage. McKenna is growing up so fast. (It made me feel older.)

Jan. 31, 2008 We are no further ahead than before after seeing the hematology oncologist today. Natalee's hemoglobin, which had been improving, has dropped to 4.8. The doctor again asked her how she is even functioning with her level so seriously low. He reconfirmed that Natalee has SAA, and discussed another treatment beside a stem cell transplant - an IV immunosuppressant called ATG (anti-thymocyte globulin) made from horse serum. It would be given along with an oral immunosuppressant. He wasn't sure if it was safe for someone on dialysis and said he would need to check into it before implementing treatment. Natalee stated she will be the guinea pig to find out if ATG works with dialysis patients! (Ever the positive attitude.) There is a 50/50 chance her bone marrow would respond, but it would take several months to know for sure. If it is deemed safe, they will call her to be admitted for treatment. She would be in the hospital at least a week. (Nothing with Natalee is ever easy! So, again we are waiting. Inhale, exhale…BIG SIGH!)

Her kidney transplant coordinator called later on and said all her doctors had a conference meeting about her. I am grateful for all of them and their genuine concern and quest to find what plan of treatment will work best for her well being. Now we are waiting to hear what was decided. (Hoping she hasn't "stumped the doctors" - we're running out of cards and signs!)

Chapter 9

Nothing's Ever Easy

Feb. 11, 2008 Natalee was approved for med-van transport and today was the first day they took her to dialysis. She informed them she leaves home at 9:30 a.m. to arrive by 10:00 a.m. to have her treatment on time. They showed up at 9:00 a.m. Two other people, who go to another dialysis center, were picked up on the same run. The van never came back for Natalee until an hour and a half after her treatment finished. (Natalee was not happy with the arrangements, but is at their mercy.)

Feb. 12, 2008 To have med-van services pick you up, you must call before noon the day prior to schedule a ride. Natalee had to have an extra dialysis treatment today due to remaining excess fluid after her treatment yesterday. She didn't know about the extra treatment until the afternoon yesterday, so I was the designated chauffeur today. (Good thing it's my day off.) If McKenna has a day off school transport won't take her along. That's a major problem, as is the scheduling policy, so med-van transport for all intents and purposes is not going to work out. (Back to "GO" and DO NOT COLLECT YOUR SANITY! Sigh.)

This summer will definitely be a challenge when McKenna is out of school. We can't expect her to go to dialysis with Natalee three days a week. David is a very dedicated employee, but someone at his workplace made a comment about him leaving work to take or pick Natalee up, even though he is using his alloted lunch time, or making up time by working extra. (All I can say is I hope that person never has a situation like we have.) At least where I work they are willing to support my taking her as long as I put in my eight-hour workday. That still doesn't solve making sure McKenna is cared for while Natalee is at dialysis. (I have enough to currently think about, and can't think about this situation until it's closer to school letting out for the summer.)

Feb 21, 2008 Natalee was to have the long overdue colposcopy procedure today. Due to her low platelet count putting her at risk for bleeding, her gynecologist had to use cryotherapy this time. He said there were no cancer cells evident, just abnormal tissue, but the biopsy will be the conclusive factor.

Feb. 22, 2008 I received good news from my friend, Carol, whose mother goes to dialysis with Natalee. Her mother received a kidney transplant this week from a cadaveric donor. She had been on the list for three years. We're happy she received a kidney and can start living a life of not being tethered to a dialysis machine several times a week for hours at a time.

March 3, 2008 Natalee's hemoglobin dropped to just above 4. I told her to call her PCP to ask if a blood transfusion is being considered soon. (The only way she is functioning is surely by the Grace of God.)

Some good news....the biopsy result was negative for cancer.

March 6, 2008 I dropped Natalee off at out local hospital for a transfusion of two units before I went to work. The transfusions took until around 3:00 p.m., so I had to pick McKenna up when she got off the school bus and take her with me to my office - my workday wasn't over, and McKenna's still too young to stay home alone. Too often McKenna never knows where she'll be going next, or with whom. David works across the street from the hospital. He picked Natalee up when he got off work at 3:30 p.m., then stopped at my office for McKenna on the way to take Natalee home. Such a juggling act! Our lives, most days anymore, are like a three-ring circus. "The Cirque du Natalee's Challenges" is complete with elephants, juggling, overloaded spinning plates, and the unexpected! It sometimes has jumping-through-hoops acts to get things accomplished. I'm sure no one would want a ticket to this circus. (Oh wait, you bought one...you're reading this book!)

To add to the circus, Natalee had a visit from CYS. The mother of a girl who rides McKenna's bus reported Natalee for leaving McKenna home alone. The bus drops McKenna off in front of her house and the girl told her mother McKenna was using a key to get into the house. Bring in the clown - the mother assumed no one else was at home. When CYS came to investigate, they found that to be far from the truth; without a doubt. McKenna had a house key to let herself into the house when Natalee was too ill to get off the chaise and let her in, but McKenna was never home alone. The matter was dropped. (People need to verify facts before assuming things that can get other people into serious trouble.)

Natalee felt and looked better after the transfusion. I can tell she is feeling better.....she is her very chatty self when she feels well! Chattiness seems to be an inherited thing on my mother's side of the family. (Guilty!) My mother always said her side of the family was "vaccinated with Victrola needles," referring to the 1905 Victor <u>Talking</u> Machine Company phonographs!

Chapter 10

God Had a Much Better Plan

April 3, 2008 Natalee saw her hematology oncologist in Pittsburgh today. He is pleased that she hasn't had to have any transfusions for the last month and stated she appeared healthier overall. She does have more color and doesn't look so pitifully thin and literally on the brink of death's door like she did months ago. Lately she has been able to tolerate more activity than just resting on the chaise. Today he felt he didn't want to put her at risk with a stem cell transplant. Risks include: graft-versus-host disease (donor transplants only), graft failure, organ damage, infections, new cancers, and even death. The decision was made to keep her on the Procrit injections for her red blood cell production and possibly continue the Neupogen for the white cells, and continue monitoring her blood counts for now. If her counts return to normal and stay there without the injections, she can be cleared to go back on the list for a kidney. A return to Hillman in three months is scheduled. All in all, I see that *God's* plan is coming to fruition - God's plan has no risks. Prayers are being answered for another miracle. (She's on the way back to occupying the throne and being the "Queen of Beating the Statistics.")

May 8, 2008 Time for celebraton. After applying for it, then waiting a couple months, Natalee received an insulin pump and started wearing it after attending a class for reinstruction in its use. Now she will have another adjustment period to get her insulin dose and blood sugars in sync.

Natalee has been improving overall since April with the help of the injections she is receiving. She is feeling stronger and has been able to

Faith, Hope, and a Lifetime of Beautiful Scars

schedule a few more tests that are required to be approved for the active kidney transplant list. We're so thankful for God's plan for healing the SAA without the need for a stem cell transplant - A MIRACLE. God is surely watching over Natalee. (Natalee is even able to drive herself to dialysis again.)

Chapter 11

Good News, Bad News

May 9, 2008 Natalee has continued complaining about her ears - feeling pressure and having the sensation that there is "something in there." Due to nothing being visible on a physical exam, an MRI was ordered last week. Today the ENT doctor called and wants to see her next week instead of next month. I'm certain that means it won't be good news. Just have to hold on….we're back to the roller coaster ride of waiting and wondering now what?)

May 15, 2008 No more wondering. Natalee was referred by her ENT to see a local neurosurgeon. The ENT doctor said there is a "spot" showing up on her brain on the MRI, but he can't specifically identify what it is at this time. Another stump-the-doctor moment. More things on the list of things we don't want to think about. (We are definitely out of cards and signs.)

June 18, 2008 The injections to improve her RBC and WBC counts are being continued, and her levels are stable and within normal limits. Her blood sugars have improved with use of the insulin pump…..her new BFF. Now she is just waiting for the appointment with the local neurosurgeon and to see the hematology oncologist to have a follow-up bone marrow biopsy to confirm her wonderful miracle.

Aug. 10, 2008 Natalee had another MRI of her head. The neurosurgeon is not sure what the "spot" is, but feels it *may* be a tumor. How much more can crop up for Natalee to have to deal with? The Cirque du Natalee's Challenges already has too many plates precariously spinning in the air to keep up with and too many elephants to herd into submission. (Some people say they want to run away to join the circus, but I doubt anyone would want to join this one.)

Aug. 21, 2008 Today I took Natalee to Hillman for the bone marrow biopsy. The tech today was not as proficient as the previous one, so Natalee experienced some pain during the biopsy. I really don't know how she unflinchingly endures so much discomfort during the many painful procedures she has to tolerate. I was only watching the procedure and wanted to cry. (And maybe give out a little yelp, too.)

The oncologist was pleased at how much better Natalee looked and also with her improved lab results. She is to continue the injections for now since her levels are where they should be. He said he will talk with the head of transplant about releasing her to be officially back on the kidney transplant waiting list, if they also agree.

HOLD ON! Up one minute, down the next....

So much for the short-lived good news. Seems like bad news is always there to follow it. (It's like finding a dollar, then losing a twenty.) Now the neurosurgeon wants to see her ASAP, which never means good news. (In Nataleeland, ASAP means Always Speculate A Problem.) Unfortunately we have to anxiously wait until Tuesday and try not to think about what he wants to urgently tell her. (Why is it, when there is something you don't want to think about, all you can do is think about it?)

Aug. 26, 2008 The neurosurgeon informed us the radiologist reported the "lesion" is a tumor. However, he went on to say that he himself wasn't totally convinced it is a tumor. It's small, and would be hard to biopsy easily to establish a conclusive diagnosis. For now, he ordered another MRI in three months and will order one every three months to compare for any changes. We asked if she could be released by him to back on the kidney transplant list and he answered a welcome, "Yes." (At least that was a glimmer of good news to make Natalee happy.)

Later in the afternoon Natalee got a call from Hillman saying her bone marrow is "good" now. The hematology oncologist will be talking to the head of transplant to clear her for the active transplant list. (Confirmed - Blessed with another miracle.)

> He is the one you praise; he is your God, who performed
> for you those great and awesome wonders you saw with

your own eyes. (Deuteronomy 10:21 NIV) By faith in the name of Jesus, this man whom you see and know was made strong. It is Jesus' name and the faith that comes through him that has completely healed him, as you can all see. (Acts 3:16 NIV)

May 3, 2009 It's been an unbelievable ten months with no *major* issues for Natalee. The emergency during that time frame was my own broken ankle five days before Christmas, which kept me off my feet for two-and-a-half months and off work for over three. It took a plate and ten screws to put it back together. The surgeon called it "a difficult" surgery. (I can stump doctors, too!)

Natalee had a minor scare with her blood count in March due to a heavy monthly cycle causing a scary big drop in her red blood count. It was thankfully corrected with doubling her Procrit injections. (I can only pray this is not going to be an ongoing problem.)

May 14, 2009 Natalee saw her local neutropenic oncologist today, who is pleased with her blood counts and is discontinuing her Procrit injections. (The recent drop in her red blood cells was not related to SAA. God already healed that problem.) Healthy kidneys produce a hormone called erythropoietin (EPO), which prompts bone marrow to make increased red blood cells. People with ESRD have lower red cell counts due to the kidneys not producing sufficient EPO. Anemia worsens as kidney function declines. Blood loss to any measurable degree will lower the count drastically if not treated. The Procrit Natalee received is one of many EPO stimulating injectable medications. (Now you know in case it should come up in conversation sometime!)

Chapter 12

Triple the Trouble

Aug. 28, 2009 Hard to fathom, but thankful that Natalee's had three months with no *major* issues....until this week when several issues developed all at once, disrupting the short-lived, but welcome streak. Now it seems like she's making up for lost time. Natalee saw her gynecologist due to continued abnormal cycles, and is to have a pelvic ultrasound and uterine biopsy in a few weeks to determine the cause. (I didn't miss "Wait and See" the past several months, but "Now what" is back.)

An extended episode of her GP erupted last week, and today she had an onset of acute abdominal pain accompanied by vomiting with some blood in it, so we chalked up another "bonding" time in the ER this morning. (More cloned comfortless waiting room chairs to get acquainted with.) A CT scan didn't show much nor did an abdominal x-ray confirm any reason for the blood in her emesis. (Here's your card!)

Since she missed her dialysis treatment this morning, Natalee was scheduled to have one at the hospital after being processed for admission for further testing. An elevated blood pressure and blood sugar >500 also had the doctors concerned. Hopefully Natalee will not be in the hospital long. (Poor McKenna will have to be shuffled around unless I take time off work.)

A call was placed by the ER physician to her nephrologist for dialysis orders, but being the caring doctor her nephrologist has always been toward her, he instead came to see her. Her PCP, who is also extremely solicitous, came to the ER to see her, too. They collaborated and decided she would have dialysis tomorrow *after* an EGD. The blood thinner, heparin, flushed into her fistula after dialysis would put Natalee at greater risk for having bleeding during the EGD. (What time is it? Why, it's "wait and see" time! They're baaack!)

Aug. 29, 2009 The gastroenterologist said he thought the bleeding and pain were related to her gastroparesis bout - she may have vomited so hard it caused bleeding due to a small blood vessel rupture in the esophagus. Natalee told him this was different from the way her GP acts. She has never had associated pain or bleeding. The revised plan, he decided, was to hold off on the EGD and treat her with medication first. He then named a few he could order. Natalee reminded him she had tried all those meds in the past and they had no impact on her GP. Strike one. Then he suggested a liquid diet for a few days to give her stomach a rest. Natalee reminded him she was on dialysis and has restricted fluid intake. She is only allowed 30-ounces of fluid a day. (I get thirsty just thinking about it.) Strike two. Finally, he said he would just go ahead with the EGD! A good choice before he struck out. (I think he may have sighed here.) Thank goodness Natalee is not afraid to speak up! The scope revealed her stomach lining is inflamed and she has bleeding duodenal ulcers, which he biopsied. (Doctors eventually learn to listen to her!)

Sept. 30, 2009 Busy day. Natalee saw her local neurosurgeon, and he wanted her to reconsider having the mysterious lesion in her head biopsied. We discussed it, and Natalee told him she wants to wait until the results of the next MRI scheduled for March 2010, then decide. (Right now she is very much against having a hole drilled in her head.)

Next she saw her gynecologist and had a uterine biopsy (BX). The doctor discussed medical and surgical options to resolve the abnormal bleeding problem. Natalee is okay with a surgical option if needed for this problem because she can't afford her blood counts bottoming out every month. Nothing will be decided until the biopsy results are final. (More "wait and see.")

Oct. 15, 2009 Good news! The BX was negative for cancer. Treatment options are - 1) having a hysterectomy, which is not a preferred option due to Natalee being a high surgical risk, 2) an IUD device, which Natalee flatly decided against, and 3) NovaSure ablation, which involves destruction of the uterine lining, which can be the cause of her problem. No incisions are required, and it only takes about five minutes in the doctor's office. That was the only option she was left with, but sounded like the ideal one. The procedure is scheduled for December 15.

Dec. 15, 2009 The NovaSure ablation is canceled because her Hgb is only up to 8.0 and they wanted it at 9.0 for the procedure. So, she will have to reschedule and hope the Procrit will raise her level enough by then. (Sigh. What else is new?)

She is to go to Pittsburgh January 7 for her evaluation to be back on the kidney transplant list. Sometimes I can't remember if she is on or off the list! (I think I need a weekly memo.)

Chapter 13

Patience and Perseverance

Dec. 18, 2009 My turn. I was in the hospital with Atrial Fibrillation. Maybe the stress of my job, extended family member issues, and worrying about Natalee all these years has caught up to me. All I know is I have to be healthy so I can be there for Natalee. Thank goodness nothing major is going on with her right now. (What is it with me and hospitals the week before Christmas?)

March 16, 2010 Weather-wise it was a rough winter. Snow in abundance seems to love to visit the area where we live and is occasionally accompanied by its friends, Sleet and Ice. (None are my friends.) Thanks to Snow and friends coming to stay, we had to cancel Natalee's appointment in January for her transplant evaluation in Pittsburgh. It was rescheduled for March 9, and thankfully Snow and friends took the day off.

The staff at clinic all thought she looked great! Some of the newer docs were amazed at the difference in what they perceived her to look like from her very thick paper chart and actually seeing her in person. Natalee's coordinator was upset that many of the test results Natalee has kept up to date to get back on the list were never forwarded to her. We found out it was because of one tech at the dialysis center not doing her job and forwarding them. For whatever reason, she always gives Natalee a hard time. It's upsetting to know there are staff who fail to do their job, which can then result in a negative impact on someone else's life and health. Natalee's coordinator at clinic said she will closely follow up to make sure the test results are forwarded and received by her. We should know soon if Natalee will be back on the list. Transplant encouraged her to try and find a living donor again. (If it was only easier said than done.)

Natalee's hemaglobin still isn't high enough to have the NovaSure ablation. It has to be above 9.0. If nothing else, we have learned patience and perseverance dealing with the Cirque du Natalee's never-ending health challenges!

> Therefore, since we have been justified through faith, we have peace with God through our Lord Jesus Christ, through whom we have gained access by faith into this grace in which we now stand. And we boast in the hope of the glory of God. Not only so, but we also glory in our sufferings, because we know that suffering produces perseverance; perseverance, character; and character, hope. (Romans 5: 1-4 NIV)

July 17, 2010 Natalee had a critically low potassium level of 1.0, scaring the staff at her dialysis unit. (Normal level is 3.5-5.0.) They were concerned because low potassium can cause weakness, irregular heartbeat, elevated blood pressure, muscle spasms, nausea/vomiting, and dizziness that can lead to passing out. One of the staff immediately called Natalee when they received the results, and was relieved when Natalee answered the phone! Her level had been above normal a couple weeks ago, and she did too good a job avoiding foods high in potassium to bring her level down. It is a balancing act to keep her blood levels of potassium, phosphorus and other blood elements in acceptable range while on dialysis. The renal diet and fluid restriction to help with achieving the balance is more than I think I could manage to follow, but Natalee faithfully does. Being diabetic, with GP and high blood pressure added into the mix, makes her food choices even more challenging. (We joke that when she buys food she should - 1) take it out of the box, 2) throw away the food, 3) eat the box!)

She had an EGD this past week, and it showed inflammation only; no further ulceration. (Thank you God for answered prayers.)

The next thing to tackle on her list of things to put behind her is to have the NovaSure ablation. It is scheduled for August 24. Hopefully her Hgb will be above 10.0, where they now want it to be for the procedure, but Medicare is denying coverage for the Procrit injections at the moment saying it is not medically necessary! (Big eye roll here!) She is now getting Epogen (same type of med, just different pharmaceutical company) which they will pay for her to have. Go figure. (I can only pray it will be effective.)

Aug. 15, 2010 Well, here we go again! Natalee's insurance is not paying for the Epogen now. (I wonder who makes these decisions?) Natalee's Hgb dropped to 7.0 and she had to have two units of blood….and more unwanted antibodies. Unfortunately, since she cannot get her Hgb level up without the Procrit or Epogen injections, and she continues to have a heavy cycle for over a week (further depleting her red blood cells and Hgb levels); without having the NovaSure ablation, the transfusion was necessary. Praying she will achieve a Hgb of 10.0 and stay there until she can have the procedure which is paramount at this point to end this reoccurring cycle. (Prayer is free. No insurance to deal with, just guaranteed assurance.)

Aug. 24, 2010 Hallelujah, prayers answered. Natalee was able to have the NovaSure ablation today and all went well. She's glad the procedure is finally over. Hopefully, her Hgb will be more stable now, and she won't need any more blood transfusions and only occasional injections. (So thankful God hears our prayers.)

Chapter 14

Deflating News

Jan. 10, 2011 The New Year is starting off with great news! This Thursday, January 13, Natalee's case will be presented at Transplant for review. Her tests are up to date with acceptable results and have all been received by her coordinator. They will review all the tests and her case in general, then decide if she is a candidate to be back on the transplant list. After the review, we will hear via a letter if she is accepted. (But this is Natalee we're talking about, so we'll pray nothing else crops up that will continue to keep her off the list.)

Jan. 14, 2011 Natalee had a surprise call from Pittsburgh. A surprise because we were expecting a letter with the results after her case was presented. (I hate thinking negative, but per usual, this can't be good.)

I hate being right in some instances, and this is one of them…..the call from Transplant was to tell her they wanted her to see one of the UPMC neurosurgeons regarding the unspecified brain lesion before she can be back on the transplant list. Natalee questioned why she had to see a neurosurgeon there since the lesion has not changed from the time it was discovered in 2008, and was being followed by her neurosurgeon here. She mentioned to them that no one really knows how long the lesion has been there - it could have been there when she had her previous transplants since she never had a CT of her head prior to when they found it. For all we know, she could have had it all her life. The reply, however, was a simple - "So he can be familiar with your case." Now she has to wait to get an appointment. She is praying they will not want to biopsy the lesion before they will put her back on the transplant list. (Deflating news, but not defeating.)

Chapter 15

We Need a Break from Never-ending Problems

Jan. 25, 2011 David requested today day off work and took Natalee to her appointment with the neurosurgeon at UPMC Presby. She stopped at her local neurosurgeon's office yesterday to pick up a CD to take with her today of all the CT scans and MRIs of her head she had done here.

The neurosurgeon at Presby compared the scans and said they showed where there was some growth of the unexplainable lesion. Much to Natalee's displeasure he wants her to have another MRI. Rather than biopsy the lesion he wants to remove it. Right now it has no "tentacles" and could be removed more easily, plus it is not impinging on any major areas right now that control cognitive function, speech or motor skills. He would have scheduled everything today but she wanted to talk it over with me some more before making such a big decision on the spot. (One of those elephants in the room....the one you don't want to address until you absolutely have to acknowledge it.)

The UPMC neurosurgeon we chose has an impressive resume, so we both feel confident with him and his decision that removing the lesion would be for the best in the long run. The office nurse is to call tomorrow to find out her decision and schedule a date, if Natalee decides to have the surgery, which right now looks like scheduling the surgery will be the wise thing to do. Her main concern...of course, this is Natalee we are talking about....is having her hair shaved off. Just another act in the "Cirque du Natalee's Challenges" to get through, but hopefully a step closer to transplant. (A very big scary act she'll need God to get her through.)

Out of curiosity I asked Natalee if the person who failed to send her completed test results to Transplant still worked at dialysis. Natalee said she was fired for not sending the test results, which was part of her job. Two others who worked at dialysis were fired in the past for not reporting abnormal symptoms and problems Natalee was having that caused her to end up in the hospital. Job duties should never be taken lightly by people who work in health care. Lives are at stake. It's frightening to think that there are staff who don't seem to care, working in places where caring is critical; they're seemingly only there to collect a paycheck. (I know, I've unfortunately worked with some of them.)

Feb. 7, 2011 Natalee and I both started coughing last Tuesday. (We probably caught a bug at the ER last week from the person who was coughing relentlessly while occupying the cubicle next to Natalee.) As the week progressed, we both developed major coughing and fever. Natalee was ordered an antibiotic by her nephrologist who saw her at dialysis. So far it's not doing her much good. Her cough is unabating. I have better immunity, so I'm toughing... and coughing... it out. (Clorox wipes are out in full force!)

Feb. 13, 2011 Natalee's terrible cough is lingering. We had to cancel the scheduled MRI in Pittsburgh this past week since she was unable to lay flat without coughing. (One definition of delay is "wait." Not one of our favorite vocabulary words.)

This morning, I got a call from a mother whose son received a second kidney this week as part of the Paired Kidney Exchange Program that began in 2008 at UPMC. His father had given him a kidney in 2005. As the donor on his behalf, his mother-in-law, who was not a match for him, donated to someone in Wisconsin who was her match. He received a kidney in exchange from someone in Tampa, Florida. He is already out of the hospital and doing well. There were a total of sixteen transplants and thirty-two surgeries with twelve medical centers and ten states involved in the exchange. It's astounding how far the transplant process has progressed in the six years since he and Natalee had their first kidney transplants. We are so happy for him and his family and pray he and all the others involved will do well. (My head hurts thinking about all the complex in-depth logistics that go into the planning for the multiple pairings and surgeries.)

Natalee received a letter from Transplant this week that she will be *considered* for the exchange program. All she would need is a donor on her behalf and they will match up the exchange. Great news, but easier said than done to find a serious live donor. She's had many offers, but when poeple find out what is involved she never hears from them again. (But first.....she needs the MRI and clearance to be even be eligible for a transplant.)

(By the way, I survived my coughing and fever beyond six minutes! Prayer in action!)

Chapter 16

Sigh...is Anybody Listening?

March 23-24th, 2011 I hate getting up early. Natalee was scheduled to be in Pittsburgh for an MRI with contrast at 6:45 a.m., so I reluctantly crawled out of my warm bed at 4:00 a.m. and we were out in the cold and on the way by 4:30 a.m., thankful that the weather was cooperating. (And thankful for the remote car starter to get my car warmed up.)

After the MRI, she had the usual four hours of dialysis to rid her body of the contrast dye and its dangerous non-reversible side effects if not removed timely. While I waited I had lots of stereotypical waiting room chair choices to become familiar with today - plain blue or tan ones, ones with stripes and some with polka dots, some with arms and some without. (Decisions, decisions.)

I noticed a little more pink coloration than usual and very slight swelling on the lower part of Natalee's fistula. I pointed it out to the dialysis nurse, and she agreed. I thought it looked like it could be the start of inflammation or infection. Her fistula wasn't sore or showing any other symptoms. Just something to keep a watchful eye on for now. There was no choice but to go ahead with dialysis. Her fistula didn't look any worse after dialysis and will be checked again at her dialysis treatment in the morning.

We got home from our long day in Pittsburgh around 4:45 p.m. At 7:30 p.m., Natalee called and said she spiked a sudden fever of 103.8 with shaking chills. Now what? I immediately left the house to go check on her. With the symptoms she was exhibiting, I was worried she had a systemic infection brewing. I decided it was too risky to "wait and see," so we went to a local ER. Natalee was feeling too ill to travel two hours back to Pittsburgh to be seen, and I was too exhausted to drive in the dark that far. McKenna came with us to the ER, and David picked her up there. It would have wasted more time waiting for him to get across town to Natalee's house to get her. (Another Cirque du Natalee's Challenges hectic juggling act.)

From the minute we arrived at the ER, Natalee and I informed the attending staff what transpired that day and how important it was for her to have her scheduled four hours of dialysis in the morning, already scheduled at her dialysis center, which I named, for 7:30 a.m. They would need notified if she was going to be admitted to the hospital. I'm sure I sounded like a broken record, repeatedly telling them about the importance of making sure she had dialysis in the morning as scheduled. The reply was, "It's being arranged." I also pointed out to several people I thought there appeared to be a cellulitis or other infection possibly beginning in her lower fistula. Much to my frustration, no one looked at it.

After being admitted to a room at 3 a.m., Natalee emphasized to the staff on that unit the importance of receiving her crucial four hours of dialysis daily for two more days. She restated the need to notify the dialysis center to let them know she was admitted and then make arrangements for dialysis at the hospital.

The next morning, no indication of dialysis was on the horizon. Out of curiosity, Natalee called her dialysis center at 8 a.m. to see if anyone had contacted them. The nurse Natalee spoke with said they were wondering where she was, that no one had called and told them she was in the hospital. Natalee was told by the hospital staff that they left a message saying she would not be there, but the dialysis center said there was no message on their machine. As the morning progressed, Natalee repeatedly inquired about when she was going to have dialysis and was appeased with "arrangements are being made." (HMMMM? Someone's nose should be growing very long.)

I arrived just after lunch and still no inkling of dialysis happening any time soon. I marched out to the nurses' station and asked what was going on, and was told the same thing….. it was being arranged and they had a call out to her nephrologist for orders. I asked to talk to her assigned nurse and was told he was in a meeting. No one else seemed interested in finding anything out for me, so I returned to Natalee's room feeling none too happy. About forty-five minutes later, I returned to the nurses station and politely asked again to see her nurse, even though I wasn't feeling in any way like being polite. Someone said they would find him and send him to Natalee's room. Finally, he appeared and said he was not informed at report that morning about the dialysis need! (So much for good communication, especially about something SO critically important.)

I was tired… and angry… and cranky… and disgustedly said, "We'd be in Pittsburgh right now if circumstances had been different, and we would not have to put up with this incompetent run around!" I was no longer feeling polite by that time! (Close your eyes so you don't have to see my head exploding.) After telling him how many people had been informed of her paramount need for dialysis, I went on to point out Natalee had been nauseated since we arrived at the ER, and asked why she still had not received anything to counteract it. When I arrived today, she was vomiting. He was very nice in spite of my blatant irritability and placated me by saying he would check into it right away. And he did! (Maybe I scared him! Could have been the steam coming out of my ears.) He came back with welcome news that he got an order for something for her nausea and dialysis was definitely being arranged. Kudos to him for coming through with flying colors for Natalee. We were told by other staff they couldn't get hold of her nephrologist earlier; that's why the delay. One of her nephrologists came to see her and told Natalee he had not received any calls and told about any of this. (I did apologize to her nurse.)

> In your anger do not sin: Do not let the sun go down
> while you are still angry. (Ephesians 4:26 NIV)

Natalee was given medication for the nausea before being taken to dialysis at 4:00 p.m. The dialysis nurses didn't work for the hospital per se, but were contractual and on call. Had Natalee's dialysis been arranged when it was supposed to have been, the nurse could have come earlier and not had to work late.

During dialysis, Natalee started shaking uncontrollably. Her temp was slightly above normal initially, but toward the end of the treatment, her temp was climbing. The renal nurse was very concerned and called the nephrologist several times to keep him informed regarding what was going on and how Natalee was doing. The doctor decided to stop the treatment at three-and-a-half hours due to Natalee's continued shaking and chills, which mysteriously subsided soon after the treatment was stopped. (The nurse was able to reach him on the phone right away all three times she paged him!)

I was allowed to stay in the room during dialysis and pointed out I thought it looked like Natalee was developing a cellulitis in her distal fistula, and the nurse agreed. At the end of the treatment, we noticed a small yellow pustule had surprisingly and suddenly developed on that area. While the nurse was putting pressure on Natalee's fistula to quell any bleeding after the dialysis needles were pulled, the small yellow pustule popped and started to bleed profusely. It's ironic that an AV fistula is a lifeline for a dialysis patient but can be the cause of death within minutes if more than normal bleeding isn't stopped. Normally the dialysis nurse and Natalee would have been isolated in that room and away from any immediate help, which could have been a big problem. The nurse knew I was also an RN, so while she kept pressure on the area she directed me to get sterile dressings from the supply cupboard across the room. Once the bleeding was under control the nurse paged the doctor again. He ordered a culture of the discharge from the pustule. (Another dedicated renal nurse saves the day!)

March 25, 2011 The preliminary culture report showed a Staph infection. (No surprise to me.)

How to have a frustrating day....

10:15 a.m. - Natalee is to have dialysis today at noon, so she told us not to visit until later. She may be able to come home after dialysis and will call us.

2:00 p.m. Natalee called said she has not had dialysis yet. She was told she would have dialysis at 3:00 p.m.

4:00 p.m.- No dialysis or word yet. Natalee did not order lunch thinking she would be at dialysis at noon. She ordered a dinner tray for 6:30 p.m., counting on being through with dialysis by then.

5:30 p.m. - No dialysis yet. I told her to call for a dinner tray *now* before she has low blood sugar problems, ask what the hold-up with having dialysis is to see if she can get a definite answer.

6:00 p.m. - Finally. The dialysis nurse told Natalee she had called and told *Somebody* she would be starting dialysis at 3:00 p.m., *but* there were two other patients to be put on the machine before Natalee. Unfortunately that was not what got relayed to Natalee by *Somebody*. I guess *Everybody* thought *Somebody* told Natalee, but it was actually *Nobody* who relayed the message to her. (Thank you, *Nobody*.) There were to be two renal nurses on call, but one had called off work. The one working had been there since 6:00 a.m. by the time she got to Natalee. (God Bless that nurse and her dedication.)

March 27, 2011 Natalee was released from the hospital today. (Visualize fireworks and a happy- dance celebration.) She is to have her regularly scheduled dialysis in the morning and is to continue to receive the IV antibiotic after her dialysis treatments for a couple more weeks.

Chapter 17

This Takes a Rocket Scientist (at Least a Brain Surgeon)

May 19, 2011 Natalee saw the neurosurgeon at Presby today. During the four-hour appointment he reviewed her past and recent MRIs and noted there was a slight increase in the tumor the past year. It is about 1.5 cm (roughly 0.6 inches) and horseshoe shaped. Due to the tumor location the possible ramifications of the surgery include speech, cognitive, and right-sided motor deficits as before. Of course, if she doesn't have it removed the tumor could grow and engender the same problems, especially after receiving another kidney transplant and taking immunosuppressants. A risk either way. Right now she has no symptoms from the tumor's presence, which is a plus. She didn't say so, but I know she is concerned about any possible residuals associated with the surgery becoming permanent. We have to remember the key word is *possible,* but with prayer all things are possible and we will believe no residuals will occur. The nurse who was present told Natalee she is really strong to go through all she has and what she is facing now. (She doesn't know the half of it.)

> Jesus said unto him, if thou canst believe, all things are possible to him that believeth. (Mark 9:23 KJV)

The neurosurgeon called her transplant doctor and nephrologist to make sure they are on board with the surgery. We have faith in her doctors and like the fact they confer with each other to make sure Natalee will have the best outcomes. (Better yet, God is on her side.)

Natalee only had two questions related to the surgery, seriously asking: 1) how much of her hair would have to be shaved, and 2) if the removed piece of skull would be replaced. Laughing, I told the surgeon that she is more concerned about having some of her hair shaved off than she is about the surgery itself. He told her it will be a small incision with minimal hair removal. I could see Natalee heave a sigh of relief. She will be able to part her hair on the opposite side and cover the incision until the hair grows back. Yes, she will get the piece of skull back, plus some tiny titanium plates and screws to keep it in place. (No, she will not set off any metal detectors.)

I will schedule my vacation time for the week of her surgery. Natalee and I were laughing at calling it "vacation" time. No beach vacation for me… again. I guess I won't need my sunscreen. I will instead relax in insufferable waiting room chairs while basking in the glow of fluorescent lighting, and enjoy fine dining in the hospital cafeteria. (At least I can have French fries.)

Natalee will be in the hospital from two to seven days, depending on her progress, and could be back on the transplant list two months after her surgery, aside from any problems. However, if all of the tumor can't be removed, and depending on the biopsy report, chemo and/or radiation may be on the agenda. That would keep her off the list. She will definitely need follow-up MRIs periodically. We can't think that far ahead right now though. As always, we have to take one step and one day at a time or our brains would self-destruct…mentally staggering under the magnitude of…well, just everything. (Too many contingencies to juggle in my head all at once.)

The surgery to remove the brain tumor is tentatively scheduled for July 12 pending clearance from her PCP, nephrologist and other doctors, and barring any other problems that may crop up. We will have to travel to Pittsburgh sometime before the surgery for pre-op testing.

June 19, 2011 Natalee has never been afraid to have surgery before, but she says the thought of brain surgery makes her nervous. I don't think it's the actual surgery she is scared of, but more so of the possible residual side effects that could be permanent and life-altering. I reminded Natalee that God has brought her through countless past surgeries and we are trusting Him for this one, too. (God is with us today and already waiting for us when tomorow comes.)

> Those who know your name trust in you, for you, Lord, have never forsaken those who seek you. (Psalm 9:10 NIV) When I am afraid, I put my trust in you. In God, whose word I praise - in God I trust and am not afraid. What can mere mortals do to me? (Psalm 56:3-4 NIV)

July 7, 2011 Pre-op testing day. The neurosurgeon recapped the details of the surgery, possible complications, and residual side effects. Natalee met with an anesthesiologist, then had an EKG and MRI without contrast. The surgery is confirmed for 7:30 a.m. on July 12. Natalee is as ready physically and mentally for this as she'll ever be. (It's in God's hands.)

> Cast all your anxiety on him becasue he cares for you. (1 Peter 5:7 NIV)

I know Natalee's surgery is scary for McKenna, too. She doesn't want to be there the day of the surgery. It's better for her not to be there since there is nothing she can do but wait and worry with only what her imagination can supply. She prefers to see her mom after she is awake and on the other side of the surgery. Arrangements were made by Natalee for McKenna to stay with a nurse who worked at dialysis and kindly offered to help out. She is distantly related to me on my dad's side of the family. McKenna knew her from the times she had to go to dialysis with Natalee. At least McKenna will be distracted with activities, enough not have to think about what is going on at the hospital. (So, now we count down the days…. and pray.)

Chapter 18

Why is There Always Drama?

July 11, 2011 Natalee had dialysis this morning before heading to Pittsburgh for her scheduled 4:00 p.m. admission. Within the first two hours of admission, she was seen by doctors from neurology, renal and endocrinology, in addition to the Residents, Fellows and PAs. What's funny is, when doctors who have never met her come into her room, they look at her and quizzically ask, "Are you the patient?" They are astonished that she looks so "well" and not like the person they have read about in her extensive medical history. (Could be because she is always happy and smiling.)

She is always a challenge to get blood from due to her poor veins, and only the arm without the fistula is able to be used for blood draws. The good news was the lab tech got it without any difficulty on the first try, which made Natalee, and the tech, happy. Sometimes I think the lab techs who know her draw straws as to who will be the unlucky one to draw her blood. Bad news was that her potassium (K+) level was critically high at 5.5; too high to safely have surgery since elevated K+ can cause irregular heartbeat and even heart block. Now what? (Why is there always drama?)

To make sure it wasn't a problem with the lab process or the blood hemolyzing in the collection tube, a renal nurse was called to redraw blood from Natalee's fistula. (They are the only ones allowed to access a fistula.) The result came back 5.1, a little less alarming, so they decided to do a 2K bath - two hours of dialysis with specific settings and dialysate to lower the potassium level. (Praying it resolves the problem so they can proceed with the surgery.)

I could see Natalee's emotional barometer rising and her smile fading before she blurted out, "If this doesn't bring the level down and surgery is canceled, I am not going to go through all this again at a later date." I know how frustrated she gets being poked and prodded, and having unexpected delays compound her stress level. I know she just wants to get this surgery over with…. tomorrow. I was trying hard to be positive, trying not to allow *my* visibly climbing stress level show, for her sake. Calm needed to prevail. I doubt if I could be as positive as she generally is, and go thorough all that she does without whining….BIG time! She does have her moments though, and justifiably so. This was one of those moments, but that's what it was - a moment of venting her frustration. I knew she would be okay in a short time, and eventually be ready to move forward with the surgery..… whenever. (Praying for her K+ level to drop to where it needs to be for the surgery to take place…tomorrow! Amen!)

Once she was settled, David and I returned home with plans to be back for the surgery in the morning. (It's going to be a long restless night for all of us.)

July 12, 2011 Natalee called us at 5:30 a.m. to inform us that her potassium level is normal and the surgery is on again. The nephrologist decided the potassium level was elevated because her blood sugar was >300. He explained: hyperglycemia lowers osmotic pressure in cells, K+ is driven out of the intercellular space and builds up in the blood of those with renal disease who don't make urine. Therefore, after treating her with insulin to bring down the blood sugar level, the 2K bath, *and prayer*, the potassium level came down.

David and I waited in the surgical waiting room in the way-better-than-normal chairs and counted down the minutes until we got word everything went well. The surgery took around four and a half hours, which passed seemingly longer than "normal" hours pass. (Time only flies when you're having fun.) Afterward, Natalee was taken to recovery and eventually to ICU. When we spoke with the surgeon, he relayed he was able to safely remove 90-95% of the tumor; he didn't want to be too aggressive and risk causing problems resulting in loss of speech, motor or cognitive skills. Anti-seizure medication is being prescribed as a precautionary measure. Seizures post neurosurgery are quite common. They may occur immediately or even months to years after the removal of a tumor due to incongruous electrical activity in the brain. Natalee will be required to take it for several weeks to months. The pathology report won't be final until next week. We called McKenna with the good news, and she was relieved everything went well for Natalee.

Natalee was awake when we were permitted to go in to see her in ICU. We were thankful that her speech, motor, and cognitive skills seemed to be intact. We were startled when we noticed there was a telfa non-stick dressing stapled…. yes, surgically stapled …over her incision. I was surprised that all her hair was intact except where the bandage covered the incision. (I knew she would be ecstatic when she saw it was minimal.)

Natalee's problem with anesthesia making her sick was not any different this time, even after being given medication to hopefully control it. On top of that misery, she had a headache, which I'm sure all the retching didn't help. The nurse gave her morphine IV for the headache. (I pray the medication for the nausea will take effect soon - I don't like seeing her this miserable.)

The nephrologist came to see her and jokingly said, "I stopped by because I heard you had a date this morning, and I wanted to find out how it went!" (Even doctors know a sense of humor is good medicine.)

> A cheerful heart is good medicine, but a crushed spirit
> dries up the bones. (Proverbs 17:22 NIV)

Tired, but relieved, David and I left Pittsburgh in the early evening and headed for home with plans to pick up McKenna. We were grateful for Natalee's friend caring for McKenna, taking the time to take her to cheerleading practice, and keeping her busy in general. Going to practice gave McKenna a little bit of normalcy. There's refuge in normalcy. (McKenna was happy she will see Natalee tomorrow.)

July 13, 2011 David had to go back to work, so only McKenna and I are visiting Natalee today. Two things McKenna loves about going to Pittsburgh: 1) playing car games, and 2) the Squirrel Hill tunnel. She reminds me, if she falls asleep on the way, to be sure to awaken her when we reach the tunnel. (I like the games better than the tunnel.)

Natalee had a bad night due to ongoing nausea/vomiting and an unrelenting headache. She had an MRI this morning, which was very uncomfortable for her - having to lay flat and still so long. She is unusually quiet today; staring a lot. I'm not sure if she is focused on anything in particular or only deeply ensconced in her thoughts. The right side of her neck is bothering her where the central IV line remains in place. The dressing over it is taped down tightly and pulls uncomfortably when she moves her head. Developing a tolerance for discomfort is something she has mastered to a great degree, but this was not one of those times. We mostly just sat there in her room in quiet introspection until the dialysis nurse arrived to begin Natalee's treatment. (McKenna and I took that time to visit the cafeteria. It's still a novelty for McKenna.....and I needed French fries.)

After dialysis, Natalee perked up. I gently brushed out the bottom of her tangled hair and helped her brush her teeth. A nurse came in and assisted her out of bed, into a well-padded chair. (Unlike the pervasive visitor chairs.) Moving Natalee and all the paraphernalia she was attached to was no small feat. The nurse made sure Natalee was comfortable by placing several pillows around her for support and warm blankets over her to ward off the chill from the air conditioning. The nurses in ICU were attentive, frequently asking Natalee if she needed anything. I hope they know that they are not only taking care of the patients, but their actions reassure families that their loved ones are being well cared for when they are not there with them. As the afternoon wore on, a barrage of doctors had all made rounds and agreed she was doing well enough to be moved out of ICU tomorrow.

July 14, 2011 McKenna and I arrived at the hospital this morning and arrangements were being made to move Natalee to the 6th floor neuro unit. The vomiting has subsided, but she still had nausea that isn't being relieved, even with medication. All she has eaten since surgery are a couple of dry crackers with some sips of Ginger Ale. I told her she should try to get something more in her stomach and maybe she would feel better. She gave me a stop-bugging-me-already-mom look. Then, she ate a few more crackers. (Probably to keep me from harping about it. I'm good at harping.)

McKenna had to be back in Johnstown for cheer practice at 5:00 p.m., and wanting to keep things "normal" for her, we said our good-byes at 3:00

p.m. Natalee called later on and said she ate some mashed potatoes that stayed down. A little progress. She was happy all the doctors who made rounds are pleased with her progress, and indicated she may be able to come home tomorrow. (God is good!)

> For whatever is borne of God overcomes the world. And
> this is the victory that has overcome the world - our faith.
> (1 John 5:4 NKJV)

July 15, 2011 Natalee was at dialysis when we arrived to bring her home. McKenna was happy we got to have lunch in the cafeteria while we waited. Me, too! I never order French fries anywhere else, but theirs are the best, and irresistible! (I may be addicted to them.)

One of the neurologists was in to see Natalee before she was released and said it would be a while until she is back to normal. I'm not sure she knows what normal is anymore. She mentioned to him that she has a lingering headache, a feeling of having fluid in her head with a "pop-rocks" sound - which he said would all eventually subside. After the doctor deftly removed the stapled-on dressing, the incision was left open to air. You can hardly tell the incision is there unless you look closely.

Natalee was nervous about the long ride home and asked for medication to suppress any nausea before we left - "just in case." She did well on the drive home, and later on, was even able to eat a few bites of supper. I know Natalee felt better just being released from the hospital with the surgery behind her, and no residual complications have surfaced.

July 16, 2011 Natalee had a good night's sleep and even slept in. Restful sleep in the hospital is fleeting at best. In the morning, Natalee took a shower with me standing by. She said she felt much better after "washing the hospital off."

We are so thankful to God that He heard our prayers. Now we'll pray the pathology report is a good report.

July 21, 2011 Natalee had an appointment today to have the sutures removed. She was anxious about it, but when it was over, she said she really never felt it because the top of her head is numb. According to the preliminary path report, the tumor was labeled a grade 2 diffuse Astrocytoma, which is slow growing. Not the best news, but we will wait and see what the neuro-oncologist has to say. They had scheduled her to also see him today, but the path report wasn't final, so they canceled the appointment until next week. (Oh joy, another trip to Pittsburgh.)

July 28, 2011 Appointment with the neuro-oncologist at Hillman today. He spent a lot of time explaining the pathology report, research studies on similar brain tumors, and treatment options. Long story short.....no other treatment was recommended at this time, only follow-up MRIs. He feels she can be cleared to go back on the active transplant list after talking with the transplant team and neurosurgeon. (More prayers answered!)

Chapter 19

Decisions, Decisions

Oct. 20, 2011 MRI day at Presby. I was glad I brought a book with me so I had something to do for the extra four hours I was going to spend in the stuffy waiting room in a quintessential none-too-comfortable chair while she was receiving dialysis. (Having French fries gave me some much needed gratification.)

Oct. 27, 2011 Just returned from Hillman. Natalee had a very thorough neuro exam, and no residuals or neurological changes were noted. The neuro-oncologist said the MRI showed a margin of tissue - the remaining 5-10% of tumor not able to be safely removed - evident along the edge of the cavity where the Astrocytoma was removed.

He and the transplant team have discussed her case in depth and even called the director of the National Organ Procurement and Transplantation Network (OPTN). The prospect of Natalee's eligibility for getting back on the transplant list was the topic de jour. Long story short, she is *not* cleared for a kidney transplant, and those involved in the decision making process are still deliberating if she will *ever* be a candidate. The fear is that she will be immunosuppressed after a transplant which could proliferate tumor growth. So, it is all up in the air right now pending further discussion by an assembly of very intelligent minds. On a positive note the neuro-oncologist did tell Natalee the head of transplant would like for her to be able to have a transplant. (Now to pray the others involved in the decision making are equally convinced.)

The one reason Natalee agreed to have the surgery in the first place was so she could stay on the list, so she was beyond disappointed, but she didn't obsess on the discouraging news for long. It was what it was and only prayer could change things. After her neuro-oncologist left the room, Natalee started to smile and said to me, " I guess he doesn't know I always come through! God is on my side." She is scheduled for another MRI in late January with a return to Hillman a week later. Until then we shall wait to hear back what all those in the know have discussed and agreed upon. (Challenge on! It's out of our hands, so we will put it into God's.)

Chapter 20

Niggling Frustrations

Jan. 26, 2012 Today was Natalee's second least favorite day….MRI day in Pittsburgh with contrast and four hours of dialysis. (Dialysis is numero uno.) I finished a whole novel today occupying a dreadful chair in the tiny waiting room. It was waiting for me with open arms, literally. At least the book took me somewhere else in my head for a while. (And, of course, I had French fries.)

Feb. 2, 2012 Natalee is still not approved to be back on the transplant list. Discussions with the head of Organ Procurement continue, so we are told. Some things just can't be hurried along. (Pause for a deep sigh here.) All we can do is patiently await their decision and pray it is a "yes" to be back on the transplant list.

March 3, 2012 This past week, Natalee got a letter from transplant with the familiar laundry list of tests she needs to update to be on the active list again. (Prayers answered!)

April 28, 2012 Natalee received an unexpected letter from Medicare. *They* are denying a transplant for her based on the type of tumor information that was submitted to them. After investigating, we learned that the information they received regarding the exact tumor type was coded incorrectly, so Natalee is appealing the decision. (Another frustrating and tedious thing to have to address ASAP.)

May 6, 2012 Hooray. A letter arrived stating Medicare is now approving Natalee for a transplant. Apparently the appeal of the coding issue was promptly addressed and corrected. Now she just needs her letter from transplant to say she is back on the active list.

FYI: all diagnosis/surgeries and medical procedures are assigned alphanumeric ICD codes to describe diagnoses for billing purposes - found in the International Statistical Classification of Diseases, Tenth Revision, Clinical Modification by the World Health Organization. For example: 250.00 is the code for Diabetes, without complication. Additional tens and hundreds place numbers are assigned for each type of Diabetes and existing complications - e.g. Diabetes with retinopathy is coded 250.5. Diabetes with ophthalmic manifestations is coded 250.50. Background Diabetic retinopathy, however, is coded 362.01. Coding the specific number for a particular diagnoses is complicated and just plain mind-boggling. One wrong number or number placement can cause denial of payment. ICD Coding is an actual college course and occupation. I worked with the codes on my job and was rather amused there are even codes for falling off a horse, being struck by lightning, being burned due to water skis on fire, being bitten by a cow…well, a code for just about everything. (I wonder if " niggling frustrations overload" has a code?)

Chapter 21

Here We Go Again

Sept. 25, 2013 It's hard to believe sixteen months have passed with no major issues, surgeries or anything out of the ordinary occurring in Natalee's life - just the usual issues, which are a given. Being on dialysis, along with other health issues, is a full time job ....with no pay. During the week, Natalee is at dialysis Monday, Wednesday and Friday, and on a Tuesday or Thursday you can find her at a doctor appointment or having a test on her list for transplant completed. No rest for the weary, so to speak. All her doctor appointments have been going well, and her test results are returning as acceptable to allow her to stay on the active transplant list. This just might be a streak worthy of *Ripley's Believe It or Not*. (When things are "normal" for her for more than a week, I look at her and ask, "Who are you? What did you do with my daughter?")

Nov. 19, 2013 Here we go again. Natalee had surgery today at Windber hospital to excise lesions (vulvar hyperdysplasia) noted during a routine gyne exam a couple weeks ago. The BX showed the lesions were a class III and considered precancerous - class IV is cancer. Her gynecologist set up an appointment with a gyneoncologist in Pittsburgh for January 21 at Magee Hospital for further input. (I guess her "good" streak is over, but was much appreciated while it lasted.)

Dec. 12, 2013 Natalee is feeling depressed after receiving unwelcome news at her gyne post-op visit yesterday. New lesions have already started to appear. Her appointment at Magee was moved up to January 5.

Natalee does get depressed at times. It's harder than anyone can imagine for a parent to watch day by day as their child's multiple health challenges rule their life. I wish I could close my eyes and have it all go away; that Natalee would be 100% well. There's only so much one person can be expected to take at a time, let alone when things happen in a flood of endless waves trying to drown you. What she goes through on a daily basis would test the patience of a saint. Even I was shocked the first time she admitted she has questioned God and asked, "Why me?" Episodes of feeling low do engulf her at times, crying at night when she is alone with her thoughts, sick of being sick, tired of dialysis and surgeries, and… well, all of it. (Everyone is entitled to have a pity party once in a while.) Very few are ever privy to seeing this side of her feelings and emotions; she hides those from others quite well. Remembering that God has a plan for her life and He will be there for her to get her through her trials lifts the bouts of depression. She wants others to see her as inspirational, not as someone whose life is depressing, requiring others to feel sorry for her.

> For the Lord your God is the one who goes with you to
> fight for you against your enemies to give you victory.
> (Deuteronomy 20:4 NIV)

Jan. 6, 2014 The gyneoncologist saw nothing on her exam yesterday to warrant immediate concern or further surgery at this time. She is to return on April 3 for a follow-up, or sooner if she has any of the symptoms he told her to watch for and report. (Yay, prayers!)

Jan. 20, 2014 A major winter storm arrived and we had to cancel our trip to Pittsburgh to see the neuro-oncologist for the follow-up after Natalee's MRI earlier this week. (After twenty-nine years in home care, driving all over in some very horrible winter weather, I choose not to drive in snow and ice now unless it's absolutely, positively, necessary.)

April 3, 2014 Natalee saw the gyneoncologist at Magee. One of the lesions has increased in size, but he opted to continue monitoring it and for her to return in four months.

Chapter 22

More Frustrations, Irritations and Setbacks...O, Joy!

April 23, 2014 After contending with severe GP symptoms the past couple weeks, Natalee had an EGD yesterday. Her weight loss from not being able to tolerate eating much or retaining it when she can eat is noticable. The EGD was negative for any abnormality that could be causing the symptoms, other than the dogged GP. He ordered Tigan capsules after Natalee told him that was the only medication that helped her with controlling the nausea in the past.

April 24, 2014 Natalee had an endometrial biopsy at Magee today. I felt bad that the procedure was so painful for her. The biopsy result won't be back until next week.

The pharmacy called her today and said insurance no longer covers Tigan, except for patients on chemo. It would cost $100 for the prescription to be filled. Say, what? I guess we'll have to enter an appeal and try to get it covered as being medically necessary. (Big sigh here…..but I really want to scream!)

May 2, 2014 The EGD BX was negative for pylori bacteria. Check. The endometrial BX was also negative. Check. The GP symptoms are not as severe now and she is able to eat and retain food again. Check. The appeal requesting the Tigan to be covered has been submitted. (Three out of four checked off in the plus column all at once is probably a record.)

June 24, 2014 Natalee obtained the waiver from Medicare and was able to get the Tigan paid for with the help of the gastroenterologist's nurse who kindly filed the necessary paperwork. (God Bless her for tackling that.) Natalee is feeling better already and has been able to tolerate eating normally again. (She can't afford to lose any more weight or a big dog may just cart her off.)

Natalee had a recent offer from a *possible* kidney donor. Many people have offered to give Natalee a kidney over the years, and I know people have good intentions when they offer to be a donor, but I wish people understood how disappointing it can be to have someone say they really want to donate, then never hear from them again…… not even an "I'm sorry, I don't think I can be a donor at this time, but I'll pray you find one." At least this person, unlike so many others, was noncommittal from the get-go.

> A person who promises a gift but doesn't give it is like clouds and wind that bring no rain. (Proverbs 25:14 NLT)
> Be not rash with thy mouth, and let not thine heart be hasty to utter anything before God…. (Ecclesiastes 5:2 KJV)

Aug. 30, 2014 Natalee's platelet count has dropped sharply in the past few weeks. (Platelets are what help blood to clot and prevent bleeding) Preferably, she is still not to have any transfusions due to antibodies making matching her for a transplant harder. Of course, if it becomes the only alternative, then she will have to have a platelet transfusion. For now, since her blood is already too thin for lack of platelets, they will be cutting back on the heparin dose she receives at dialysis that helps prevent blood clotting in the extracorporeal circuit - the apparatus carrying blood outside the body and through the machine during dialysis. When I've been with Natalee during dialysis it's eerie to watch her blood course through the clear tubing and make it's circuit - leaving her body, filtering through the machine and returning back to her again. (Usually if your blood is being let outside of your body, for whatever reason, you risk death. In this instance, it is life-saving.)

I am always amazed at her ever-positive attitude in spite of all her ongoing health issues that never seem to end and the strength she musters to face them. I know she has faith that God will give her strength to help her through them all, and she strives to stay positive for McKenna's sake. I was totally shocked once when she was having one of her "moments" and frankly told me if she didn't have McKenna she wouldn't care if she lived or not. Sad to say, but I understand her feelings. (I want to die after being ill for only 6 minutes.)

Oct. 27, 2014 We had to have a reprint of our dwindling supply of "signs and cards" since no one seemed to know what caused Natalee's platelets to drop to 75,000 (150,000-350,000 is normal) in August and September, but we prayed for the level to come back to normal without a transfusion and it is now 135,000. (Nothing is too hard for God....no signs or cards needed.)

> Behold, I am the Lord, the God of all flesh; is there anything too difficult for Me? (Jeremiah 32:27 AMP) But He said, "The things that are impossible with people are possible with God." (Luke 18:27 AMP)

Dec. 15, 2014 Natalee has been looking into home kidney dialysis the past few weeks. Unfortunately, her dialysis center does not participate in home dialysis. There is another center in the area that provides it, so she called them to schedule an appointment for us to go there and learn more about it. Arrangements were finalized for Natalee to have dialysis there five days in a row using the home dialysis unit while concurrently being shown what all is involved. Natalee not only wanted to learn more about it but wanted to see how she would feel after doing dialysis five days out of seven with less time on the machine than she currently weathers. Today was the first day. There's a lot to learn - almost daunting. (I had umpteen questions.)

McKenna and I would have to learn how to proficiently set up the machine and hook Natalee up. One of us would need to be present during the treatment in case anything would go wrong - with the machine or Natalee. It's a huge commitment for all of us, but if it would make Natalee feel better in the long run, it would be worth it. For now, Natalee has decided she is changing dialysis centers and will continue dialysis at the new center until she decides if she wants to execute the home dialysis. (Big decision requiring big time prayer.)

Jan. 27, 2015 Home dialysis is on the back burner. She decided the commitment for home dialysis is too great to ask me or McKenna to take on that responsibility right now, but will keep the option open.

Chapter 23

Take a Step Forward, Two Steps Back (No Do-si-do)

Feb. 24, 2015 Today Natalee saw a new endocrinologist in town. He told her about a subcutaneous glucose monitoring device and its benefits, then surprised her by asking her to come back in the afternoon to have one applied to try out. That afternoon a tiny electrode - a glucose sensor - was inserted subcutaneously on her abdomen, similar to how her insulin pump catheter is applied. It measures glucose levels in interstitial fluid. It will be removed in a week and connected to a computer to download the minute-by-minute blood glucose levels the sensor recorded. She is to keep a log of what she eats and when. The log will be compared with the recorded levels to make adjustments in her insulin so she can achieve better control. The doctor told her she is doing everything right considering all her health issues affecting her glucose control. That was good for her to hear since she tries so hard. Natalee was excited that they also gave her a new glucose monitor because hers was an older model. (Only a diabetic could get excited about that.) The doctor said he would like to obtain a newly developed insulin pump with a corresponding sensor for her that can read glucose levels. It will automatically give insulin for a high reading and stop giving insulin for low readings until the level is corrected. It can take months of dialogue about medical necessity with insurances to gain approval for payment, however. ("Wait and see" time.)

May 20, 2015 Yesterday we went to Pittsburgh to see the

neuro-oncologist for the results of the MRI she had two weeks ago. (While she had dialysis, I had a reunion with the waiting room chairs, and some French fries. I love the movie *Groundhog Day*, but sometimes I feel like I'm living it. Different day, same scenario with a few subtle nuances…... and repeat….and repeat….and repeat…...)

The MRI showed what he called a "cloud" on one edge of the cavity where the brain tumor had been removed almost four years ago. There was a noted slight increase in the white area from her MRI in January 2014. (As happens all too often, it was not news we wanted to hear.)

The neuro-oncologist spent a considerable amount of time discussing what it could or could not be and the possible treatment options. The first option was waiting and repeating a scan in four months to rule out if the "cloud" could be showing up due to a difference in the actual MRI technique. The second choice could be radiation alone or combined with chemo. He did mention, though, some studies showed that chemo was not that effective in low-grade astrocytoma gliomas. The third possibility is awake brain surgery with mapping since her tumor is close to the area that controls cognitive functions of memory, motor control and speech. Awake mapping is done to prevent damaging critical areas of the brain during surgery. We happened to see intraoperative brain mapping being performed years ago on *Discovery*. I found it quite fascinating. (Natalee didn't think so then, and doesn't now.)

The doctor seemed surprised that Natalee was not more upset at the news, even though the gravity of the situation was very obvious. I think we have become almost desensitized to bad news over the course of Natalee's challenges. Having a defeatist attitude when facing problems is not in her nature. She is always up for the challenge and forges ahead trusting God. She assuredly said to him, "Worry won't change anything, and I have the utmost trust in you and whatever you recommend I should do."

The neuro-oncologist expounded that the tumor board meets weekly on Mondays to discuss cases. He and others, including the neurosurgeon who did her surgery four years ago, will review and discuss this recent development, then get back to Natalee with a plan of attack. This could mean she would be off the transplant list…again…which compounds the bad news. (Just more trauma to shake Natalee's world, and all the more reason to remain steadfast in the Lord.)

We knew there was a possibility the tumor could regrow. Something we knew was a possisbility, but chose not to think about. For now, we can't do anything about the returning elephant in the room trumpeting a repeat challenge. I feel bad for McKenna and know she is worried after hearing this news. (As always, we'll just have to go on with life day by day, be glad we have each day we are given and continue to face what lies ahead with prayer and faith.)

> I have been crucified with Christ and I no longer live, but Christ lives in me. The life I now live in the body, I live by faith in the Son of God, who loved me and gave Himself for me. (Galatians 2:20 NIV) So that your faith might not rest on human wisdom, but on God's power. (1 Corinthians 2:5 NIV)

June 25, 2015 Natalee has decided she does not want surgery, but would agree to radiation.

Sept. 16, 2015 Monster GP has been acting up the past two weeks with the usual symptoms, but this time she also has gastric pain when she eats anything. Needless to say, she has not been eating much at all. Natalee saw her gastroenterologist and he informed her about an implantable gastric pacemaker available now to help control GP symptoms, but it's not known if having one would interfere with having a transplant by increasing the risk for infection which could lead to rejection. (It's time to get out the "signs and cards.")

> My comfort in my suffering is this: Your promise preserves my life. (Psalm 119:50 NIV)

Chapter 24

Here We Go Again

Sept. 30, 2015 Gyneoncologist appointment at Magee hospital today. No more watching and waiting. Two of the hyperdysplasia lesions are bigger in size now, so she is scheduled for outpatient surgery November 4.

Nov. 6, 2015 Natalee's gyne surgery went well, and she was released to come home late in the afternoon, tolerating the car ride home better than expected. (My feelings for The Chairs hasn't changed.)

Nov. 16, 2015 Natalee and I went to the funeral home today to pay respects to a teacher from the Christian school Natalee and McKenna attended in the elementary grades. Natalee is friends with her daughter. The teacher was diabetic, on dialysis and had other health problems, too. (Going to the funeral home adds a heaping dose of reality to chronic illness. An ever-present elephant taking up space in an overcrowded room.)

A few hours after I returned home, Natalee called and said she spiked a fever. Now what? I had her call the gyne doctor on call and let them know since she isn't to be seen until the 19th. The doctor on call never saw Natalee before and was surprised that Natalee gave her such a detailed description of her surgical site and her symptoms. Natalee explained to her that she is very dialed into her health issues. (Years of experience.) The doctor didn't feel that the fever was from a post-op infection. Natalee was instructed to take Tylenol for the fever, and call in the morning. If her symptoms worsened, she would need to be seen. (Praying it is not a post-op infection.)

Nov. 17, 2015 I got a call from Natalee at 7:15 a.m. saying her fever was up to 103 at 3:30 a.m., but is back down to normal now. No other symptoms have accompanied the fever as of yet. ("Wait and see" time.) At 11:30 a.m. I called Natalee, and the fever is back. She feels achy all over with some chest tightness now. (Flu? More "wait and see".)

Nov. 18, 2015 Natalee missed dialysis today; not feeling well enough to be at the mercy of the machine for three-and-a-half hours. Her temp is still fluctuating. Natalee touched base with her gyneoncologist and was told if the temp persisted to come to the ER at Magee. At 3:30 p.m., she called me and said her temp went up to 104.4. I went to her house straightaway. As soon as I saw her, I decided I needed to pack some things for her, and we were on the road heading to Pittsburgh by 5:00 p.m. (I knew deep down inside she would be admitted.)

I couldn't get David on the phone to let him know we were leaving for Pittsburgh. Where he was at had no cell service. (Of all the days!) At least McKenna knew what was going on and could tell him in more detail when he got home and heard the messages I left for him. McKenna had classes scheduled in the morning, so she stayed home. There was nothing she could do at the hospital except join me in the unbearable waiting room chairs. (Is that what is meant by misery loves company?)

Natalee and I arrived at Magee at 7:00 p.m. It was dark and rainy; a miserable drive on top of everything else, but at least it wasn't snowing. The staff in the ER were beyond efficient and addressed not just the fever and finding the cause, but were concerned because she had been too ill to go to dialysis today. They immediately scheduled her to have dialysis in the morning. She was admitted into an isolation room and awaited results of the tests that were done in the ER. I left at midnight to return home since I was not prepared to stay in Pittsburgh. I knew she was in good hands. (The drive home was lonely and equally miserable.) Natalee is okay being there without family around, and she just wanted to try and sleep through the night. I will return tomorrow morning. (And also try and sleep through what will be a seemingly long, but actually short night.)

Nov. 19, 2015 The nephrologist, medical doctors and the gyneoncologist all saw Natalee this morning. She felt a little better after dialysis. Her surgical site is healing normally and not the source of the problem as far as anyone can tell right now. The blood cultures she had showed a Staph B bacterial infection, which is a serious bloodstream infection that can progress to sepsis, which can be fatal from complications if not treated in a timely fashion. They are not sure of the primary cause of the infection, but they will begin treatment with IV antibiotics. It's time for Natalee's favorite game of "stump the doctor." (I'm ready to pass out the cards! How many days until we have a winner with an answer to the mystery? I wonder if anyone wants to venture a guess?)

I visited with her most of the day before returning home. A Transesophageal Echocardiogram (TEE) is scheduled for tomorrow to check if the infection has done any damage to her heart valves. Say what? This is one test she has never had, which is hard to imagine there are any she's missed. The end of the tubing has an echo transducer that produces sound waves, making detailed images of the heart which is close enough to the esophagus the valves can be seen in more detail than with a standard echocardiogram. (She doesn't need any additional problems.)

McKenna came for supper this evening rather than eat at home alone. I assured her Natalee was being well cared for, and told her I was proud of her for helping out at home when Natalee needed help. I can't imagine how McKenna would even begin to come to terms with even the thought of losing Natalee. (Another elephant in the room no one wants to confront.)

Nov. 22, 2015 Natalee's fever is gone, but the elusive primary source of the infection still hasn't been established. Further tests are planned for this week, but the TEE is on hold for now. Hoping she gets home for Thanksgiving, but if not, the turkey will get a reprieve for the time being. (Resolving Natalee's infection is more important.)

Nov. 23, 2015 Her blood cultures remain GM+, meaning the pesky bacteria are still present. The cardiologist was in this morning and decided to go ahead with a CT scan of her abdomen today and the TEE tomorrow. (More poking and prodding.) Today is her usual dialysis, but at least they do that in her room and I can visit while she is on the machine.

Nov. 24, 2015 On a positive note, the TEE was normal and the blood cultures are negative today. (Natalee did a little happy dance in her hospital bed!) She may be discharged in the next few days if the blood cultures continue to be negative.

Nov. 25, 2015 Mystery solved….in seven days! (Maybe we should think about prizes to award to those who solve stump-the-doctor issues.) The infection was coming from her gut - the abdominal CT showed inflammation in the colon. Now they want her to have a colonoscopy, so it looks like we will be spending Thanksgiving at the hospital. Won't be the first holiday (or birthday) we've celebrated at a hospital.

Between work and college classes, McKenna has not been able to come to Pittsburgh with me to visit her mom, and due to her work schedule she won't see Natalee on Thanksgiving either. In any case, we are thankful they are being thorough and found the source of the infection. We'll have a belated family Thanksgiving when Natalee gets home. (The turkey is defrosting in the fridge, making friends with the condiments. If it hasn't flown the coop already, it's probably doing a reprieve turkey-trot happy dance with the cranberry relish.)

Nov. 26, 2015 Happy Thanksgiving! Not so happy for Natalee. She is not thankful for the liquid diet for Thanksgiving lunch, and tasteless Miralax to drink in preparation for her colonoscopy. She was in good spirits today in spite of not being able to have solid food. David and I had Thanksgiving lunch savoring fine dining in the utilitarian ambiance of the hospital cafeteria. (No fries today though.) We are all giving thanks just the same. A glimmer of good news today to give thanks for - the blood cultures are negative again.

> Enter his gates with thanksgiving, and his courts with praise! Give thanks to him; bless his name! (Psalm 100:4 ESV)

Nov. 27, 2015 The doctor said he excised a small ulcer and removed a polyp during the colonoscopy, and found no other abnormalities. No word as to when she can come home.

Nov. 28, 2015 David and I visited Natalee today and arrived to great news. Her blood cultures have been negative for the past five days, and she was being discharged today after she finishes her dialysis treatment and a dose of the IV antibiotic, which will continue for two more weeks at dialysis. Tomorrow we will celebrate a belated Thanksgiving since McKenna has the day off of work. It's our favorite holiday and reminds us of all that we have to give thanks for. (The turkey has been chilling for a week, so I'll be thankful if it's still safe to eat.)

Dec. 10, 2015 Went to Magee today for Natalee's post-op follow-up. The biopsies of the colon ulcer and polyp they removed were negative. No problems noted, new or old. The doctor said he will release her to be back on the active transplant list.

Dec. 14, 2015 Natalee saw the infectious disease doctor today at the Kauffman building in Pittsburgh. Another coveted transplant clearance granted. (Just one more appointment to go for Natalee to be released to be back on the active transplant list and then we'll hope she can remain on it without any further problems causing her to be off the list.)

Chapter 25

Just More of the Same

Dec. 22, 2015 At UPMC Shadyside hospital in Pittsburgh for Natalee's MRI of her head today. The doctor ordered it on short notice, and Presby didn't have an opening. She was not ordered contrast, so no dialysis afterwards. After the MRI we walked from the hospital, via the connecting bridge, to Hillman Cancer Center to see her neuro-oncologist. Her appointment time came and went and we waited two more hours "bonding" with the compulsory waiting room chairs. (I might like them better if they had a footrest. And maybe a soft pillow.)

One of the views the doctor wanted to see on the MRI was not scanned, so he asked if we could come back another day, even though everything else on the MRI looked the same. That particular view is usually done with contrast, and contrast wasn't ordered, so it wasn't scanned. We explained it is a two-hour trip one way, and if we can actually make it there depends on the weather. (Snow, no go! My sled dogs are retired!) Natalee told him we would have to reschedule a day depending on her dialysis schedule and other appointments. As we were leaving the main waiting room we heard someone calling, "Natalee." It was the doctor rushing to catch up with us! He said he made a call over to Shadyside and if we could go over right away, they could do another MRI at no charge. So, we hiked back over to the hospital; saving us another trip to Pittsburgh. We left the hospital in time for rush hour traffic. (Why is it called rush hour when nobody's rushing anywhere?)

April 7, 2016 Natalee saw the gyneoncologist in Pittsburgh today. Not good news. She has another lesion. The surgery date is set for April 20. (Downside: The surgery will take her off the active transplant list for now.)

April 24, 2016 Natalee had received a call last week from her PCP saying her pre-op chest x-ray appeared to show an enlargement of one of the upper chambers of her heart (right atria) when compared to her last x-ray. Now what? A CT scan to further investigate was ordered and her April 20 surgery was canceled. The CT result was normal, so the surgery was rescheduled for May 4. Now Natalee got a call re-rescheduling her surgery for May 11 because the doctor is going to be out of town on May 4. (The circus is alive and well.)

May 7, 2016 Natalee texted me early this morning to let me know she awoke at 3 a.m. with a dangerously low blood sugar of 34, manifesting in classic symptoms - shakiness and drenched in sweat with trouble thinking clearly. She said she managed to eat one of the snacks she keeps at her bedside for just such occasions. However, she couldn't remember if she needed to do anything with her insulin pump. She later discovered she gave herself 1.3 units of insulin. (Her pump keeps a log she can view.) Something she shouldn't have done for a low level - insulin will lower it more. She said she felt like passing out. (Low glucose levels cause brain cells to malfunction, leading to fainting or even a seizure occurring.) Thank goodness she didn't lose consciousness and was able to recheck her level and eat more food to compensate the low level.

McKenna is no longer living at home, and it greatly concerns me that Natalee is alone at night. When she has low glucose episodes, she could pass out and couldn't call for help. Trusting God will watch over her is all I can do. (She doesn't want a "help, I've fallen and can't get up" gizmo.)

May 11, 2016 Surgery day. We left home at 11:30 a.m. and arrived at 1:00 p.m.! (Traffic was moving…and so was I! Natalee calls me "Mario", as in Andretti!) They informed us the doctor was ninety minutes behind schedule. No biggie, we're used to waiting. (I just love bonding with those chairs even longer. Sarcasm, of course.)

As always, we laughed and carried on while we waited. A little later her doctor appeared between cases, apologized for running late, and estimated how much longer it would be until her surgery. A little after 4:30 p.m. she went to the OR. I went to the waiting room. (Different chair, same sentiments.) After the surgery was over, the doctor came to the waiting room and told me everything went well.

Sometime after 6:00 p.m. a nurse came to the waiting room and led me to the second phase of recovery unit. Natalee was awake and alert, reclining in a comfy blue chair like she was queen for the day, munching on soda crackers. The nurse gave her a some pain medication so she could tolerate the ride home more comfortably. Even so, she was more than glad when we arrived home and she could lie down. She'll be staying at my house until she's able to drive. (Now we'll pray she heals quickly..... with no problems.)

May 13, 2016 I heard Natalee get up at 4:00 a.m. to get ready to go to dialysis. I also heard her vomiting three times while she was getting ready. There was nothing I could do for her but pray it would stop. Even though she wasn't feeling well, she managed to get ready, swallow her meds with some juice - hoping they'd stay down - and still managed to be cheerful. Cheerful would not have been remotely in my vocabulary if that was how my morning was going. (Inserting a sad face here as I return to bed. David is the chauffeur today.)

May 17, 2016 This evening Natalee began having burping with a sulfuric after taste, which she sometimes gets when her GP is starting to flare up. An hour later she went into the bathroom and I heard the commode flush *five* times. I checked on her, but there's nothing more I could do. (Praying her GP will let her get some sleep.)

May 18, 2016 Natalee excitedly told me she met a girl, Charlene, who is on dialysis at the same time, is close to her age, on the kidney transplant list, is diabetic with GP, legally blind, and has a pancreas graft. She had a kidney transplant, but it rejected years later due to other health issues she was having. It will be good for Natalee to have someone to talk to who *really* understands what she goes through. (Natalee is by far not the only one with multiple challenging health issues.)

May 27, 2016 This morning Natalee was able to drive herself to dialysis. I took her to see her gyneoncologist this afternoon and no problems were noted. The GP is in check for now, so we stopped for lunch at our favorite Panera Bread on the way home. When we got back to my house, she packed her things to return home. (I'll miss having her here.)

May 29, 2016 Today Natalee had a two-hour phone conversation with

Charlene. Natalee never thought she would meet a virtual mirror image of herself.

June 21, 2016 The past few days Natalee has had a plaguing pain in her lower left leg and foot with no visible signs indicating a cause. The pain started to move up her leg causing it to feel "tingly." Her PCP wanted to order vascular studies of her leg, but her insurance won't cover them. The insurance also won't cover a Dexa scan to screen for osteoporosis because of her age. Her doctors have tried several times to obtain approval to no avail. Osteoporosis runs in our family and she is a prime candidate due to her additional health issues. She has had extremely high PTH (parathyroid) levels in the past which contributes to bone loss. (Her PCP is seeing her this week, and the stump-the-doctor challenge is on.)

June 26, 2016 Her very diligent PCP somehow was able to get the vascular studies approved and scheduled them for July. He also scheduled her to see a neurologist for EMG studies on her legs to detect if neuromuscular abnormalities are the pain source. (More poking and prodding.)

July 15, 2016 Today was the EMG. The tech who did the procedure was very jovial and kept us laughing. The test involved stimulating her leg muscles with an electric prod and needles. (Only Natalee could laugh, make jokes with the tech and have fun during a pain-inducing test.)

July 20, 2016 I took Natalee for the vascular study on her legs this afternoon. Pressure cuffs that pump up like a blood pressure cuff were applied on her feet and at various places on both her legs…ankles to thighs. She said it was uncomfortable when they were pumped up and squeezing her legs. Natalee had marks on her legs for several hours after the testing where the cuffs had been tightly pumped up.

Chapter 26

A Trip to Texas

July 15, 2016 Natalee's birth father (whom I shall name X rather than write out biological or birth father every time I refer to him) bought her an airline ticket so she could visit him in Texas this coming week. A huge concern is she will be flying there alone. (I think she is more nervous about it than facing surgery.) Arrangements were made for assistance to take Natalee and her carry-on across the airport to her next flight once she arrives at Dulles, since walking that far and carrying her bag is too taxing. The same arrangements were made for when she arrived in Houston.

Plans for sightseeing, shopping and going out for dinner were mentioned by X during several phone calls to make plans. Natalee reminded him that eating at regular mealtimes can be challenging some days due to her GP, plus being diabetic and on dialysis add to her dietary restrictions. She reiterated she is not interested in sightseeing or shopping, which is too taxing for her. (Besides, she hates shopping!) It's hard for people who don't live with someone with a chronic illness to fully understand their limitations. (She will have to be firm with X about them when planning things to do.)

X is aware and agreeable that he will have to pay for part of her dialysis treatments while she is there because she will be out of state. Her dialysis center here will fax orders and machine settings to the Center where she will have treatments. Natalee said X keeps asking her if she called the Center there to set up an early morning time so they could have the rest of the day to do whatever. She reminded him: 1) a Center doesn't make the final schedule until late in the day prior due to not knowing who will be in the hospital or who died (reality check) and won't be there the next day, and 2) they aren't going to give her a regularly scheduled patient's morning time slot and bump them to another time for her. Natalee will be fit in where they have an open time slot since she is only going to be there for four treatments over ten days.

I will be praying extra hard she stays "well" while she is in Texas and that her flights and dialysis go smoothly. (She may be over forty and independent, but I'm still her mom and worrying about her will forever be part of my being!)

Good news today, sort of! Natalee received a call that the results of her vascular study and EMG were normal! Bad news is she's back to "stump the doctor" as to what is causing her leg pain.

July 26, 2016 "Stump the doctor" is solved. The earlier good news, however, was short-lived. Natalee saw her cardiologist today for a routine check-up and he told her that the vascular studies showed narrowing of the veins in her legs and that the ultrasound she had recently of her carotid arteries showed a narrowing. (The carotid testing was part of her transplant check-list.) We already know Natalee has some minor degree of arterial blockage (4 vessels) in her heart and a leaky valve. He is prescribing Lipitor for her since her cholesterol level has increased compared to the last test results. That can contribute to the narrowing. (Hmmm, I wonder who called her with the "normal" results and how they came to that conclusion? Another mystery.)

Natalee said the cardiologist had a new medical resident with him today and the resident heard the heart murmur she has when he listened to the left side of her chest, but he looked puzzled when he listened to the right side. The cardiologist smiled and told him he was hearing the bruit from Natalee's fistula in her right upper arm. It is so strong it can be heard in the right side of her chest. (I guess the resident learned something today from Natalee - "the living textbook.")

July 28, 2016 Natalee spent the night at our house and David took her to the local airport at 5:15 a.m. for her flight to Texas. She called when she arrived at Dulles airport to say all was going well and that she was met with transport when she got off the plane to get to her next flight. (So far, so good.) I was glad to get her call when she arrived in Houston, too, where transport also met her. Now I pray she can enjoy her stay. (She deserves a vacation away, although she never has a vacation from dialysis or health issues.)

July 29, 2016 Natalee had dialysis at the Center in Texas today and said the staff were very nice, interested in where she was from, and fascinated by her health history. Ill luck won out, though, and she was scheduled for 2:30 p.m. and won't get out of there until at least 6:30 p.m. All is going well otherwise, so far.

August 6, 2016 Natalee returned from Texas safe and sound. She had a nice time and didn't have any major health issues. X lives on a lake and Natalee said she enjoyed just being a passenger in a canoe, relaxing in the sunshine and enjoying the calming scenery without Dr. office vists and testing procedures. I'm glad she got away for a little vacation and was able to enjoy it, but I missed her. (Hard to tell if her cat missed her. Cats are like that.)

Chapter 27

Back to the Same Old, Same Old

Sept. 9, 2016 Natalee called me and said she kept smelling nail polish remover, but there was none anywhere around her. I worried she may possibly have DKA. A quick test to confirm DKA is by dipping a test strip into urine and assessing the color change, then comparing it to a chart on the test strip canister for the results, but Natalee doesn't make urine, so testing is not an option. (I am stunned at how many people don't realize Natalee has no urine output due to her non-functioning kidneys, thus the reason for dialysis.) Her blood sugars have been elevated since she started on Lipitor; one of the side effects for diabetics. Very high blood sugar levels cause ketones to rise to unsafe levels. One of the by-products of ketones is acetone which causes a nail polish smell. I told her to stop the Lipitor her cardiologist prescribed, and to call and let him know.

Sept. 11, 2016 After stopping the Lipitor, Natalee's blood sugars are improving. (Moms, that are also nurses, know best!)

Sept. 12, 2016 Natalee and I had a scheduled "bonding" day yesterday for a follow-up MRI of her head followed by four hours of dialysis. (Yes, me and The Chairs meet again. They were just sitting there waiting for me, glaring at me and daring me to choose one of them!) After the MRI we had enough time to have lunch in the cafeteria before dialysis. (It was long day, so I had French fries twice!)

I read two thirds of a new mystery book I started while freezing air was briskly circulating from the vents in the small waiting room that was, according to the thermostat on the wall, 65 degrees. (The Chairs didn't seem to be my worst problem today! Where's a heated chair when you need one?) Much to my dismay, there was no way to access the thermostat to reset the room temp. It was covered by a locked plastic shield to keep prying fingers, like mine, off. On a good note, I was glad I had a jacket with me so I didn't turn into a popsicle. On a bad note, a guy entered the waiting room and chose one of The Chairs and sat down. He didn't smell very pleasant, to put it nicely. (I thought saying he was reeking of nauseating body odor may too harsh. I think I saw the chair frown.) At that moment, I was glad it wasn't overly warm in the waiting room or the smell would have been even worse! I had to vacate the room until he left, so I took a walk to the gift shop. (Okay, so I went back to the cafeteria for dessert, too.)

Natalee will return to Hillman in two weeks for the MRI results. Next week she has an appointment at Magee for a check-up. Nothing like visiting a different hospital in Pittsburgh every week. I could be a certified hospital tour guide. (My fee: French fries.)

Sept. 19, 2016 Natalee had a good check-up today at her gyneoncologist appointment....no new lesions. Now we are waiting and praying we get more good news next week at Hillman. Hopefully she's on a steady roll of good news and achieves a trifecta. (But I wouldn't bet on it.)

Sept. 24, 2016 Natalee is excited. She is starting and heading up a "Care Team" at her church. She has always had a beneficent heart for helping others and this is something she can do that only requires brain power, phone calls and the help of volunteers. Natalee previously coordinated clothing drives for the local Victims Services and Women's Help Center, and collected donations for the food bank. People brought donations to her house, and Natalee had them delivered to the various agencies. (I know one of the reasons God blesses her is because she is compassionate toward others in need and a cheerful giver when it comes to helping others in whatever way she can.)

> A generous person will prosper; whoever refreshes others
> will be refreshed. (Proverbs 11:25 NIV) Give, and it will
> be given to you. A good measure, pressed down, shaken
> together and running over, will be poured into your lap.

For with the measure you use, it will be measured to you.
(Luke 6:38 NIV)

Several people at the church have commented how inspiring it is for Natalee to be involved in spite of all her health issues. I am glad she has found something to do that doesn't require a taxing effort or a set schedule she couldn't meet. (She feels very blessed.)

Chapter 28

Deja vu

Sept. 27, 2016 Another long day at Hillman. Her appointment with the neuro-oncologist was scheduled for 11:00 a.m. and we weren't called into the exam room until 12:30 p.m. where we "bonded" and waited some more. After many years of doing this I guess we are programmed to always come to appointments prepared to wait a while. (If we see the doctor on time, it's a bonus!) Some people in the waiting room were grumbling about the long wait, but we are grateful Natalee has such a competent and brilliant doctor who takes all the time he needs; never rushing us out of the exam room before he covers everything we need to know and answers all of our questions. It's worth the wait.... without complaining. (And they have good coffee!) A word to the complaining people - go watch the fish in the aquarium. Watching them will make you feel more relaxed while you wait.

No trifecta. The earlier run of good news was cruelly overshadowed by further existential bad news. The Astrocytoma shows definite growth since the last two MRIs. He called it a "flare." Long story short and sparing the detailed technical medical jargon discussed with us, the remedies are either removal of the tumor during awake brain surgery or chemo and/or radiation. The neuro-oncologist is going to confer with her neurosurgeon regarding any further testing he may want to suggest, and his thoughts on surgical removal. He then said this news will have to be presented to Transplant and he also wants to discuss Natalee's case with some of the other neuro-oncologists at Hillman during the tumor board meeting. We trust her doctors without reservation, but other opinions are more than welcome since this will impact her life in more ways than one. My brain doesn't even want to begin to process this news. There doesn't seem to be a limit on trials or challenges where Natalee is concerned. (Sigh, how I wish there were.)

I know I have alot to say (mostly in jest) about The Chairs, but what I endure while spending countless hours bonding with them is nothing compared to what Natalee endures physically, mentally, and emotionally.

Natalee was, of course, highly disappointed with the news. On a good note, her neuro exam was normal, so the tumor is currently not affecting any vital functions. We are thankful for that. As usual, Natalee immediately announced, "I'm giving it to God. Me and God've got this." Worry won't change anything and until we know more, there's no point in stressing over what might be in store. (Even with good planning you can't look around the corner in life to see what's next. You have to take life day by day as it comes…..and trust God to get you through it.)

> The steadfast love of the Lord never ceases; his mercies never come to an end; they are new every morning…. (Lamentations 3:22-23 ESV)

Natalee's biggest worry is being taken off the transplant list permanently. If surgery is her choice, she would be off the list again and may have to fight to get reinstated like the last time. Chemo and radiation would also keep her off the list as long as she was receiving treatments. As far as Natalee is concerned, the *only* option she will acquiesce to is the one that will keep her on the list. Emphatically, Natalee said to me, "I am not going to do dialysis the rest of my life!" She has stated before that she would never have brain surgery again, but now says if it would keep her on the list, she will unhappily agree. Natalee is to call the neuro-oncologist within the next two weeks on his private office line or email him directly to find out what decisions were collectively made. Lots to consider. (It's a wonder our heads don't explode.)

In true Natalee fashion, one of her biggest issues with having the surgery is being in ICU post-op and having to use the commode that swings out from a cupboard under the sink in the room. There is no additional privacy around it - just the closed door to the room itself and the curtain over the window. Only Natalee would be more disturbed about that than facing brain surgery. (Just another one of Natalee's unconventional concerns.)

Unexpected news like that makes you realize the truth about your own mortality. As I am writing this I am trying to think how I feel about today. Numb, an emotional vacuum is a good description; and tired… just tired. I can't let this occupy any real estate in my head right now and begin to stress about it. I have to trust God that it will all work out favorably. It's in His hands….mine can't do anything but pray. (I'm glad God doesn't get tired of hearing prayers.)

> Cast your cares on the Lord and he will sustain you; he will never let the righteous be shaken. (Psalm 55:22 NIV) When I am afraid, I put my trust in you. (Psalm 56:3 NIV)

Oct. 18, 2016 Natalee was talking about how she wants to be cremated and she's decided she wants a mosaic cremation urn; death is a reality she accepts. Every day I am aware that she has reached her average life expectancy for a diabetic on dialysis with multiple health issues, but I hold on to the fact some live longer and pray she will continue be one of them. (That factual elephant is always lingering in the shadows. I try not to dwell on it, or I wouldn't be able to breathe and function.)

Oct. 19, 2016 The neuro-oncologist called Natalee today and suggested she go ahead and make an appointment with the neurosurgeon. So far, the treatment of choice being recommended is the awake brain surgery with mapping. Natalee has agreed she would rather have the surgery and be done with it, but not until spring of 2017. She doesn't want to worry about travel to Pittsburgh in the winter and unpredictable weather. (Plus, she wants to have the surgery over, and be recovered enough to be able to open her pool in June. A priority for her!)

Oct. 25, 2016 Natalee's transplant wait list appointment was today. The PA and transplant coordinator confirmed that all her required tests for the past year are completed and acceptable. We learned something today we didn't know. There is a National transplant registry open to everyone that is hard match due to the level of antibodies they have. Say there is a kidney available in Arizona, and it would be a match for Natalee and also a match for someone in Arizona; they would allow the kidney to go to Natalee due to her being such a next-to-impossible match. Natalee is on that list….when she's on the active list. Bad news is, however, it's practically a one-in-a-million chance to get a cadaveric match for her. Right now she is back on the inactive list and will remain inactive until she has the surgery and is cleared post-op. So, we'll pray that 2018 will be the year she gets a kidney. (Never give up hope.)

We arrived in Pittsburgh in enough time to get French fries in the cafeteria before her appointment. (One of *my* priorities!) We didn't leave Pittsburgh until after 4:00 p.m., so we stopped at Panera for supper. (A priority for both of us.) Great "bonding" time today and good food! I told Natalee the only reason I take her to her appointments is to get fries in the cafeteria and to eat at Panera. (I think she believed me.)

Nov. 7, 2016 Natalee called and wanted to know where online I saw a cremation urn that looks like a brass book with an elephant carved in relief on the front! Natalee loves elephants. (Can't be because there have been so many of them in "Cirque du Natalee's Challenges" over the years.) Natalee said, "It would match Jimmy's urn." Not a typical mother-daughter conversation, for sure, but one based on Natalee's reality that we face. She decided that's the urn she wants. (For now anyhow!)

Nov. 9, 2016 The neurosurgeon's office called today to schedule Natalee for a high-definition fiber tracking MRI (HDFT), plus a functional MRI of her head in preparation of the tumor removal. The HDFT is a 3D image that allows the surgeon to see the detailed wiring of brain fibers so the best way to remove a brain tumor can be determined. (It was developed by the Learning Research and Development Center - University of Pittsburgh.) The functional scan does brain mapping and measures brain activity, precisely which part of the brain handles critical functions such as speech, movement and sensation. She will also need to be scheduled for a magneto encephalography (MEG) to map brain activity in the motor cortex. The testing is scheduled for the end of February.

As a nurse I find it quite fascinating, but as Natalee's mom, I can't think about all this right now or it would overwhelm me. I am just so thankful she has a doctor who is thorough and on the cutting edge. (No pun intended.) I know Natalee can go into the surgery with confidence in him. And most importantly, with many prayers and God on her side. (We'll let the docs deal with the technical stuff.)

Nov. 10, 2016 I keep many of my feelings and innermost thoughts to myself, but ….

Lately, I've had the feeling from their reactions, some people don't believe all that Natalee has endured and continues to endure. It does seem unbelievable. Even I can't believe it sometimes, although I see all her struggles right before my eyes on a daily basis. Natalee has even heard a few people have said she's faking being ill. (How do you fake brain surgery, dialysis, and wearing an insulin pump?)

David and I are both retired now, and we don't have to be concerned about taking time off work any more to be there for Natalee. That takes some of the pressure off. I know Natalee feels bad that we don't go on vacations so we can be there for her if she needs us, and that we spend a lot of time and money taking her to appointments here and in Pittsburgh, but we don't mind. We know the actuality of her situation and want to be there for her as much as we can, in every way we can.

Do I get weary of it all? Of course, I'm human after all. There are days I am weighed down by sensory overload related to her ongoing health issues that are on a seemingly never-ending loop running through my head. But then I think about how weary Natalee must feel living it day in and day out, and still she soldiers on. It's certainly not easy over the long haul, but taking one day at a time makes it palatable. Her fortitude and faith humbles me and makes me proud. (I can't say it enough.) I tell people who have healthy children they need to be *very* thankful every day.

Jan. 20, 2017 Natalee called the neurosurgeon's office yesterday to begin scheduling her HDFT and MEG. On a good note, there is no dye involved in either test, so no follow-up dialysis afterward. (The Chairs at the dialysis unit will just have to miss me. As much as I dislike them and dis them, The Chairs are quietly reliable, and always there for me.)

Jan. 23, 2017 I woke up to find a text from Natalee on my phone asking me to call as soon as I got up. Reminding myself not to panic until I talked to her, I immediately called her. She didn't sleep much last night because she wasn't feeling well - complaining of feeling shaky, heart racing over a hundred, and a headache - but couldn't put a finger on just what the problem was. Her blood sugar was okay when she checked it, so that was not the problem. Being that it was a Sunday night she also had extra fluid on her since her last dialysis was finished at 9:00 a.m. Friday. That in itself causes her some shortness of breath with any activity, but she now had shortness of breath while resting. In typical Natalee fashion, though, she went to dialysis in the morning. When they put her on the machine and checked her blood pressure it was 237/112. Big problem. The nurses exclaimed they were amazed she hadn't had a stroke or MI. Natalee said it finally dawned on her she missed taking her evening meds. By the end of her treatment her blood pressure was down to normal, for her, and she felt better, just really tired. (Crisis averted.) I asked Natalee if she felt okay to drive home; if not, her dad and I would come get her. She said she felt able to drive and would call when she arrived home.

I told her she needs to set her phone alarm in the evening as a precautionary reminder to take her meds, even though she rarely misses a dose. I haven't noticed her forgetting anything else, but I have observed in conversation she repeats things she already told me the day before; more than usual. It worries me that the brain tumor could be impinging into the area that controls her cognitive skills. I haven't detected any other neuro deficits though. (Natalee has a blood pressure cuff at home and assured me she will keep an eye on her pressure and make sure she doesn't forget her bedtime meds.)

Jan. 24, 2017 The MEG and HDFT are scheduled for February 2. We are fortunate to have a MEG scanner close to us. (There are less than 40 in the U.S. and around 100 worldwide.) The test is done in a magnetically shielded room, and takes three hours. Brain activity is mapped by recording magnetic fields the brain naturally produces. Natalee will be sitting up for the test, positioned below a tube-type structure with a soft helmet-like end that will cover her head; open in front so not to block her visual field. Positioning coils will be taped to her head to help to determine the precise position of her head, and electrodes will be attached to her head for an electroencephalogram (EEG) study. (Sounds sci-fi - without the tin foil!) During the study, she will be presented with some stimuli or asked to perform specific tasks, such as pushing a button or reading something out loud to check her sensory skills. We found the cost for the MEG is around $10,000! (Having a brain tumor isn't cheap.)

After the MEG, we will have time to go to lunch before the high-definition fiber tracking scan. (I hear French fries calling my name.) The scan makes the detailed wiring connections in the brain visible to the human eye in 3D and vivid color to determine the best way to remove a brain tumor while preserving brain function. On average, a standard MRI in the U.S. costs over $2600, so I can't imagine what an HDFT costs. (Just glad insurance covers the tests.)

Feb. 1, 2017 Natalee saw her endocrinologist this afternoon to have her stored pump readings downloaded. The nurse noticed a small crack in the pump's case. Natalee inquired where things stood with obtaining the new pump with a sensor. The nurse told her that she would only be eligible right now for an upgraded pump replacement since hers was cracked, but she would email the company and ask if it could be replaced with the new one with the sensor instead.

Shortest "wait and see time" ever! Natalee received a call at 8:30 p.m. from the clinical coordinator of the company that Natalee's pump and supplies come from. She asked why Natalee thought she would benefit from a pump with a sensor instead of just an upgraded pump replacement. Natalee started to explain her medical problems and was stopped after mentioning three of them; no doubt enough to justify having the pump with a sensor. She should hear next week if it is approved by her insurance. *If* it is, the coordinator said she will be the one to train Natalee on using the pump and sensor. (Praying it all comes to fruition sooner rather than later.)

Feb. 2, 2017 Today was Natalee's MEG testing and HDFT. For the MEG, Natalee said electrodes were adhered to her head and face with glue that was stored in a locked biohazard cabinet! She was required to respond to visual, motor and voice stimuli, with each portion of the test taking about 15 minutes. The HDFT was similar to having an MRI.

Now we'll wait to hear from the neurosurgeon to set up an appointment to discuss the test results and upcoming surgery. I prayed for good weather for our trip today and it was sunny and dry; a cloudless blue-sky day for this time of year. A long day, which seemed even longer to Natalee during her testing, and equally so for David and I while enduring the multiple carbon copy, less-than-comfortable, waiting room chairs. David is not a fan of The Chairs either. (Getting French fries almost made up for hours of enduring them!)

Feb. 15, 2017 The neurosurgeon's nurse called to schedule Natalee for another MRI with contrast and four hours of dialysis on March 8. The less-than-welcome news was a complete surprise. She will also be seeing the doctor that day and have pre-op testing. The surgery is scheduled for March 16. (The ball is rolling now.)

Chapter 29

Additional Frustrations

Feb. 21, 2017 Same old sideshow…..bring in the clowns. Natalee is more upset than usual with her DME company regarding…you guessed it…. her pump supplies. She has only been able to get "emergency" supplies sent to her until she satisfies a requirement to have a fasting blood sugar and fasting C-peptide test. She was told by her supplier that the tests are required now by Medicare. Problem is…. she had the tests done….. *twice.* She was told a repeat was necessary because the final result of the first test reported the C-peptide as non-fasting while the blood sugar was marked fasting, so they wouldn't accept the results. (Considering Natalee was fasting when they were drawn… *at the same time… in the same tube…* how is that even possible?)

When she went to have the blood redrawn, Natalee specifically told the lab techs to mark that both tests were fasting, and even watched them write "fasting" on the *one* tube used to draw *both* tests, then also wrote it on the request. Same problem again, only this time the results were unacceptable because the results reported the C-peptide was fasting and the blood sugar was marked as non-fasting; the opposite results of the first test. (Color me astonished.) Again, Natalee told the supplier that both tests were drawn at the same time, while she was fasting - in one-lone-single-solitary tube. They still won't release the supplies until both tests are repeated, again! Third time's a charm, hopefully. (Insert a head shake and a frustrated eye roll here.) I told Natalee to call Medicare directly if the problem is not soon resolved. (Not having any extra insulin delivery sets for her pump is adding to her stress level on top of all this nonsense.)

On a good note, she received instructions for the appointment with the neurosurgeon, the MRI and pre-op testing on March 8. Another long day. We probably won't get out of Pittsburgh until after 7:30 p.m. (Looking on the bright side, at least we'll miss rush hour traffic! And I can have French fries…twice!)

Feb. 22, 2017 Unbelievable! A month's worth of Natalee's pump supplies mysteriously arrived today. She had called Medicare two days ago to find out their actual policy about the testing she is being required to have before her supplier will release her pump supplies. The person she spoke with was very helpful and read her the Medicare policy about requirements for obtaining DME supplies. Surprise, surprise. What the DME is telling her is NOT what's in the actual Medicare policy! (Interesting.)

Natalee then called her DME supplier and asked to talk to a supervisor; explaining all that was going on with not getting her pump supplies on time, the problem regarding the test results, and what she found out from Medicare. Apparently the problem is their *interpretation* of the Medicare policy differs from the actual Medicare policy. A matter of semantics at best. He promised her more supplies would be delivered ASAP and that he was sorry she was having to jump through hoops every month to get her supplies on time, and for all the problems she has encountered recently. He did tell her he saw in her record that it appears things have been approved for her to get the new pump with the sensor that will be available soon. (We'll see….soon isn't an actual time frame.)

Chapter 30

What Could Possibly Go Wrong?

Feb. 25, 2017 At church service this evening, Natalee was anointed with oil and prayers were offered for the surgery to go well. When people ask her about her upcoming surgery she just says, "God has this." People are amazed she is so calm about it. (I call it faith in action.)

> In the same way, faith by itself, if it is not accompanied by
> action, is dead. (James 2:17 NIV)

March 6, 2017 Sad news today. A truly remarkable man, Dr. Thomas Starzl, passed away at age 90. The transplant center at UPMC is named after him. He initially pioneered liver transplant and anti-rejection medications; later becoming involved in other organ transplants and improving outcomes. He was referred to as "the father of modern transplantation." Thank you, Dr. Starzl, for your exceptionally brilliant, ingenious contributions to medical science. A truly inspiring life benefiting mankind. (We felt blessed when he consulted on Natalee's case several times.)

March 8, 2017 Natalee stayed at my house overnight so we could leave from here for Pittsburgh, and save time by me not having to pick her up. (Okay…and for me not to have to get out of bed any earlier.) Natalee questioned why the water in the commode in the upstairs bathroom was running. I told her I didn't know; it never did that before. I did the only thing I knew to do.…..I called for David to check it out, but he couldn't get the water to stop running. We decided to shut off the water supply line and deal with it when we got home from Pittsburgh. Good thing David went back into the bathroom to get something before we left ...... there was water all over the stone-tiled floor! To add to the expanding mess, the water leaked from the line into the downstairs bathroom, too. Needless to say, a not-so-happy David stayed home and spent the day bonding with our plumber while Natalee and I were on our own for a day of bonding in Pittsburgh. (The supply line valve had ruptured and that's what caused the flood.)

Due to the catastrophe in the bathroom, Natalee and I ended up leaving a little later than planned, arriving in Pittsburgh just in time for rush hour traffic. We made it to the hospital with only ten minutes to spare before Natalee's appointment with the neurosurgeon. (Mario was driving!) The PA, who had never seen Natalee before, smiled and said, "I didn't have hours to read through all your medical history, so I got a shortened report from the Doc.!" (He was joking, of course.... I think!) The neurosurgeon showed us the films from the hi-def fiber tracking and MEG. So incredible! They were highly detailed and showed the fibers and pathways in brilliant living colors....different colors for different areas and functions. The tumor is irregularly shaped with some tentacles evident. (For the curious, MEG scan images can be viewed on Google.)

Natalee and I were encouraged to ask questions and the doctor gave in-depth answers to our concerns. After all the t's were crossed and i's dotted, Natalee reminded him she was on dialysis and diabetic with an insulin pump. (He made the comment that Natalee was a "delicate" patient due to all her health issues.)

Next, we took the long walk via the bridge to Montefiore for her pre-op testing. I was worried about Natalee walking that far since this was a Monday and she was fluid overloaded, not having dialysis yet today. Walking even a short distance was taxing for her, but she refused a wheelchair ride. Taking our time, she managed the trek okay. After the pre-op testing, we had time for some lunch at Montefiore's cafeteria. (Yes, they have the same yummy French fries! Priorities!)

After the MRI with contrast, the last thing on the day's agenda was a hike back over to Presby for dialysis. Natalee began experiencing chest tightness and shortness of breath halfway there, so we took a few rest stops. She said lying flat for the MRI pushed all the fluid she was retaining upward. (This was one time Natalee was overjoyed to arrive at the dialysis unit and couldn't wait to get hooked up.)

I spent the day doing the usual….. waiting in various waiting rooms adorned with varying décor and a variety of varicolored chairs - causing me the usual varied vexations. I was enjoying reading on my Kindle, until my Kindle died later in the day, so I had to read on my phone's Kindle app to pass the time, hoping my battery wouldn't run out on my phone, too. By then I was reminding myself that real hold-in-your-hand books don't run out of battery…..and to bring my phone charger along next time. I was also thinking again that hospitals should have an arcade of sorts for people to pass the time while waiting long periods…. where I could play Skee ball. (I need to find the hospital's Suggestion Box.)

March 14, 2017 To start with, I have been sick with some kind of virus since we got back from Pittsburgh. I have a dry cough and my temp is 99.5. I have been feeling tired and yucky all week and was hoping Natalee wouldn't catch it, but she came down with it, too. I felt terrible, and am 99.9% sure she caught it from me. Neither one of us has been sick all winter. Now is certainly not a good time. I can't remember the last time I had a cold or flu. (Why now? Sigh, cough, sigh.)

Natalee called Pittsburgh to let them know what symptoms she developed. We thought they might cancel the surgery, but here's where we are….long story short…..sort of: Natalee is on her way for STAT blood work locally; the results to be faxed ASAP to Pittsburgh. A temp <100 is not considered a fever, so if her WBCs and RBCs are within normal range, she is to be admitted tonight and have the surgery tomorrow instead of Thursday. After a mad scramble to be ready to drop everything and dash off to Pittsburgh, here we sit, waiting for the lab results and a call from Pittsburgh. David and I packed a bag and prayed we can get a room at Family House at the last minute. Oh, to add to the jolting change of plans, there is a major snow storm with a possible Nor'easter blizzard predicted. Natalee heard on the news that Pittsburgh has no snow, so far. One minor plus on a day of uncertainties and a stressful roller coaster ride of last minute plans. The three-ring circus, as always, is alive and well. (It may even have an extra ring today.)

Natalee received a call at 6:30 p.m. - The STAT labs are not back yet, so no trip to Pittsburgh tonight. (Breathe.) Natalee is to get a call in the morning to find out what time she is to be admitted tomorrow, pending the not-so-stat results. She has dialysis in the morning and we can't leave for Pittsburgh until she is back from her treatment. Natalee is still coughing, but we are both feeling a little less under the weather this evening; a plus to this frenzied roller coaster ride of a day. (If you call feeling like your head is stuffed with cotton qualifying as better. Please pass the tissues. Sigh. Sniffle. Cough.)

March 15, 2017 Pittsburgh called Natalee and all of the blood work was acceptable. She is to be there around 2:00 p.m. to be admitted. We'll be heading to Pittsburgh in the arriving and intensifying blizzard named "Stella." High wind and blowing snow piling up are making the roads and driving hazardous, so we'll take the truck, and pray for safe travel. (David will do the nerve-wracking driving, Mario isn't fond of driving in a snowstorm.) "Stella"….last name "Snowmageddon"…. is to head out of the area later in the day to spread havoc elsewhere. (Can't say our life is never exciting.)

We arrived on time in spite of the storm; driving out of the heavy swirling snow and slick, white-knuckle-inducing road conditions once we passed Blairsville. There was little to no snow in Pittsburgh. (Insert humongous sigh of relief here.) Natalee was admitted on 5G at Presby and settled in. She didn't want us to come early in the morning to see her off to surgery, but to come later. We prayed with her and said our good-byes before heading home. The weather man was right, and the roads were passable to clear the whole way home. (Good riddance, "Stella".)

I called Natalee later on to say good-night and to pray for the surgery to go well tomorrow. She will go to pre-op holding at 6:30 a.m. with surgery scheduled for 7:15 a.m.

March 16, 2017 6:00 a.m. I called to pray with Natalee and talk for a little while. As usual, she isn't nervous at all; just ready to get it over with. (After all, God's got this.)

7:30 a.m. Fasten your seat belts…..the roller coaster ride begins again….. surgery is canceled. The neurosurgeon saw her in pre-op holding, and because Natalee is still coughing, he didn't want to chance her coughing while he was operating and woke her up for the mapping. Also, her latest labs showed a low platelet count, which increases the bleeding risk during surgery. Time to play "stump the doctor"….here's your card. (I found it strange that my platelet count was low this week, too. I am blaming it on whatever virus we entertained.)

Natalee is highly disappointed, as are we. She just wants this surgery to be done and over with….today. It's hard to anticipate something for so long, be ready for it, and then in a twinkling it doesn't come to conclusion - even if it is a brain surgery. No use stressing about things we can't control, however. God apparently has a plan, so we'll trust Him and continue taking a day at a time. (Ones with less stress, excitement, and frenzied emotional roller coaster rides.)

David and I left for Pittsburgh thinking Natalee would be released since the surgery was canceled. Wrong! They kept her to recheck her platelets and continue an IV antibiotic. After dialysis in the morning she may possibly be released. We stayed with her the rest of the day. (A Chairs and French fries day!)

She is to call us after dialysis in the morning and let us know what the plan is before we head to Pittsburgh. (No use occupying The Chairs in her room while she is at dialysis for three-and-a-half hours.)

March 17, 2017 Natalee was released to come home today. We're all feeling drained, recovering from the intense adrenaline rush and the disappointment of the past few days. It's not like we haven't been there before, but it doesn't get any easier. Natalee is to call in two weeks to reschedule the surgery. Praying Natalee will no longer have a cough….or anything else. Test results proved she contracted Influenza B, so I guess that's what I had, too. It can lower the platelet count as a side effect. Mystery solved. (It's good to be home and get some much needed rest after a nightmarish few days.)

March 20, 2017 Another trip to Pittsburgh today. This time to Magee for Natalee's gyne appointment. She has two new lesions, but he wants her to have the brain surgery before scheduling gyne surgery, which would have to be at least a month after the brain surgery. (So, more waiting while life goes on….looking ahead to two surgeries now.)

Chapter 31

Beautiful Scars and Badges of Honor

March 21, 2017 This morning, a Monday, I went with Natalee to her church. The pastor is beginning a series in April entitled *Beautiful Scars.* As part of the series, they are filming Natalee answering questions and talking about her faith in the face of her ongoing health issues, and how God has brought her through so much. She is one of several people to be interviewed. Today's interview will be edited to an eight minute segment (LOL! Good luck with that!) to be used during one of the series sermons. She is excited that it could be an inspiration to others going through trying times.

March 22, 2017 Natalee received word the brain surgery is scheduled for April 27. We're in a cosmic holding pattern until then. (With no coughing).

April 2, 2017 Today is Natalee's forty-sixth birthday. (And I am only 39.) When people ask if I have any children, I say, "Yes, I have a daughter who is somehow older than me now!" I am thankful God has given her to me for these forty-six years. I try not to think about that lurking statistical elephant in the room…the one that wants to sit on my chest some days and suffocate me…the one that whispers, *"Diabetics on dialysis have a life expectancy of around ten years."* Then I remind myself Natalee *is* the Queen of daring to beat statistics. The statistics, I'm sure, don't account for a longer life when you take care of yourself the best you can, and trust God to be in control. One of the great human drives is to be in control, but God can do a better job…..when you let Him. Once you give God your burdens, don't try to take them back - let go, let God. (He doesn't need backseat drivers either.)

> Many are the plans in the mind of a man, but it the purpose of the Lord that will stand. (Proverbs 19:21 ESV) For I know the plans I have for you, declares the Lord, plans for welfare and not for evil, to give a future and a hope. (Jeremiah 29:11 ESV)

That being said, I just want to be there for Natalee every day we have to share. I want good memories to outweigh bad ones. I don't want to mull over what the future may possibly hold, but make today count for something good in the memory department. You can't buy memories...or time. You make them. Natalee doesn't dwell on her pain and suffering, but looks for joy and happiness in her daily life. I'm glad that, no matter what comes her way, there is always room for laughter, and that makes good memories. By God's grace, Natalee *chooses* to be very inspiring to others.

> But he said to me, "My grace is sufficient for you, for my power is made perfect in weakness." Therefore I will boast all the more gladly about my weaknesses, so that Christ's power may rest on me. That is why, for Christ's sake, I delight in weaknesses, in insults, in hardships, in persecutions, in difficulties. For when I am weak, then I am strong. (2 Corinthians 12:9-10 NIV) For our light and momentary troubles are achieving for us an eternal glory that far outweighs them all. (2 Corinthians 4:17 NIV)

Today, David and I went to church with Natalee. Pastor Brad started the new series and Natalee's video was part of the first sermon. Both were very moving.....how our mental, emotional, and physical scars we are wounded with in life can become beautiful scars which are signs of victory - "badges of honor" - that show how God has brought us through difficult times. (All for His glory.)

Chapter 32

Brain Surgery - Take Two

April 20, 2017 Natalee's platelets were still low on her blood work results last week….88,000. A repeat level was drawn yesterday and she is awaiting results. If the results remain low, she may be ordered a platelet transfusion next week, so she can have the surgery as planned. In no way does she want to have another delay. The countdown has begun with surgery in one short week! (Prayers in full force - that it's a for-sure event.)

I called Family House and made reservations to stay the day before her surgery and after her surgery. That way, we will all be less stressed before the surgery, and David and I will be more rested not having to drive back and forth.

April 27, 2017 Today is obliteration-of-the-brain-tumor day, but we know with Natalee it's not a done deal until she's finally in the OR and asleep on the OR table. (*Finally* is never a sure thing in Nataleeland, though.) After she checked in at the second floor surgical desk, we were escorted to the pre-op unit. Two doctors from anesthesia came to see her and asked if she had any concerns or questions. One said he would be there for "take off and landing," and the other one would "be there for the rest of the flight!" (Off to La La Land on Anesthesia Airlines.)

The neurosurgeon popped in and spoke with us for a short time. He asked Natalee if she was ready. Natalee resolutely replied, "More than! Let's get this over with!" A girl (I don't remember her title), came and said she was the person who would be asking Natalee questions during the awake mapping part of the surgery. She proceeded to describe some of the tasks she would be asking Natalee to perform. One of the things she said she'd ask Natalee to do was counting to ten. We knew they would probably ask her to count and had joked beforehand that Natalee should tell them she could count to ten in three languages - English, French and Spanish! When the girl mentioned she would have Natalee count, I looked at Natalee and we both started laughing. The girl looked puzzled, so we confessed what we had joked about beforehand.

Before they whisked Natalee off to the OR, we said a prayer. Everyone was amazed at how calm and upbeat Natalee was. David and I went to the surgical area waiting room and settled in; prepared to mark time for many long hours. At least the chairs were in a league of their own - high-backed, padded, glider rockers, and we had a footstool! Bonus! (No redundant complaints from me this time.) We left the comfort of the exceptional chairs long enough to go the cafeteria to get some breakfast. Following Natalee's progress on the computer screens located in the waiting room and in the cafeteria, we saw she was listed "in OR" when we left the waiting room, and when we returned, "procedure started" was beside her identifying number. (It's definitely a go!)

The past few months, many people were curious and asked us about awake brain mapping. They mostly wanted to know if Natalee would be able to feel pain when awakened. Interestingly enough, there are no pain receptors in the brain itself. Only the brain covering, the scalp, and bone covering have pain receptors. Ironically, the brain is the tool for other body parts to detect pain! Natalee will be asleep for the painful part of the surgery.

Brain mapping 101: The images from the MEG and HDFT will help with the mapping. The surgeon will stimulate areas around the tumor with small electrodes to determine areas that need to be avoided to prevent damage to functional areas of the brain. That's where the awake part comes in…..asking the patient to answer questions and perform tasks while the surgeon is mapping the area. If there is loss of function when an area is stimulated, it is mapped and no tissue in that area is cut out, ensuring as much of the tumor that can be excised is safely removed.

Around 9:15 a.m. "Dr. Take-off-and-landing" came to tell us they had completed the removal of the piece of Natalee's skull, and were ready to wake her up for the mapping part. He reassured us that all was going very well. (It's hard to wrap my head around being able to talk with people and perform verbal and visual tasks, while knowing a piece of your skull is missing.... and the doctor is poking around in your brain.)

I called McKenna to tell her the news. She couldn't be at the hospital today, but the timing couldn't be helped. She is in the middle of college finals. Truthfully, I think it is very hard for her to be present while Natalee has surgery. All she can do is wait and worry at the hospital, and I know she worries that she could lose Natalee one day after almost losing her in 2007. Having other things away from the hospital to occupy her mind takes less of a mental and emotional toll on her. It's her way of coping.

Around 11:30 a.m., "Dr. Take-off-and-landing" alighted in front of us again. He asked if the surgeon talked to us yet, and we tentatively replied, "No." He became quiet, looked like he wanted to say something, but didn't. After a pause, he softly said, "I shouldn't tell you this, *but…..*". When I heard "but," my heart literally stopped for a second and plunged rapidly into the pit of my stomach. I steeled myself, thinking he was going to tell us some dreadful news. Then he smiled, and told us the surgery was over, and Natalee did very well. He then, conspiratorially, said, "You didn't hear this news from me!" (I wanted to punch him and hug him at the same time!) She was being transferred to ICU and they would let us know when we could see her. (Now I can breathe.)

Not long after hearing the good news, we were directed to a closet-sized conference room for privacy where we spoke to the neurosurgeon over the phone. He told us everything went according to plan. (We didn't let on we already received the good news.) When he was mapping toward the back of the tumor area, he said Natalee lost function of her right arm, so he didn't remove any more tissue there. A post-op MRI will be done tonight (no dye), and dialysis is scheduled for tomorrow. I called McKenna right away with an update, and she was relieved. One less thing to stress her out today. (Now she can breathe, too.)

On arrival to the ICU, before entering, I called the number for her assigned nurse as instructed on the sign that was posted by the phone outside the unit. I asked if we could come in to see Natalee, but he said they were just getting ready to take her for a CT scan, and if we waited in the hall by the elevator we could see her for a minute, and visit with her when she returned. (The CT would show if there was any bleeding post-op that could cause problems.)

When they wheeled her bed out into the hall, she was semi-reclined, fully alert, and smiling. After giving her a hug and kiss we resigned ourselves to more sitting and waiting in the ICU waiting room. (Different room, but the usual unmistakably miserable chairs that make my usual hours-long discomfort more uncomfortable.)

When she returned from the CT scan, her nurse immediately came to get us. As we entered her room, as expected, she was tethered to the bed in a tangle of IV lines and other paraphernalia. (As often as we've seen her in that situation, we never get used to it.) The first thing Natalee told us was that she remembered everything while she was awake for the mapping part of the surgery. Before the surgery, she debated if she wanted to remember being awake or not. The answer, after the fact, is definitely NOT. Natalee remembered not being able to move her right hand or arm momentarily during the mapping. (How frightening that would be for even one second.) She said she could feel pressure, but no pain. Natalee said, "I wanted to cry." I asked her why. She said because it was such a long process, and she was getting tired having to perform the tasks asked of her. She laughed, and said one of the verbal tasks she was asked to perform was to count to ten......in all three languages! (Only Natalee could be a big show-off during brain surgery!)

Natalee has a telfa dressing stapled to her head over the sutures; covered with a beige, beanie-type surgical cap. I, however, think they should give patients Steeler, Pirates or Penguins beanies. (They are in Pittsburgh, after all!) It looks like they shaved her hair off in a two-inch wide swath from above her left ear, up and over her head to the right side.

The nephrologist set up dialysis for tomorrow morning, in her ICU room. The time for the post-op MRI was not firmed up, as yet. It could be tonight, or early tomorrow morning. After visiting for a while, David and I left her so she could get some rest. We walked the two blocks back to Family House to also take a break for a while. (And lie down.)

Natalee's supper tray came just as we arrived back in ICU. I fed her before we went to the cafeteria to get our own meal. (Okay...... French fries.) Feeding herself was awkward due to being semi-reclined in the bed. Sitting up any higher caused pressure in her head, and she was not allowed to lay flat. She was hearing a "pop-rocks crackling" sound in her head from the fluid shift, and complaining of a slight headache post-op. (That will all go away eventually, but Natalee knew it was coming, and was not looking forward to any of it.) The medication ordered for nausea was working, and she was able to eat almost all of her supper. The neurosurgeon came to see her and reiterated all went well. The MRI she is to have will reveal how much, if any, of the tumor is remaining. He said he took as much as he could, without causing loss of any function. Lots of prayers answered today. So thankful for them all, and for the words of encouragement and support we received. (**God is good!**)

April 28, 2017 Natalee was able to sit up in bed and eat breakfast without any help. She had an MRI at 3: 00 a.m.! (I guess you could say that was early morning!) No contrast, so that made her happy. She was able to walk, with help, to the dreaded commode in her room. The most difficult part of that was not getting her there, but maneuvering all the equipment she was connected to there without tangling all the lines, pulling something out, or disconnecting something. Of course, much to her dismay, the thing she was most concerned about happened - a male nurse from dialysis came into the room to program the dialysis machine…. while she was being queen for the day on the throne! (C'est la vie! Color Natalee mortified.)

Natalee will be taking oral anti-convulsant medication for a while as a precaution like she did in 2011. She is doing well enough to be moved out of ICU later in the evening. (Hoping Natalee will be discharged tomorrow.)

David and I are exhausted. Waiting and sitting. Sitting and waiting. The overall stress of the day itself, and more waiting makes me more tired than being active. Add to that, getting up early is not in my normal routine …..I'm retired. Today I'm just plain tired. Not complaining though. (I'm energized in the sense that prayers continue being answered.)

I called Natalee at 7:00 p.m., and she was upset because she couldn't remember all the steps to program her insulin pump. Her hands are slightly swollen, especially her right hand, which made it difficult to use them. The nurse had to assist her. I reminded Natalee after surgery there is some expected swelling in the surgical area, which can cause some of the neuro symptoms she is experiencing. She seemed less upset after I said I didn't think it would be a permanent residual problem. I reminded her why she had all those preliminary tests and the awake mapping...so only the tumor would be resected, not healthy brain cells. Most importantly, prayers are on her side. (I didn't really want to consider any other explanation.)

April 29, 2017 Natalee is still in ICU, but will be discharged today from there. David and I arrived at the hospital at 11:15. Her nurse said Natalee would be getting lunch soon and she could stay and eat before we left, if Natalee wanted. She wanted. David and I decided to go to the cafeteria to grab some lunch, too, before heading home. We both got an order of French fries to go. (What else?) We brought them back to ICU and ate lunch with Natalee. That saved us having to stop anywhere to eat on the way home. (At least that was my reasoning. *Wink, wink.*)

Natalee seemed more subdued than usual. She said she is having difficulty getting her limbs to move the way she wants, especially the right side. I had to help her get dressed. I noticed her balance was a little off, and she was listing to the right. I kept reminding her it is temporary. (I also kept reminding myself... and praying it is.) She hasn't verbalized any concerns out loud, but I'm sure it's a thought somewhere in the recesses of her mind. Who could blame her? The neurological ramifications are scary. It has to be very frightening, weighing on her ruminations. The implications of permanent residuals are life-altering.

Chapter 33

Stumping Mom and Frantic Panic (Here's Your Card!)

After we arrived back in Johnstown, Natalee needed help to walk from the car to the house. Natalee laughed at herself as she listed to the right while I tried to steady her, hoping we both didn't fall down. She was really tired when I got her settled on the chaise in the living room, so she took a nap for a couple hours. (David and I took naps, too.)

I had to help her check her blood sugar since she had difficulty using her hands. Shocking result....567! She started laughing out of frustration when she couldn't remember how to program her pump to give a bolus dose of insulin, or even how much she should give. I wasn't laughing. I was in a state of major-frantic panic since I am not all that familiar with her pump and adjusting the settings. She has handled that on her own for years. Unfortunately, the pump's operational manual was in her head. Now it's stump-my-mom time. (Thanks, but I already have several cards.) She kept telling me the wrong things to do, but I finally figured it out, and got a number programmed in for a bolus dose of insulin.

When I rechecked her glucose level an hour later, it was still up...565. I'm still stumped. (Apparently I need another card.) Natalee then decided she needed to change her set - the insulin reservoir that fits into the pump with attached tubing connected to the needle inserted subcutaneouly in her abdomen to deliver the insulin. I changed the set, and she remembered enough to tell me most of how to do that, but she forgot how to reset the pump. It was manic-frantic-panic time now. (I prayed instead… a better option!) We finally got it figured out, and hopefully it will deliver the right amount of insulin, and bring her level down. (Prayers answered…. for the moment!)

I had to help her get ready for bed. Her right arm and hand are more swollen than before, and she can barely use her arm. She has to really concentrate to perform some tasks. Her balance is off even more. She isn't safe to walk without one of us walking beside her with hands-on assist so she doesn't fall, or bang into furniture and doorways. Typical Natalee, she kept laughing and making jokes about not being able to remember things and not being able to walk a straight line. Emotional regulation in a serious scenario. (More prayers needed.)

Gigantic-manic-frantic panic overtook me later in the evening when I realized she did not program her pump to cover the food she ate at supper. I had asked her earlier if we needed to do that, but she said, "No." In the back of my mind I didn't think that was right, but I took her word for it because I was so exhausted I couldn't think straight either at the time. (And I didn't even have brain surgery, just brain drain.) I checked her blood sugar, and it was coming down due to the bolus dose I programmed, which turned out to be enough to also cover what she ingested at supper. I like to think it was a stroke of genius that I programmed the right amount of insulin, but it was a stroke of God answering my prayers and guiding me. (God never needs a card.)

I got up a few times during the night to check her glucose level, and it continued coming down. Relief for now! In the morning, I hoped she remembered how to program her pump to cover what she ate. (Where is the paper instruction manual when you need one? I am not fluent in pumpese.)

April 30, 2017 Natalee spent the day on the chaise with her right arm elevated on a pillow. Her hand is a little less swollen now, but not her arm. She is doing better with directing me in the steps for programming her pump to cover the carb grams she eats. (I'll soon be a master programmer.) There were a few times where she couldn't retrieve a word she wanted to say, but didn't have to focus so much to talk today. Miniscule progress, but progress nonetheless.

McKenna came to visit. She is visibly very concerned, but Natalee reassured her everything would be fine. Now if Natalee can just convince herself. I'm sure Natalee is unsettled by the symptoms she is exhibiting. (Even though she still doesn't say so out loud.)

Natalee had some bills she wanted to pay by check, but is currently unable to write her name with either hand. David and I have POA for her, and have for the past ten years. One of those elephant-in-the-room kind of decisions you hate to face, and then make, but know you will need to have it at some point. (Today is the day.)

Chapter 34

Making Progress

May 1, 2017 Dialysis day. I am getting her ready since she needs help getting dressed - no bending over allowed, her right arm is not fully functional yet, and she still has difficulty remembering what she needs to do at times. Getting up at 4:30 a.m. throws my retirement schedule out the window for now! (David is driving her today. I'm going back to bed.)

I called the surgeon's PA, explaining the neuro problems Natalee is having. Decadron, a steroid, is being ordered for Natalee to help reduce any brain swelling. Decadron had not been ordered sooner because steroids raise blood sugar levels. Now she will have to monitor her blood sugars more frequently. (Natalee is not happy about that; she hates being a pin cushion!)

May 3, 2017 As requested, I called the PA back this morning with an update. Natalee is allowed to begin gradually reclining her position, but not too much at a time. She's happy about that. If any neuro symptoms or increased headaches occur, she is to go back to being upright.

At 10:00 p.m. Natalee remembered to tell me that she had a call from Pittsburgh this afternoon. Unfortunately, she didn't remember what it was about, or who called. Sigh. Can't do anything about it now. (I'll have to put on my sleuthing hat in the morning.)

May 4, 2017 After much pondering on my part, I deduced it was probably the neuro-oncologist who called. I was told they had indeed called to coordinate the neuro-oncologist and the neurosurgeon appointments so we only had to make one trip to Pittsburgh. (So thoughtful and accommodating.) Now Natalee will see the surgeon's PA at Presby at noon on the 9th to have the dressing and staples removed, and then head to Hillman to see the neuro-oncologist, with blood work scheduled beforehand.

May 5, 2017 Progress. Natalee was able to dress her upper body today without assist. Her right arm and hand are 90-95% functional now. I helped her dress her lower body since she is still restricted on bending over. A little unsteadiness and some memory problems are still plaguing her at times. If her memory doesn't improve, there is no way she could safely drive, live alone, or manage without assistance. (That's the looming uninvited elephant always on the loose.)

Natalee has been a little uncharacteristically irritable at times, but who can blame her. It could be a side effect of being on the steroid, being tired of having to sit and sleep upright, and not being able to be fully independent in everyday tasks - although she tries to do as much as she is able for herself. She's tolerating gradually laying a little more reclined, and is looking forward to being able to lie flat again. Natalee remarked how we take little things we are able to do for granted every day, and don't appreciate what we are able to do, until we can't. So very true. Guilty as charged, although I think of that more often now, and try to appreciate what am able to do. Focus on the positive, not the negative. (Negitivity breeds stress and anxiety and can affect your mental and physical health. Negative people bring others down.)

May 6, 2017 Today is one of our memorable event days, complete with some unseasonably cold, and dismally rainy weather. McKenna graduated from college with a degree in Business Management....the bright spot of the day. Natalee was up to attending the graduation, and sharing the memorable day with McKenna. She did well getting to and from the car, then in and out of the building with assist, and tolerated sitting through the very lengthy proceedings in the overly chilly auditorium. (I won't say out loud that it was boring.) We are proud of McKenna, and it was a good memory.

Chapter 35

More Elephants That Can't be Ignored

May 9, 2017 The neurosurgeon's PA removed the bandage and staples today. Natalee bought wide, colorful headbands to cover the area. No one would ever know she was missing a swath of her hair.

If anything, over the years we've learned life is a journey that can be detoured and rerouted in an instant. It was a welcome sunny and warmer day out for our trip to Pittsburgh, but the news Natalee received greatly overshadowed it. The PA had that sad-news face we have become all too familiar with, and was to be the harbinger of startling life-changing news…..empathetically relaying it to us. The tumor, which was a grade II Astrocytoma in 2011, is now a grade III *malignant* Anaplastic Astrocytoma. We were told five to eight out of 100,00 people are affected with this type of rare, high-grade, fast-growing tumor. The full force of this revelation hit us like a totally unexpected thunderbolt. The immediate momentary silence following was deafening. The shock in the room was palpable. It was one of those moments where you feel like you're trapped in a nightmare, wanting to open your eyes and wake up so it would go away, but you know your eyes are wide open. (I was trying not to let the 2000-pound elephant of hopelessness invade my thoughts.) The PA said the neuro-oncologist would discuss Natalee's prognosis further at our appointment with him later today. (For what it's worth, there was a glimmer of positive good news…she can begin tapering off the Decadron since her post-op neuro symptoms are gone.)

We left Presby and drove over to Hillman without discussing the newest unexpected challenge Natalee is facing. We traveled mostly in stunned silence, each lost in our own thoughts. What was there to discuss until we knew more? No use speculating about what the news held for Natalee's future. Natalee had been subdued when she first heard the news, but after mulling over the sequela and it's latest challenge she snapped out of it, brightened up, and convincingly announced, "I can't worry about what I have no control over. God has a plan." (I happily said good-bye and good riddance to the 2000-pound elephant trying to occlude my faith.)

After waiting a very long and trying one-and-a-half hours to know more about how this would affect Natalee's future, the neuro-oncologist started out by saying he was waiting for the results of the genetic markers to return. The markers would further determine more about the tumor, how it would respond to treatment, and her subsequent prognosis. Most statistics say life expectancy is 2-5 years. (But this is Natalee - the reigning Queen of defying the statistical odds.) There is no real cure for Anaplastic Astrocytomas, but they are treatable to prevent further growth, and to keep the tumor under control. He proceeded to discuss the treatment options and settled, for now, on radiation five days a week over a six week period - thirty-three treatments in all. Radiation wouldn't be started for a few more weeks, though, to give her more time to heal, and would be immediately followed by at least six months of chemotherapy. (I can't think that far ahead right now.) Her doctors in Pittsburgh will continue to discuss their findings and the best plan of treatment, then coordinate them with the doctors here at home at the UPMC Cancer Center that is affiliated with Hillman. (Color me and Natalee elated not having to stay or drive to Pittsburgh for the radiation treatments.)

When the doctor finished discussing and explaining everything, I threw a monkey wrench in the established plan. I reminded him that the original intention was for her to have gyne surgery a month after the brain surgery. He thoughtfully looked at Natalee for a second, smiled, and then remarked, "You have a lot going on!" After considering that disruption in the plan further, he said he would talk to her gyneoncologist to schedule her surgery during a break between completion of the radiation and starting the chemo. (If you could call having another surgery a break.)

The most devastating news for her was that she may be permanently off the transplant list now in light of the findings. The next unwelcome news she didn't want to hear was that she can't drive until she sees him for follow-up on July 18. And the final straw was that her pool definitely won't get opened for the summer with all this going on. (Other than the decadron being discontinued, not more than a miniscule crumb of good news today. Color Natalee sad.)

Natalee called McKenna with news of the latest challenge. McKenna is understandably very upset. It's too much for her to think about since memories of her dad's death still haunt her. I heard Natalee reassuring McKenna that she would be okay. (I don't think McKenna felt as sure as Natalee tried to sound.)

While reading about high-grade anaplastic astrocytomas, I was given a reality check upon learning that these types of tumors can recur over time near the original site. Sometimes the cells can migrate to other areas in the brain. One good thing, if there's anything good to consider, they rarely migrate and develop outside the central nervous system. (Praying not to go there.)

Chapter 36

Radiation Implementation

May 10, 2017 Natalee got a call from radiation oncology at the UPMC Cancer Center here in town. She will be seen on the 12th for a preliminary evaluation. (Nothing like jumping right in.)

The 2000-pound elephant of hopelessness had gone, but left a disquieting friend…..the resurfacing one regarding the possibility of Natalee selling her house and living with us permanently. David and I would like her to move in now, but Natalee wants to maintain her independence. We want to respect that for as long as she can manage. On the other hand, David and I are getting older (not old!), and it is more difficult to maintain two houses. Lots more running between houses, and elsewhere, especially now that she won't be allowed to drive for a couple months. Financially it would be more beneficial, for all of us. I'm not complaining about it, just stating facts to consider. I'm just glad we are able to do all we can for her. Lots of elephants to keep in line and from running amok along with a plethora of decisions to make, and prayers to pray. (And sighing to do.)

May 12, 2017 Get-to-know-you appointment day with the radiation oncologist. She was very thorough and explained everything in depth that Natalee needed to know. Today was the first anyone actually said the big "C" word, instead of saying malignant, when referring to the tumor. For some reason, hearing that word and what Natalee is facing, hit me with an out-and-out flood of stark reality. It unexpectantly overwhelmed me. All at once I felt like I was drowning in a sea of what-ifs. I gradually shook myself out of my reverie, and had to keep reminding myself to only focus on getting through today. You can only swim to shore and reach firm ground one stroke at a time. Natalee was doing a better job of it than I was. (Like Dory says, "Just keep swimming!")

> When he calls to me, I will answer him; I will be with him in trouble; I will rescue him and honor him. (Psalm 91:15 ESV) I sought the Lord, and He answered me and delivered me from all my fears. (Psalm 34:4 ESV)

(Psalm 34:1-10 is my favorite bible passage to read when I am feeling down. It lifts me up and restores hope.)

Natalee has an appointment on the 16th for a CT scan to map out the area to be treated with radiation and determine the best approach to targeting malignant cells without destroying good brain cells. She will have a mock treatment a day prior to the first actual treatment to confirm the predetermined calculations are precise. In order to assure the treatment is pinpoint accurate, a ventilated mask will anchor Natalee's head in position by being bolted to the table to make sure there is not even the slightest movement while the treatment is in progress. To make the mask, a lattice-like piece of thin plastic, soaked in warm water to make it pliable, will be applied over Natalee's face and molded to attain the shape of her face and head. It hardens as it dries to retain the created shape.

Radiation can cause some swelling in the brain, so Natalee will be back on Decadron while she is undergoing radiation to prevent the possible return of the neuro symptoms she had after surgery. She will start the Decadron the day before the first treatment. It's a no-brainer trade-off: neuro symptoms or having to check blood sugars more often. Side effects of radiation to report and how they would address them were explained. Hair loss in the radiated area was one expected side effect mentioned. What was unexpected was what was said next.... the hair loss *may* be permanent. Natalee looked more stricken at that statement than she was at the news the tumor was malignant. The look on her face couldn't have been any more horrified. That struck right at the heart of the one thing Natalee didn't want to hear. She is always so positive, but that put a big negative spin on things. Natalee has never been vain, but having ALL her hair is important to her, and she hates wearing a wig. (I reminded her that she's the undefeated Queen of defying the odds. We'll start praying now her hair will grow back.)

To say I'm not feeling anxious for her and the new challenge she's about to embark on would be a lie. This, I think, is the hardest battle she has faced overall. Too many variables and unknowns in the equation, especially with all the enigmatic concerns she can sometimes present due to her other health issues adding to the mix. The fear of the unknown, and the fear of her fate, can weigh heavily on my mind. But, there is no room for fear in this battle. I can only pray for an extra added measure of strength and faith to get Natalee, McKenna, and us through this, hang on to hope, and relinquish control over to God. (The battle is not ours, but God's.)

> Have I not commanded you? Be strong and courageous. Do not be frightened, and do not be dismayed, for the Lord your God is with you wherever you go. (Joshua 1:9 ESV) For the Lord your God is the one who goes with you to fight for you against your enemies to give you victory. (Deuternomony 20:4 NIV)

May 14, 2017 Mother's Day. Natalee was excited to be able to attend church for the first time since her surgery. McKenna came this afternoon and brought gifts for Natalee, and me. We discussed the plan that is unfolding for Natalee's treatment. McKenna seemed less upset today after hearing the plan, and seeing firsthand that Natalee is doing well.

May 17, 2017 Busy and blessed week! The evening of the 15th, at our monthly bible study fellowship meeting, we were surprised, and very blessed, after being given a card containing a check for $200 from the class. We were overwhelmed, to say the least. It's comforting to know there are so many people praying for Natalee, and supporting her (and us) in so many ways. We will gratefully use the thoughtful gift for travel expenses to and from Pittsburgh.

Yesterday morning, David and I took Natalee to radiation oncology for her mask fitting and CT scan. She had sci-fi, waffle-like imprints on her face from the mask. She said it fit very tightly over her face and head so she couldn't even open her eyes, but it wasn't uncomfortable. (Was saying she looked like "Lizzie Lizard" mean, even though she laughed, too?)

In the afternoon, I took her to an appointment with her endocrinologist. His office is now aggressively pursuing getting her a new insulin pump and sensor, but with a different company than she has now after Natalee recounted an unbelievable conversation she had earlier this week.....

Natalee called the person who had contacted her in February concerning the pump with the sensor. She never called Natalee back as she had promised. The tone of the conversation in February led Natalee to believe she would definitely be getting the pump and sensor relatively soon, but now this person told Natalee she didn't even remember talking to her in February, and had no record of any such call! (Natalee had her name and number to be able to call her back.) Now she says the insurance will not pay for a new pump with a sensor, only an upgrade of her current pump since there is a crack in the battery case. (If she never talked to Natalee, how did she know about that? Seriously? That's all I can even begin to say, I'm so flummoxed.)

MAY 23, 2017 One of the women from church asked Natalee if she wanted to get another kidney some day. Replying she would love to eventually get a kidney and be off of dialysis, Natalee explained having radiation and chemo will take her off the eligibility list - possibly permanently - pending the outcome of the treatments. This person then told Natalee she was seriously interested in giving her a kidney, if Natalee qualifies to be back on the list. She even verified that she is the same blood type as Natalee. How ironic is that? Natalee has waited for years to get a call that a kidney was available, or to find a sincere donor when she was on the active list. Now she is off the list, and here is a genuine serious donor offering the priceless gift of a kidney. Natalee will have to discuss all this with her transplant coordinator and doctors when her radiation and chemo treatments are completed. For now, it's something to remain hopeful about. (Until then, we'll put it in God's hands to work it all out.)

May 24, 2017 Another day, another waiting room, and another assemblage of waiting room chairs. I really should have taken pictures of all of them that have faithfully supported me over the years, and made a commemorative scrapbook to remember all the long boring hours we spent together.

Natalee's medical oncologist has been conferring with her neuro-oncologist regarding the best option for her chemo. IV chemo is restricted in crossing the blood brain barrier that is meant to protect the brain from harmful substances, so an oral chemo drug was decided on. The schedule for administration of the chemo will be daily for five successive days, once a month, for six, to possibly eight months....or more. The side effect that concerned us the most is the potential for a drop in Natalee's blood count triggering a return of Aplastic Anemia. After acknowledging he was aware of that, he asked who the hematology oncologist was who treated the SAA. He will discuss our concern with him before Natalee begins treatment.

Surprise! Natalee received an insulin pump replacement today in the mail, but not one with a sensor we have long been hoping would arrive, only an upgraded replacement of her current pump. (Don't know whether to have a happy or sad face.) Her endocrinologist is still trying to obtain a sensor from another company that will work compatibly with her pump. (It seems like this has been dragging on forever.)

May 24, 2017 Today was the the mock run through. Most of the mocking - in fun only - was of Natalee's "Lizzie Lizard" face! (It definitely isn't a good look.... unless you're green.)

Chapter 37

The "Play and Pray Game"

May 25, 2017 First radiation treatment today. One down. With a sigh of relief, all that she said afterward was, "I didn't feel a thing!" (As for me, one thing I had feelings about was getting acquainted with the new-to-me waiting room chairs that will be in my life for the next six weeks while she has her treatments.)

I made a sign before she embarked on the radiation treatments titled: COUNTDOWN TO 33 TREATMENTS with a radiation symbol in the center and numbers 1-33, in calendar fashion, around it. I purchased an array of colorful fun stickers to cover the numbers as each treatment is completed. On the bottom of the sign it says: I can do all things through Christ who strengthens me. (Phil. 4:13 NKJV)

After returning home from her first treatment, we posted a photo on Facebook of Natalee holding the sign, and an explanation of the rules of our "Play and Pray" game I devised for our FB friends and family. Each day I will post her picture holding the sign, and a fun question. For example: your favorite movie, your favorite car you owned, your favorite food, and so on. After posting their favorite thing, I asked them to say a prayer for Natalee. The next day, I will post Natalee's answer to the prior day's question, then post a new question and picture. At the end of the thirty-three days and questions, we will count up who matched Natalee's answers the most. That person will receive a small gift. So far, there are many people who are playing and praying. (A few doses of medicinal laughter will be fun, and garnering more prayers will be a blessing.)

June 15, 2017 Yesterday Natalee completed a third of her treatments. David and I wait near the aquarium and watch the fish swim in endless circles, like they're looking for a way out. I occupy the same waiting room chair each day since we have become so familiar. The other ones will have to be jealous. (I already have a favorite feisty fish.)

Natalee had to reschedule her appointment for the MRI and the follow-up appointment with the neuro-oncologist July 18. We are now told she can't have an MRI until six weeks after the radiation is completed. The long-awaited gyne surgery is tentatively scheduled for August 2. Chemo won't begin until some time in late August, or early September.

June 22, 2017 Last evening I noticed that Natalee's face looked puffy for a post-dialysis day. The puffiness extended into her neck and collar bones. She wasn't having any swallowing or breathing problems, so we decided to "watch and wait," and address it with the oncologist today at radiation. The doctor felt it was a side effect of the Decadron, so she decreased the morning dose. If any neuro symptoms start to develop, the morning dose will have to be increased back to what it was. (Another balancing act in the Cirque du Natalee's what-else-can-happen Challenges.)

Here's a what else: Natalee is at the much dreaded traumatic point with her hair. This past weekend she started shedding profusely and there are areas were her hair is very thin. My Swiffer is working overtime trying to keep up with all the long hair that has escaped to the floor. (I'm glad I have hardwood floors, otherwise my vacuum would be coughing up a hair ball that would make a cat jealous.) Tomorrow she has an appointment to have it all cut off. Natalee is, as usual, taking it all in stride now that it's time to face that inevitable elephant.

June 23, 2017 Hair today, gone tomorrow…. so to speak! Our former stylist no longer works at the salon. Natalee had not seen our new stylist yet. (How weird is it that Natalee had a new hairdresser when she had her hair cut off in 2007?) The stylist asked how Natalee wanted her hair cut and was obviously confounded when Natalee replied in all seriousness, "A buzz cut!" From the waiting area, I witnessed the stunned stylist suddenly sit in the adjoining empty salon chair! (Evidently, a hair raising shock for her!) Natalee explained why she wanted to have a buzz cut. The hairdresser sympathetically listened. While her hair was being cut off, Natalee asked if I was crying yet, but I managed to keep my emotional cards in check through the whole process. At least her beautiful head of hair will grow back eventually. (We're already praying.)

June 26, 2017 One of the radiation staff approached Natalee today and offered her some caps and wigs her sister had when going through chemo, but no longer needs. When we got home we immediately looked through the three boxes she gave her. It was like Christmas! Natalee was elated there were many cute cadet-style caps, some with price tags still on them. The wigs, unfortunately are blond, and since Natalee has black hair, she will return those. Someone else may benefit from them. (I told her that she should have kept one blond wig so she could tell people her hair grew back a different color!) We came up with fourteen reasons having a shaved head is a good thing:

1. Don't have to worry about windy days.
2. Can sleep in since she doesn't have to style her hair.
3. No more shedding!
4. Don't have to buy shampoo or conditioner.
5. Get to wear cute scarves and hats.
6. Don't need a comb, brush, straightener, or hair dryer.
7. Cooler in hot weather.
8. Don't have to worry about getting your hair wet in the rain, or when swimming.
9. Never have a bad hair day.
10. Won't get gum stuck in your hair, or have tangles you can't get out.
11. Save money on haircuts and hair coloring appointments.
12. Minimize the possibility of having dandruff.
13. No bed head.
14. No hat hair.

July 17, 2017 Hip hip hooray! Today's the last day of radiation! (Insert fireworks here!) Natalee was permitted to bring her "Lizzie Lizard" mask out to the waiting room for us to take a picture of her holding it. (No, she did not want to keep the mask as a souvenir!) Today was the last question in our "Play and Pray" game. We will post congratulations to the winner tomorrow. The game made the six weeks seem to go by faster. Everyone commented that they had fun playing the game. (Most importantly, the many prayers definitely helped.)

Natalee saw her radiation oncologist's partner after her treatment. It was the first time he met her. At the end of the appointment he commented how a great attitude aids the healing process, and if anyone has a great attitude, it's Natalee. She will have a follow-up appointment in several weeks, and was given a schedule to taper off the Decadron in titrating doses until then. As we were leaving, everyone wished her well, and some of the staff gave her hugs. I told them they definitely radiated smiles of hope! (I said a fond farewell to The Chairs I've rated a seven as far as waiting room chairs go!)

As much as all that that made our day a celebratory one, Natalee got other news later on that diminished the joy she was feeling. We had been surprised and puzzled when, after the surgery, she was told she needed to arrange a comprehensive driving test to be cleared to drive again. Shock of all shocks, the driving school she called charges $380 for a few hours of instruction and testing! Natalee contacted OVR (Office of Vocational Rehabilitation), but found out they will only pay for testing for someone who is being cleared to go back to work. Insurance will not cover it either. X graciously consented to pay for it when she told him about having to take the test when he called to ask her how things were going. (It's a definite blessing when someone else offers to help out in any way, and this was a biggie.) The driving school she contacted cannot schedule the comprehensive driving test until the end of August! She was looking forward to being able to have the test ASAP. They had openings sooner, but those conflicted with Natalee's dialysis schedule. (Looks like David and I will be her chauffeurs for a while longer.)

July 29, 2017 After thinking about it, I told Natalee to call her neuro-oncologist and ask if she definitely has to take the comprehensive driving test. She didn't have to take one after her brain surgery in 2011. Natalee should ask if he would just clear her to drive since she obviously wasn't turned into the state to have her license taken away, and she passed the neuro exams completed by her doctors here. Much to Natalee's elation, he moved her appointment up, canceled the driving test, and will officially clear her after he sees her. As I always say, it never hurts to ask! The first thing Natalee did when she hung up the phone was call and cancel the driving test! (Joy has returned to Natalee's world!)

This whole summer, for David and me, has been an endless whirlwind of running here and there - taking Natalee to and from dialysis, to doctor appointments and radiation, to and from church, delivering her to various other things she has going on, and going to her house every other day to help care for the cat and the house. Some days I feel like I'm on a hamster wheel, running in endless circles; different day, same scenario. I know Natalee feels the same, more often than I do. I don't think there have been more than a few days that we haven't been on the go somewhere, but when you truly love someone you do what you need to do for them, regardless of your own needs. I'm thankful we are able. At least David and I get out of the house to do a few things by ourselves, and Natalee is self-sufficient in most things. (Sad to say, there are caregivers who have little help or no relief. Remember, actions speak louder than words in offering support to a 24/7 caregiver you may know.)

Chapter 38

Next Act Before Chemo

Aug. 2, 2017 Got up at 4:00 a.m. (UGH!) and readied to take Natalee to Magee hospital for her long-awaited gyne surgery. David and I spent the day acquainting ourselves with yet another crop of waiting room chairs, and more waiting. Different rooms, different chairs, but seem to be all the same.

The surgeon spoke with me afterward and said everything went well. On the way home, Natalee felt well enough for a stop at Taco Bell for a bite to eat, which turned out to be good timing because her blood sugar dropped to 79. For sure, she needed to get some carbs into her body. (Taco Bell is definitely a great place to get loaded up on carbs, and David's favorite place to stop.)

Aug. 8, 2017 Natalee got a call that the biopsy came back unchanged, still precancerous cells. No cancer, nonetheless. She definitely doesn't need another diagnosis of the big "C" in her life. (Prayers answered once again.)

Natalee saw the medical oncologist who discussed the affirmed treatment plan - an oral med called Temozolomide (Temodar). It is able to cross the blood brain barrier. She will take it for five successive days each month, with weekly blood work to monitor her blood counts. I know chemo is going to have side effects in some capacity, but if it would trigger the Aplastic Anemia to rear it's ugly head again, it would be almost paralyzing. Remembering how ill she was battling SAA in 2007, I don't want to see her go through that again with all the other trials she has to contend with right now. I am more stressed out about the chemo side effects than any surgery she has endured, to the point it is irrepressible at times. All I can do is give it over to God, but it's proving easier said than done right now. (I wish I could be as strong as Natalee is.)

> Come to me, all you who are weary and burdened, and I will give you rest. (Matthew 11:28 NIV) Let us hold fast the confession of our hope without wavering, for he who promised is faithful. (Hebrews 10:23 ESV)

Aug. 14, 2017 Today was the much anticipated appointment at Hillman, and Natalee passed her neuro test with flying colors. (Happy dance time.) As we thought he would, the neuro-oncologist addressed the upcoming chemo. He wants to speak with her nephrologist before she begins chemo; there are considerations to address since she is on dialysis. (That's Natalee - always a challenge!)

After her neuro exam, Natalee remained sitting on the exam table. I was occupying one of the chairs in the room, and the doctor was talking with us while seated on the other chair. All of a sudden he asked Natalee to switch places saying, "You're the paying customer, you sit in the chair!" He jumped up, took a seat on the exam table, and continued talking without missing a beat!

Aug. 15, 2017 Natalee's post-op appointment with the gyneoncologist originally scheduled for the 23rd, was moved to today. She had a good report with no new problems noted. Chemo is the next act in the Cirque du Natalee's never-ending medical challenges.

Aug. 28, 2017 MRI at Presby today. After her MRI we all had a quick lunch (yes, I had fries), then David and I got reacquainted with the familiar, but always welcoming Chairs, while Natalee had dialysis. Long day today, and a longer one coming up in three days. (For right now, the only thing that matters is that the MRI result is good news.)

Aug. 31, 2017 Natalee had an extra appointment today at Magee to have some sutures removed that have not dissolved and are bothering her. Afterward, we went to the cafeteria for breakfast and then headed to her next appointment at Hillman, scheduled for 11:00 a.m. We arrived at 10:00 a.m. She was able to check in and have her blood work completed early, then we went to area C to wait....and wait... and wait.....and wait some more. She was finally called to be seen at 1:30 p.m.! It was worth the wait, though; good news for once. No evidence of the tumor was seen on the MRI. (Insert a wild happy dance here.) There was some "shadowing" that was attributed to the radiation treatments, but **no tumor**! (I would have waited all day just to hear that news. Thank You Jesus!)

> This is the confidence we have in approaching God: that if we ask anything according to his will, he hears us. (1 John 5:14 NIV) If you abide in me, and my words abide in you, ask whatever you wish, and it will be done for you. (John 15:7 ESV)

News Natalee didn't want to hear, however, was that she had to have another MRI with contrast in two months, then every two months - possibly for a year. The doctor also affirmed that he spoke with her hematology oncologist regarding our concerns about the Aplastic Anemia. The consensus was, after ten years with no relapse, it would be unlikely to recur. (We'll still pray it doesn't.)

I am more tired after four total hours in the car, and six-and-a-half hours of sitting in various and equally miserable, but cutely-patterned, waiting room chairs. More tired than when I have a very active day. Now I really need a nap! (David says when I die he will have "She finally got a nap!" engraved on my tombstone.)

Sept. 5, 2017 Natalee will start her chemo tomorrow. It's always scary to go into uncharted waters, but God will go ahead of her, and also with her.

> The Lord himself goes before you and will be with you; he will never leave you nor forsake you. Do not be afraid; do not be discouraged. (Deuteronomy 31:8 NIV) Fear not, for I am with you; be not dismayed, for I am your God; I will strengthen you, I will help you, I will uphold you with my righteous hand. (Isaiah 41:10 ESV)

Natalee has to wear gloves to handle the Temodar, as with any chemo drug. As an added precaution, she will remain upright thirty minutes after taking it so none of the medication backs up into her esophagus. Over the next five days, we'll pray the possible side effects of the chemo will be minimal to nil.… and that her GP behaves. (She was told not to take the chemo if her GP is uncontrolled.)

The past few days I noticed Natalee was not her usual chatty self. I thought it was because of worrying about starting the chemo. I was mistaken. This evening she told me she was feeling down because.…wait for it.… her pool is not only not going to be opened for the summer, but it's history! (Natalee's #1 priority of what to worry about.) It was losing water gradually, from a slow leak in the liner. A new filter was overdue, and it was getting to be too much for her to take care of both physically and financially. David and I are getting to the point it is too much for us, also. So, she came to the painstaking realization it had to go. I feel bad since it was the one thing she enjoyed during the summer that didn't tax her energy, and was relaxing for her. Now she has an 18-foot round sandy circle in the yard that is several inches deep. I told her to look at the bright side - she is the only house in the neighborhood that has a beach. She could get a kiddie pool for on it in the summer...or a fire pit...or make it a skating rink in the winter. (Grass it is!)

Chapter 39

Chemo

Sept. 6, 2017 Day one of chemo. So far, no side effects.

Sept. 8, 2017 Day three, no appetite with some nausea and a low-grade temp setting in. The Zofran is not helping to quell the nausea, which she says is more of an upset stomach with lower abdominal cramping.

Sept. 12, 2017 First course of chemo completed two days ago. The only remaining side effect is an on and off again low-grade temp. She will be having blood work done tomorrow to see if her blood counts have dropped. (Praying they stayed within normal limits.)

Sept. 21, 2017 David and I rarely get away, but our long-time friends, Steve and Judi, asked if we wanted to go to Gettysburg with them for three days. They have never been there before. We agreed. David and I always enjoy visiting there. Natalee was doing well and not having any problems (more than usual), so we were confident it was okay to leave town for a short while. However, things can change in a very short time with Natalee.....

The first night we were in Gettysburg (the 18ᵗʰ) I called to see how Natalee was feeling. She was fine when I called before we left town, but her GP reared it's ugly head full-time at the end of her dialysis treatment in the morning, and she and the bathroom were now fast friends. Unable to eat and keep anything down, she had to shut down her insulin pump for a while to prevent hypoglycemia. (Time for prayers; that's all I could do for her.)

When I called the next morning she was no better. If things didn't change, going to dialysis Wednesday morning would not be possible, which is always a concern. As she predicted she did not make it to dialysis and was still in the throes of unrelenting GP. (If her GP prevents her from being able to go to dialysis too many days, she could end up in the hospital.)

Today (Thursday) she was able to go for a rescheduled dialysis treatment, and kept down some broth with rice.

While spending so much time in the bathroom, she said she thought she'd do something useful and do some cleaning in there! Only Natalee could be so sick and still want to try to do something useful. (If you recall, I'd just be useless and waiting to die after six minutes of being sick.)

Oct. 22, 2017 Good news: She received a call from the company that was contacted regarding the sensor for her pump. They will supply it, but… (why is there always a *but?*) she will have to pay $96 up front and $50 a month for supplies! **Bad news:** On her very limited income that is not even a remote possibility. **Good news:** Giving it to God. (Maybe He has a different plan.)

Oct. 30, 2017 French fries day! (Oh, I mean MRI day at Presby.) Usual routine. You already know how I feel about The Chairs. At least the waiting room temp was seventy-three degrees this time, and not a bone chilling sixty-five.

While we were at the hospital, several staff, and even a doctor we passed in the hall, stopped and greeted Natalee by name and asked how everything was going. (It's nice to be recognized and remembered when you go places, but not so much to be well-known by the staff at the hospital!)

Nov. 7, 2017 Long day at Hillman today to receive the results of Natalee's MRI. No changes and no evidence of any tumor. Her blood counts are staying within normal range, and the doctors feel Aplastic Anemia will not be a returning problem. The third round of chemo is scheduled for next week and is to continue every month for another 3-5 months, along with an MRI every two months. I am sure the MRIs will eventually decrease as time goes on, and she is declared cancer free, which will be a big victory. As for a small victory, Natalee's hair has begun growing back in the bald areas on both sides and the middle of the back of her head. (Prayers being answered.)

Chapter 40

God had a Plan

Jan. 6, 2018 Happy New Year! Natalee is praying for a year without any surgery or major challenges. Minor challenges never go away. Natalee noticed her insulin pump is not recording and storing the normal blood glucose levels. She was directed by her endocrinologist to call the help line of the company that made the pump.

Jan. 9, 2018 While on the phone with the help line today, Natalee mentioned her inability to afford the pump with the sensor, and asked if they have an assistance program. The person she spoke with was very helpful; she said she would check into it and call back.

Jan. 18, 2018 Natalee received surprising news. A representative from another company, who the help line representative contacted, called and said they are sending Natalee a sensor that will work with her current pump....and there'll be no charges for the sensor or supplies! God bless her for going over and above her job duties. (God intervening with a better plan.)

Jan. 23, 2018 Follow-up at Hillman for the results of the MRI done on the 17th. (The Chairs were glad to see David and me. The feeling was not mutual.) There were no changes from two months ago. That was the good news. The not-so-good news was that he wants Natalee to be on the Temodar for a year, leaving seven months to go. The MRIs will continue every two months. (Color Natalee MRI weary.)

Natalee has hair again....all over! It's very short, of course, but no glaring bald spots. She may be able to stop wearing hats by April. She hasn't had short hair since she was little, so it will be a big adjustment once she retires the hats.

When Natalee was two, I had hair long enough to sit on. I decided to get it cut and went a little drastic with a "pixie" cut! When Natalee saw my very short hair, she put her little hands on either side of my face, looked at me very seriously, then said, "You look like a movie star." My mother, who had virtually sported the same hairdo as long as I can remember, countered that remark with, "Yes, Rin Tin Tin!" (Maybe I should have bitten her!) *FYI for those who are looking puzzled: Rin Tin Tin was a German Shepherd, and was an international star in motion pictures.

The hairdresser had banded my long hair in a pony tail at the nape of my neck and lopped it off. I saved the pony tail, and stored it in my cedar chest. After we got married, I asked David to get something out of the chest. He had a major panic attack because, at first glance, he thought it was a snake! Like Indiana Jones, he's not fond of snakes. When he was little his older brother, Larry, scared him with a fake one that struck out when the attached bulb was squeezed. He told David to sit down by a tree when the prank was perpetrated. It scarred David for life where snakes are involved. (Glad I didn't have a big brother!)

Feb. 2, 2018 It's Groundhog Day and Punxsutawney Phil saw his shadow and predicted six more weeks of winter. That's the bad news. The good news overshadowing that is Natalee received her glucose sensor.

Feb. 7, 2018 Natalee is euphoric she only has to check her blood sugar levels twice a day now instead of six to eight. The sensor has an attachable transmitter that sends the blood sugar readings every five minutes to a small receiver she carries, the size of a credit card, which displays the recorded levels on a screen so she can check them. Natalee can set high and low parameters on the receiver which will alert her if she is approaching those levels before she becomes symptomatic. (I feel better knowing she will be awakened before her blood sugar drops to dangerous numbers during the night.)

March 21, 2018 Today is a repeat of one year ago when "Stella Snowmageddon", came to visit. This time "Toby Ice-n-snow" showed up to interrupt Natalee's scheduled MRI. No way was I going to tackle driving on treacherous roads. Rescheduling it along with the follow-up at Hillman is on today's agenda.

April 2, 2018 Today Natalee is 47. It started out with her GP manifesting itself. To add to her less-than-happy day, she was to start chemo today, but will have to wait to see if the GP symptoms resolve. Also, Mother Nature pulled an April Fool's joke a day late with 6-8 inches of snow blanketing everything during the night. (Not a happy birthday.)

April 4, 2018 Because the back of Natalee's hair is longer than the sides, she has a mullet! It was time for a professional haircut to get her out of the eighties. She now has a cute hairstyle and no longer needs to wear her hats.

May 3, 2018 Natalee received a call from transplant to inform her she would not be eligible to be back on the transplant list until October of 2020. At least she will be (hopefully) eligible then; and her living donor will still be willing and able. (I know God has a plan! He always does!)

June12, 2018 A day for rejoicing. Natalee's "mirror image" friend from dialysis, Charlene, received a kidney from a living donor today. We are so happy for her, and wish Charlene and "Keekee" - her name for the kidney - all the best.

Chapter 41

There'll Always be Trials, but Life Goes on

I feel this is a good place to end the book - with another major health challenge we're declaring defeated in spite of the statistics. Natalee's life will go on with her daily challenges, but she will continue to meet any, and all new trials as always.........with hope, and prayer, and faith in God's promises sustaining her.

Some questions will always be on the "Wait and See" list:

1. Will she ever be able to have another kidney transplant? (We will always hope.)
2. Will Natalee have new major challenges to face? (Faith will get her through the challenges,)
3. Will she have any more surgeries to add to the list? (Praying she won't.)
4. Will I ever grow to like waiting room chairs? (No!)

Those are questions only tomorrow can answer with any certainty. Tomorrow will take care of itself, so for now we'll praise God for today's answers.

I think I have come to terms with the inevitable, but am not totally at peace with it. When that final day of Victory does come for Natalee, as it will eventually for all of us, knowing she is with the Lord we will rejoice that she is free from "The Cirque du Natalee's Challenges" - with elephants in the room, juggling and balancing acts; from sickness and suffering; from poking and prodding; from surgeries and pain; from bad news and wild emotional roller coaster rides; from endless waiting; from "Wait and See" and asking "Now what" …you get the beautiful picture. (Oh, and free from my terrible puns and jokes.)

In life, Natalee has turned her beautiful scars into badges of honor. In death, as all Christians who are followers of Jesus will, she'll be awarded five heavenly incorruptible crowns that will last for all eternity. (The Greek word translated *crown* means "a badge of royalty.")

1. The crown of rejoicing - For what is our hope, or joy, or crown of rejoicing? Is it not even you in the presence of our Lord Jesus Christ at His coming? (1 Thessalonians 2:19 NKJV)

2. The crown of righteousness - Finally, there is laid up for me the crown of righteousness, which the Lord, the righteous Judge, will give to me on that Day, and not to me only but also to all who have loved His appeariong. (2 Timothy 4:8 NKJV)

3. The crown of glory - …and when the Chief Shepherd appears, you will receive the crown of glory that does not fade away. (I Peter 5:4 NKJV)

4. The crown of life - …Be faithful until death, and I will give you the crown of life. (Revelation 2:10 NKJV)

5. The imperishable crown - Do you not know that those who run in a race all run, but one receives the prize? Run in such a way that you may obtain it. And everyone who competes for the prize is temperate in all things. Now they do it to obtain a perishable crown, but we for an imperishable crown.
(1 Corinthians 9:24-25 NKJV)

Until then, our little family will continue to make lasting memories, and put our faith, hope, and trust in God - meeting life's challenges - one day at a time.

Why, you do not even know what will happen tomorrow. What is your life? You are a mist that appears for a little while and then vanishes. (James 4:14 NIV) But thanks be to God, Who gives us the victory through our Lord Jesus Christ. (1 Corinthians 15:57 NKJV) I have fought the good fight, I have finished the race, I have kept the faith. (2 Timothy 4:7 NIV)

Epilogue

My hope is that this book was inspiring, and most of all has given glory to God for all He has done in Natalee's life. Some people will question why Natalee has suffered so much, with so many challenges. Was it a punishment from God? Natalee, or I, have ever believed that. Yes, God *allows* suffering. The Book of Job is a good example. Why, is an age-old mystery. Only God can see and knows the "big picture" for each of us from the day He gives us life to the day it is finally laid to rest for eternity. I believe if we have faith and hope during times of suffering, are obedient to His Word, surrender unconditionally to Him, and wholly trust Him to bring us through trials, we will be giving glory to Him and will receive blessings in return. As a Christian, suffering should teach us compassion for others who are going through trials, bring us closer to God, and remind us that we need to be ready to meet Him some day by having a real *relationship* with Him. (Yes, there is a difference between being religious and having a relationship.) We should not let suffering distance us from God or plant bitterness in our hearts.

> I consider that our present sufferings are not worth comparing with the glory that will be revealed to us. (Romans 8:18 NIV) I have told you these things, so that in me you may have peace. In this world you will have trouble. But take heart! I have overcome the world. (John 16:33 NIV)

How, you ask, has Natalee been blessed in all this? She will tell you she is blessed to have received so many miracles and answers to prayers, to have had compassion and support from others, to have drawn closer to God, to have been given an extra measure of faith and joy, and most importantly - knows she will assuredly be with Him one day in eternity.

> Now we see things imperfectly, like puzzling reflections
> in a mirror, but then we will see everything with perfect
> clarity. All that I know now is partial and incomplete, but
> then I will know everything completely, just as God now
> knows me completely. (1 Corinthians 13:12-13 NLT) Then
> shall the dust return to the earth as it was: and the spirit
> shall return unto God who gave it. (Ecclesiastes 12:7 KJV)
> Where, O death, is your victory? Where, O death, is your
> sting? But thanks be to God! He gives us the victory through
> our Lord Jesus Christ. (1 Corinthians 15:55 & 57 NIV)

The Word says to pray without ceasing. (Only the blood of Jesus makes us worthy to pray.)

> Rejoice always, pray without ceasing, give thanks in all
> circumstances; for this is the will of God in Christ Jesus
> for you. (1 Thessalonians 5:16-18 ESV)

Has God answered all of our prayers, you might ask. Sometimes the answer was "yes". Sometimes the answer came in a short amount of time. Other times we had to wait for a faith-testing long while. Occasionally when the answer was "yes," it was an unexpected answer - not at all what we thought it would be. (God knows just what we need.) Other times, God blessed us with more than what we prayed for. Then there were those times the answer was just plain "no." (God also knows what we don't need!) In that case, don't let the devil lead you down the treacherous path to thinking God doesn't care. Our desires may not have been God's desires for our lives, or maybe we just weren't taking the time to listen or look for the answer. Don't pray with greed over need. Have an attitude of faith in Him when you pray. We are not to be double minded - having our hearts divided between God and the world, only partly believing God for an answer.

> But when you ask, you must believe and not doubt,
> because the one who doubts is like a wave of the sea,
> blown and tossed by the wind. That person should not
> expect to receive anything from the Lord. Such a person

is double-minded and unstable in all they do. (James 1: 6-8 NIV)

I don't understand how a bumblebee flies (big body, little delicate wings), or how hummingbirds' wings can flutter so unbelievably fast, but I know they can. I see it, and I believe it. Natalee and I don't try to understand God's answers to our prayers. We believe He has a plan for our lives and will help us through *every* circumstance when we have put our faith, hope and trust in Him. (We've seen it countless times, and therefore believe it.)

> Then Jesus told him, "Because you have seen me, you have believed; blessed are those who have not seen and yet believed." (John 20:29 NIV)

Believe! If you were inspired by Natalee's story, and want to have a relationship with Jesus - ask God for forgiveness of your sins, confess and accept Jesus Christ, His Son, as your Lord and Savior. Study His Word so you can grow in knowledge and grace and have a relationship with Him, living in obedience, and being a blessing to others.

> For God so loved the world that he gave his one and only Son, that whoever believes in him shall not perish, but have eternal life. (John 3:16 NIV) If we confess our sins, he is faithful and just and will forgive us ours sins and purify us from all unrighteousness. (1 John 1:9 NIV) If you declare with your mouth, "Jesus is Lord," and believe in your heart that God raised him from the dead, you will be saved. For it is with your heart that you believe and are justified, and it is with your mouth that you profess your faith and are saved. (Romans 10: 9-10 NIV) Therefore, if anyone is in Christ, he is a new creation; old things have passed away; behold, all things have become new. (2 Corinthians 5:17 NKJV)

If you have wounds and scars in your life, I hope they become *beautiful* scars, transformed to *badges of honor,* extolling victory in and through Jesus Christ. **To God be the Glory!**

Acknowledgements

I want to thank God for giving me my wonderful daughter, Natalee, whose challenging life inspired this book, and for her allowing and wanting me to share her remarkable journey. I can't praise Him enough for all the miracles and answers to prayer He has blessed Natalee with. It's been a story in the making for many years. Writing it has been emotional at times, always uplifting, and sometimes tedious work. I've been privileged and blessed to be her mom. (And the other half of our comedy team that gets us through tough times!)

Many thanks to my husband David for understanding why I spent so many long hours in front of my computer, writing and turning my journal into a book, and again as I nervously birthed the book throughout the editing and publishing process. Most of I thank him for always being there for us without faltering....our Rock. *Love you to infinity and back.* (Because that's farther than the moon.)

Thanks to my granddaughter, McKenna for hanging in there throughout Natalee's challenges. It hasn't been easy, and has been a lifelong challenge for her, too, creating her own beautiful scars and badges of honor. I'm proud of you, but most importantly, keep on making yourself proud of you. (And ...*I love you, more!)*

Special thanks to Cindy Bruscha for providing her valuable input as an English teacher extraordinaire and for giving me encouragement and positive feedback. Cindy said the little notes I put in parentheses made it feel like I was talking directly to her, but I made her hungry for French fries. (Sorry!)

Thanks to proficient proofreader, Jim Snyder, for helping proof the manuscript he described as being "intense." He knew Natalee from church, but had no idea what she has persevered, until he graciously took on the daunting proofreading task.

Thank you, **Westbow Press,** for your all your invaluable help and guidance in publishing the book and making this a reality. I appreciate your strong Christian values. You made me feel part of a family throughout the process.

Pastor Bradley Westover... I always love your sermons, especially the one that prompted the book title. Thanks for your (and Cathy's) support of Natalee through your prayers, encouragement, and genuine caring. (You have a merry heart and always make us laugh!)

Thanks to the countless exceptional, wonderful and caring doctors and other medical staff who have always gone above and beyond to ensure the best care for Natalee. Also, to our friends (you know who you are) who provided abounding support, faithful unrelenting prayers and so much more. You are all deeply appreciated.

Last, but not least, I guess I should also thank The Chairs for their all-important supporting role in this story. They were always there... everywhere actually....when, and wherever I needed them. (Especially, my reliable padded desk chair.)

Printed in the United States
By Bookmasters